"How can the church thrive in modern day cities filled with diversity and littered with idolatry? The apostle Paul's letters to the Thessalonians provide a roadmap. Paul challenges believers to pair their faith with an obedience that will affect sanctification and spill over into the relationships around

them. Dr. Mark Howell brings fresh insight and application to these passages, showing us how believers in Thessalonica experienced many of the same challenges we face today and persevered as they submitted to the authority of Scripture in their lives, learning along the way how to genuinely love, encourage, and serve one another."

—Kevin Ezell, president, North American Mission Board, SBC

"Dr. Mark Howell has powerfully exegeted and applied the deep riches found in Paul's letter to those in Thessalonica. Like Paul, who visited this strategic city on his second missionary journey, Howell has 'reasoned . . . from the Scriptures, explaining and showing that the Messiah had to suffer and rise from the dead' (Acts 17:2). I am confident that after reading this exposition you, like the Thessalonians themselves, will welcome it 'not as a human message, but as it truly is, the message of God' (1 Thess 2:13). Read it and reap!"

—O. S. Hawkins, president/CEO, GuideStone Financial Resources

"Dr. Mark Howell has done an outstanding job in his treatment on First and Second Thessalonians. The result is the product of a scholar's mind, delivered through a pastor's heart. This material will be a welcome addition to the library of the pastor in the pulpit and the person in the pew, well documented and written in a style to be easily understood by both. ('He has put the cookies on the bottom shelf!') I further believe there is no more timely a message to our current age than this message, written to the Thessalonian Christians. Therefore, I highly recommend Dr. Howell's work and endorse it without reservation."

—Dr. Glen E. Owens, Assistant Executive Director, Florida Baptist Convention

"In these engaging expositions Dr. Mark Howell has given us a clear glimpse into a pastor's heart. The expositions in these pages are not the work of a dry exegete; rather they represent the Word of God as channeled through the heart of a pastor-shepherd. I'm grateful for these stellar expositions whose tight exegetical work and crisp illustrations bear the marks of their effective leader. I especially appreciate Dr. Howell's attention to the semantic structural analysis of each unit. May they be used to aid us in the work of exalting Christ in the text!"

—Steven W. Smith, vice president for Student Services and Communications, and Professor of Communication, Southwestern Baptist Theological Seminary

NT / COMMENTARY

AUTHOR **Mark Howell**
SERIES EDITORS **David Platt, Daniel L. Akin, and Tony Merida**

CHRIST-CENTERED
Exposition

EXALTING JESUS IN

1 & 2 THESSALONIANS

NASHVILLE, TENNESSEE

Christ-Centered Exposition Commentary: Exalting Jesus in
1 & 2 Thessalonians

© Copyright 2015
by Mark Howell

B&H Publishing Group
Nashville, Tennessee

All rights reserved.

ISBN 978-0-8054-9645-1

Dewey Decimal Classification: 220.7
Subject Heading: BIBLE. N.T. 1 & 2 THESSALONIANS—
COMMENTARIES\JESUS CHRIST

Printed in the United States of America
1 2 3 4 5 6 7 8 9 10 • 20 19 18 17 16 15
BethP

SERIES DEDICATION

Dedicated to Adrian Rogers and John Piper. They have taught us to love the gospel of Jesus Christ, to preach the Bible as the inerrant Word of God, to pastor the church for which our Savior died, and to have a passion to see all nations gladly worship the Lamb.

—David Platt, Tony Merida, and Danny Akin
March 2013

TABLE OF CONTENTS

ACKNOWLEDGMENTS

Without a doubt one of life's greatest joys is getting to enjoy the journey with my wife, Carmen, and my two daughters, Abigail and Rebekah. Indeed, God has made my life rich and sweet by entrusting to me the privilege of being Carmen's husband and Abi and Beka's dad. This side of heaven, there is no place where I would rather be than spending time with my three girls. Without their unconditional love, tireless encouragement, and personal sacrifice this commentary would never have been written. Though they do not hear it enough, I could not be more grateful for having the privilege of being the only male in a house full of girls.

I also want to express my profound gratitude to Dr. and Mrs. Paige Patterson for not only welcoming me into their family, but also for treating me as one of their own children. To say that I am blessed would be a gross understatement. Thank you, Mom and Dad, for encouraging me both to pursue my calling with passion and excellence and to love Jesus with all of my heart. To my mother, Donna Howell, thank you for your unconditional love and support even when you did not fully comprehend what your son was doing when he followed God's call to be a pastor. To my dad, Larry Howell, who is now with Jesus and will never get to read this commentary but who now knows perfectly what Paul meant when he wrote, "Since we believe that Jesus died and rose again, in the same way God will bring with Him those who have fallen asleep through Jesus" (1 Thess 4:14). A special thank you to Mrs. Patterson and Tamra Hernandez for their graciousness in reading and editing my manuscript. And finally, I am deeply grateful to the First Baptist Church of Daytona Beach for granting to me the privilege of being your pastor. Your passionate love for Jesus and His glorious gospel is obvious and contagious.

SERIES INTRODUCTION

Augustine said, "Where Scripture speaks, God speaks." The editors of the Christ-Centered Exposition Commentary series believe that where God speaks, the pastor must speak. God speaks through His written Word. We must speak from that Word. We believe the Bible is God breathed, authoritative, inerrant, sufficient, understandable, necessary, and timeless. We also affirm that the Bible is a Christ-centered book; that is, it contains a unified story of redemptive history of which Jesus is the hero. Because of this Christ-centered trajectory that runs from Genesis 1 through Revelation 22, we believe the Bible has a corresponding global-missions thrust. From beginning to end, we see God's mission as one of making worshipers of Christ from every tribe and tongue worked out through this redemptive drama in Scripture. To that end we must preach the Word.

In addition to these distinct convictions, the Christ-Centered Exposition Commentary series has some distinguishing characteristics. First, this series seeks to display exegetical accuracy. What the Bible says is what we want to say. While not every volume in the series will be a verse-by-verse commentary, we nevertheless desire to handle the text carefully and explain it rightly. Those who teach and preach bear the heavy responsibility of saying what God has said in His Word and declaring what God has done in Christ. We desire to handle God's Word faithfully, knowing that we must give an account for how we have fulfilled this holy calling (Jas 3:1).

Second, the Christ-Centered Exposition Commentary series has pastors in view. While we hope others will read this series, such as parents, teachers, small-group leaders, and student ministers, we desire to provide a commentary busy pastors will use for weekly preparation of biblically faithful and gospel-saturated sermons. This series is not academic in nature. Our aim is to present a readable and pastoral style of commentaries. We believe this aim will serve the church of the Lord Jesus Christ.

Third, we want the Christ-Centered Exposition Commentary series to be known for the inclusion of helpful illustrations and theologically driven applications. Many commentaries offer no help in illustrations, and few offer any kind of help in application. Often those that do offer illustrative material and application unfortunately give little serious attention to the text. While giving ourselves primarily to explanation, we also hope to serve readers by providing inspiring and illuminating illustrations coupled with timely and timeless application.

Finally, as the name suggests, the editors seek to exalt Jesus from every book of the Bible. In saying this, we are not commending wild allegory or fanciful typology. We certainly believe we must be constrained to the meaning intended by the divine Author Himself, the Holy Spirit of God. However, we also believe the Bible has a messianic focus, and our hope is that the individual authors will exalt Christ from particular texts. Luke 24:25-27,44-47 and John 5:39,46 inform both our hermeneutics and our homiletics. Not every author will do this the same way or have the same degree of Christ-centered emphasis. That is fine with us. We believe faithful exposition that is Christ centered is not monolithic. We do believe, however, that we must read the whole Bible as Christian Scripture. Therefore, our aim is both to honor the historical particularity of each biblical passage and to highlight its intrinsic connection to the Redeemer.

The editors are indebted to the contributors of each volume. The reader will detect a unique style from each writer, and we celebrate these unique gifts and traits. While distinctive in their approaches, the authors share a common characteristic in that they are pastoral theologians. They love the church, and they regularly preach and teach God's Word to God's people. Further, many of these contributors are younger voices. We think these new, fresh voices can serve the church well, especially among a rising generation that has the task of proclaiming the Word of Christ and the Christ of the Word to the lost world.

We hope and pray this series will serve the body of Christ well in these ways until our Savior returns in glory. If it does, we will have succeeded in our assignment.

David Platt
Daniel L. Akin
Tony Merida
Series Editors
February 2013

1 Thessalonians

Real People—Real Gospel—Real City

1 THESSALONIANS 1:1; ACTS 17:1-9

Main Idea: The gospel of Jesus Christ can transform a people and impact a city.

I. **The Gospel Motivates (1:1a) (Acts 17:1-4).**
   A. The gospel motivates us to go and tell.
      1. We become passionate about the advancement of the gospel (Acts 17:1-2a).
      2. We become passionate about the proclamation of the gospel (Acts 17:2b-4).
   B. The gospel motivates us to press on and persevere (Acts 17:5-9).
      1. The church keeps going despite adversity (1 Thess 3:1-5).
      2. The church keeps growing through adversity (1 Thess 3:6-8).
II. **The Gospel Transforms (1:1b).**
   A. The gospel transforms people (Thess 1:1b).
   B. The gospel transforms position (Thess 1:1c).
      1. Grace: our standing before God
      2. Peace: our relationship with God

A common misconception people on the outside of the church have about people on the inside of the church is that people on the inside are somehow insulated from or unaffected by the real struggles of life. Many attenders perpetuate this idea by observing the unwritten rule that when attending church, if you pretend that your life is perfect, you may just be able to convince others that it is. They could borrow a line from the old commercial on a certain deodorant: when in church, never let those in the pews around you "see you sweat."

Of course, those on the inside know from personal experience that Christians are real people who live in a real world and experience real struggles. The variable changing the equation for a believer is not the absence of these struggles, but a personal, life-changing encounter with a real God through the person of Jesus Christ. From the moment you embrace the gospel, the entire picture and pursuit of your life is radically transformed. The gospel goes far beyond reforming character or insulating you from life's challenges; it brings about the transformation of your heart.

If ever a city needed this kind of transformation, it was Thessalonica. This city was full of real people who were overwhelmed with real struggles and desperately needed a life-changing encounter with a real God. Thessalonica had a burgeoning population of more than 200,000 Romans, Greeks, and Jews. It was also the temporary home of thousands of sailors, travelers, and immigrants who visited its bustling port or traveled its busy highways. A vibrant economy, a strategic harbor, and a prime location on the Roman Empire's Egnatian Road made Thessalonica one of the most influential cities of the first century. It was the New York, Houston, or Boston of its day—yet for all its assets, Thessalonica was a lost city. The Greeks filled the temples, the Jews attended the synagogue, and the Romans paid homage to Caesar, but a pervasive spiritual darkness covered the city. As Gene Green puts it, the Thessalonians were afloat "in a sea of great religious pluralism and confusion" (Green, *Letters*, 32).

The apostle Paul knew that for the gospel to break through the religious fog of the city, it first had to shine in the hearts of the people. He was convinced that if a church could be planted in this strategically located and culturally diverse city, the gospel could spread to Rome in the West and to Asia Minor in the East.[1] He and his colleagues, Silvanus and Timothy, had personally experienced the transforming power of the gospel. They were now passionately committed to bring this good news to the people of Thessalonica (Acts 17:1-9).

The Gospel Motivates
1 THESSALONIANS 1:1A AND ACTS 17:1-4

"Be careful" are words all parents have uttered to their children. I can remember, as a child, hearing those words a thousand times, and as a

---

[1] William Barclay contends that the establishment of the Thessalonian church was vital for the advancement of the gospel and essential for the rapid spread of Christianity (Barclay, *Letters*, 181). Paul obviously recognized the strategic importance of this church. Timothy's report about the health of the church was not only a cause for much rejoicing but also a reason to be hopeful about the future advancement of the gospel (1 Thess 3:1-10).

parent I have also shared them with my children. After all, what loving parent wants a child to take unnecessary risks? In life, risk—whether it be an uncertain investment, a drive on a dangerous mountain road, or sharing a secret with an untrustworthy friend—is something to be avoided.

However, when you follow Jesus Christ you do more than choose a different life; in a real sense, a different life chooses you. This new life leads you to take big steps and bold risks. Jesus put it this way: "If anyone wants to come with Me, he must deny himself, take up his cross daily, and follow Me. For whoever wants to save his life will lose it" (Luke 9:23-24). Later Jesus would look squarely at the multitudes and challenge them to "calculate the cost" of following Him (Luke 14:28-33). Risk comes at great cost, and not everyone is willing to pay it. Denying self, taking up crosses, and following a revolutionary figure like Jesus Christ are not natural pursuits for anyone. This kind of risk-taking requires a supernatural motivation.

The Gospel Motivates Us to Go and Tell

The Thessalonian letter begins by introducing the founders of the church—Paul, Silvanus (Silas), and Timothy (1:1). They had been in the beginning weeks of their second missionary journey, and their arrival in Thessalonica was not accidental. Behind the scenes God had been supernaturally preparing the way. Through divine intervention, Paul had experienced the unmistakable call of God to take the gospel to the cities of Macedonia. His response was decisive and immediate (Acts 16:9-10). Macedonia boasted some of the most strategically located, culturally diverse, and spiritually dark cities of the ancient world. What better place to preach the good news!

Before arriving in Thessalonica, Paul, Silas, and Timothy had visited Philippi. Philippi proved to be both a formidable place to preach the gospel and a serious test of their resolve and character. Although their experience in Philippi nearly cost them their lives, it did not shake their confidence in God's calling. Far from being dissuaded from their mission, Paul, Silas, and Timothy forged ahead with a renewed sense of passion and urgency. They rejoiced that in the midst of their personal adversities, God was up to something big. Many lives were transformed, a vibrant church was planted, and the gospel was advancing.

We become passionate about the advancement of the gospel (Acts 17:1-2a). With the trials of Philippi behind them, Paul and his companions came expectantly to Thessalonica. For them, ministry was less about their own good fortune and more about the advancement of the good news. How unfortunate to view ministry as more about our comfort than about God's calling or to be more consumed about what we want God to do for us than about what He desires to do through us. We would do well to recognize a discernible link between adversity and the great purposes of God. The biblical record is replete with testimonies of how God uses the suffering of His servants to bring about His most significant work.

The pattern emerging from Paul's ministry was that whether he experienced a revival or a riot, he remained inexorably committed to his calling. Dietrich Bonhoeffer powerfully captures what it means to follow Christ in this way:

> God honors some with great suffering and grants them the
> grace of martyrdom, while others are not tempted beyond
> their strength. But in every case it is one cross. It is laid on
> every Christian. The first Christ-suffering that everyone
> has to experience is the call which summons us away from
> our attachments to this world. It is the death of the old self
> in the encounter with Jesus Christ. Those who enter into
> discipleship enter into Jesus' death. They turn their living into
> dying. . . . Whenever Christ calls us, his call leads us to death.
> (Bonhoeffer, *Discipleship*, 87)

So whether he was beaten and imprisoned in Philippi, chased and pursued in Thessalonica, or ridiculed and mocked in Athens, Paul affirmed without hesitation that he was not ashamed of the gospel (Rom 1:16).

We become passionate about the proclamation of the gospel (Acts 17:2b-4). Without question, our lives are awash in a sea of opinions. From well-meaning friends to aggressive advertisers, there is never a shortage of people who want to tell us what we should do or how we should live. However, followers of Jesus Christ do not interpret the world through the lens of human opinion; they interpret the world through the lens of Scripture.

Upon their arrival in Thessalonica, Paul, Silas, and Timothy made their way to the synagogue. It provided the perfect setting to preach the good news. Their goal was not to add another religious opinion to the already overly saturated religious climate of Thessalonica. Instead, for three weeks Paul "reasoned with them from the Scriptures" (Acts 17:2). Notice that he did not talk *about* the Scriptures, he reasoned *from* the Scriptures. There is a big difference. Faithful biblical exposition will always help people to see the text for themselves. Preachers and teachers must never assume that people will connect their thoughts with the truths of the biblical text. They must be shown what the text says and where the text says it. Biblical exposition is simply helping people to read their Bibles for themselves.

Paul's pattern of preaching provides preachers with a helpful model for faithful Bible exposition. This can be clearly seen by Luke's description of how Paul "reasoned" from Scripture, "explaining" its meaning and "showing" that Jesus was the Messiah who was raised from the dead (Acts 17:2-3). That brings together *argumentation, explanation,* and *illustration.* His approach was logical, it was thorough, and it was unmistakably biblical.

Notice carefully Paul's threefold approach in Acts 17:2-3.

- He reasoned from the Scriptures by using carefully crafted arguments to demonstrate the Christocentric focus and theological significance of the Scriptures. He engaged their minds with hopes that God would enlighten their hearts.
- He explained the meaning of the Scriptures by helping his listeners to know what was said and where the Scriptures said it.
- He illustrated biblical truth by placing it before the people in such a way that they could see the implications of its message for their lives.

Clearly, the gospel message connected with more than a few of the Thessalonians. Luke tells us, "some of them were persuaded . . . including a great number of God-fearing Greeks, as well as a number of the leading women" (Acts 17:4). The good news had arrived in Thessalonica, but this good news was about to present Paul and his companions with a big problem.

The Gospel Motivates Us to Press On and Persevere (Acts 17:5-9).

Whenever the gospel is preached, you can generally anticipate one of three responses. First, some people will get angry. This response is common in today's world when Christians are regularly labeled as hatemongers for declaring the exclusivity of Jesus as the only way to God. Second, some people will elevate that anger to the level of persecution. Around the globe untold millions of Christians live in imminent physical danger and many have lost their lives for the sake of preaching Jesus. Finally, when the gospel is preached, there will always be some people who will embrace the message and be saved.[2]

These were the exact responses in Thessalonica. The excitement of the Jews, God-fearing Greeks, and leading women who embraced the gospel was about to be interrupted by an angry mob of envious Jews and evil men who had no appetite for the message. Their initial response of anger had escalated to persecution. The gospel that had come to Thessalonica was threatening to turn their city "upside down" by challenging the authority of Caesar through the claim that there was "another king—Jesus" (Acts 17:6-7). This *serious charge* came with *serious consequences*. Simply put, the message of Jesus was counter-cultural to the Thessalonians. It hit the very heart of the city. If Jesus was the true King, then Caesar was not. If Jesus was the *only* Savior, then all the shrines and temples were worthless monuments built to worship worthless gods. If Jesus was in fact the Son of God, then God must be real. And if God was indeed real, then they were accountable to Him. The message of Jesus was therefore unpalatable to most of the Thessalonians, and they were determined to mute the message and the messengers by whatever means necessary. **When Jesus Christ is faithfully preached, you don't have to go looking for trouble; trouble will often come looking for you**. Hence, out of growing concern for their personal safety, the new Thessalonian converts implored Paul, Silas, and Timothy to leave the city. Under cover of darkness, they left the fragile new church that had been established in Thessalonica.

The church keeps going despite adversity (1 Thess 3:1-5). The decision to leave the city was doubtlessly painful for Paul. A true shepherd is driven not by personal ambition but by pastoral concern. Added to his own personal struggles, a pastor also carries the burdens of those entrusted to his care. Most pastors will tell you that even when God calls them to a new ministry, their fond affection remains for the people they leave behind. Paul may have continued on his journey to advance the gospel, but his heart was still very much in the city. He may have escaped the persecution of the angry mob, but he could not escape his concern for the new believers he left behind. Was the adversity too great? Were they still running the race? Did they feel as if he had abandoned them? When you gaze through the window of Paul's heart, you begin to see

---

[2] See Acts 4:1-4 for this same threefold response to the preaching of Peter and John at the temple in Jerusalem.

his passionate love for the church. When he finally pens his letter to the church, his words give us some indication of the inner turmoil he experienced by having to leave them so hastily.

> *Therefore, when we could no longer stand it, we thought it was better to be left alone in Athens. And we sent Timothy, our brother and God's coworker in the gospel of Christ, to strengthen and encourage you concerning your faith, so that no one will be shaken by these persecutions. For you yourselves know that we are appointed to this. In fact, when we were with you, we told you previously that we were going to suffer persecution, and as you know, it happened. For this reason, when I could no longer stand it, I also sent him to find out about your faith, fearing that the tempter had tempted you and that our labor might be for nothing.* (3:1-5)

Paul wanted the Thessalonians to be assured of his love for them. He also wanted to know how they were doing. When Timothy returned with an update, what Paul learned brought great joy to his heart.

The church keeps growing through adversity (3:6-8). The Thessalonian church was alive and well. Instead of snuffing out the light of the gospel, the adversity had the opposite effect. As early church father Tertullian so aptly affirmed in his *Apologeticus*, persecution quite often leads to a stronger church because the blood of the martyrs becomes the seed of the church. The seeds that Paul had planted in Thessalonica were growing in the fertile soil of adversity. The Thessalonian church was growing in its faith in Christ and in its love for Paul. Of course, the church was not perfect. The church was made up of real people who were living out their faith in a very real world. The gospel brought them transformation in their hearts but they had a long way to go in the sanctification of their lives. Paul would address this in greater detail later in the letter.

The Gospel Transforms
1 THESSALONIANS 1:1B

During my 25 years of ministry I have witnessed dozens of programs, campaigns, and initiatives that have promised to bring new life to the church. Many of these have been commendable and have provided valuable resources and offered helpful insights to and for pastors like me as I have sought to lead the church. Yet even a cursory survey of the ecclesiastical landscape reveals that despite the implementation of

new programs and strategies, an alarming number of churches are pla-
teaued or declining. To borrow a common phrase, it is as if we have
been "rearranging the deck chairs on the Titanic." New life does not
always accompany new programs. Perhaps the most helpful thing that
a pastor can do to breathe new life into his church is not to introduce
a new church growth model or to implement the latest church growth
strategy. Rather, the most important thing a pastor can do may be to
recall what the church really is and refocus his energy into what the
gospel really does. The key to breathing new life into your church may
not be in the discovery of something new. The key may be found in your
discovery of a passionate recommitment to proclaiming something that
is old.

The Gospel Transforms People

The word translated "church" is *ekklēsia* coming from two Greek words
(*ek kaleō*) meaning "called out." The church then is the "called-out
ones." As you have already observed, Paul's preaching impacted the
Thessalonians in such a profound way that Jews, God-fearing Greeks,
and "leading women" embraced his message. However, if you pick something up, it most often requires that you put something down. When
these believers turned *to* God, they were turning *away from* their past
way of life. One of the most fundamental truths of the gospel has been
expressed in this way. When a person comes to *know* Jesus, they will *know*
change and if there is *no* change, there is likely *no* Jesus (2 Cor 13:5).

God called many of the Thessalonians out of the legalism of Judaism,
the emptiness of idol worship, and the bankruptcy of religious ritual.
They abandoned their former lives "to serve the living and true God"
(1:9). Their lives changed and changed radically. They were called out
of darkness into light. They were called out of their sin and into sonship.
Their new standing was on the basis that they were now "in God the
Father and the Lord Jesus Christ" (1:1b), which is the essence of what
it means to be the church. I. Howard Marshall drives this truth home:

> The Christian stands in such a relationship to Jesus that his life
> is determined by his death and resurrection, both that in and
> through Christ he is a new being and that he is summoned
> to live a new life in the fellowship of the church. The church,
> then, is constituted by its relationship to God the Father and
> to Jesus. (Marshall, *1 and 2 Thessalonians*, 49)

A church is not built on the foundation of programs or strategies, but on the Lord Jesus Christ. When the gospel penetrates hearts it transforms people. Transformed people constitute the church. This concept is the essence of the believers' church, and this was what Paul founded in Thessalonica.

The Gospel Transforms Position

For many years, the American Express Company told its customers that "membership has its privileges." The privileges of a credit card company may offer some short-term benefits, but they pale in comparison to the lasting riches that are guaranteed to those who are in Christ Jesus. To be a member of God's church means that you are the beneficiary of God's grace and peace. Notice that these are not *rights* to which you are entitled, they are *gifts* that are given to the church.

Grace: our standing before God. Before being transformed by the gospel of Jesus Christ, no person, regardless of how deserving or noble, enjoys a proper relationship with God. Sin, like a thick fog on the darkest of nights, blinds our eyes from seeing God for Who He is. Even our best efforts to cut through the fog and darkness prove to be woefully inadequate. Religion can't do it. Love for our fellow man can't do it. Our best intentions can't do it. We are like the travelers on the highway wanting so desperately to speed on ahead but unable to do so because we can't see beyond the hoods of our cars. You know the feeling of helplessness and frustration if you have ever been in that situation. The fog of our sin is just that way. It is simply too thick and there is nothing we can do to lift it. We are hopelessly lost and there is no way out. We may try to ignore it and press on recklessly, but on the horizon there is a precipice that is growing closer and closer. Many people live their lives in this way. Sin has blinded them and they cannot see. The prognosis is not good. There is a cliff in the distance, and it is called "judgment." They speed down life's highway oblivious to the imminent danger ahead.

Before we can have a relationship with God, God Himself must do something about the fog. He has to help us see through it. Here *the good news* enters the picture. God offers a way out through Jesus Christ. God lifts the fog by grace. Grace in its fullest expression is revealed by the substitutionary death of Jesus Christ on the cross. God "made the One who did not know sin to be sin for us, so that we might become the righteousness of God in Him" (2 Cor 5:21). By His own initiative, God gives us a way out. The way out is a Person and His name is Jesus Christ.

His forgiveness can't be earned . . . it's a gift. The only way to get this forgiveness is to receive it as a gift (John 1:12). The only way to see God is to embrace Jesus.

The moment we receive Jesus our standing before God radically changes. We are immediately delivered from the fog and the darkness of our sin. Our citizenship is immediately transferred to a different kingdom, and we are clothed with a righteousness that is not our own (Col 1:13-14; Isa 61:10). God did not create the fog; we did. Yet because of His love for us, He provides a way out. God does for us what we could never do for ourselves. Through Christ we now stand in a proper relationship with God, and it is all because of His grace. Life's journey now takes on a new meaning. This is exactly what happened to the Thessalonians. When their standing before God changed, their lives changed because they were the recipients of God's grace.

Peace: our relationship with God. Sin not only destroys our standing before God, it also destroys our peace with God. Sin means war. You and I are at war with each other, and we are at war with God (Col 1:21). When we are at war, there is no real peace. It's no coincidence that public demand for sleep medication nets billions of dollars in revenue for pharmaceutical companies each year. Many of us can't rest peacefully at night because we aren't living with peace during the day. This includes peace in our relationships with others and peace in our relationship with God. The sobering reality is that people are looking for peace in all the wrong places. Jesus Christ offers a lasting peace—peace with one another, peace with yourself, but most important, peace with God.

Let's bring this into focus as it relates to the Thessalonians. An angry mob has stirred up their city, disrupted their fellowship, threatened their well-being, and chased away their friends. This is a recipe for sleepless nights and anxious days, right? Not exactly. You see, you could take away their stuff, but you could not take away their peace. If God's grace is real, then His peace is not only possible, but it is guaranteed. David declares that "the Protector of Israel does not slumber or sleep" (Ps 121:4). Since God is more than capable to keep watch over your life, there is no good reason why any follower of Jesus Christ should not be able to rest no matter how difficult the circumstances.

Conclusion

Indeed, Paul's time in Thessalonica was short. If we did not have access to the "rest of the story," we might readily conclude that his mission there was a failure. But as we have seen, the faith of these young Thessalonian believers was anything but superficial. They had a genuine love for Christ and a zealous passion for proclaiming His transforming gospel. Despite Paul's forceful eviction from the city, the faith of the Thessalonians persevered. Furthermore, although he was physically absent, his presence continued to be felt as he took up his pen and wrote his epistles. **Even in the midst of the most troubling circumstances, God was doing His work in His way**. Paul would never return to the city of Thessalonica, but God was going to do far more there than Paul ever could have imagined. As John Phillips insightfully notes,

> The Holy Spirit showed Paul there was more than one way to evangelize a city. If he could not go back to Thessalonica in person he could write the church a letter. . . . A new method of evangelism was born—literature evangelism. . . . Down through the ages millions have been saved through reading those letters, and millions more have had their faith strengthened. . . . God knows how to overrule our mistakes. He makes the very wrath of man to praise Him. (Phillips, *Exploring Acts*, 341)

That is how God works. No matter how routine the details of your life may appear, not a single detail is wasted by God. If God can use angry mobs (Acts 17:5) and frustrated plans (1 Thess 2:18) to bring about one of the most insightful and encouraging epistles in the New Testament, then you can be sure that He will also use your life experiences to bring about your ultimate good and His greater glory (Rom 8:28). While on this side of heaven you are afforded only an occasional glimpse of what He is doing in the world, you know that God is up to far more than you could ever imagine. The Thessalonians have long since been transported to their eternal home, but their faith continues to inspire and encourage. You stand on their shoulders. You also know that a day is coming when those who follow you will stand on yours. That's what it means to be a part of God's church.

Reflect and Discuss

1. Why do you think so many people try to hide their problems from others when they go to church?
2. What are some ways that you can encourage people in your church to be "real" with one another?

3. What was it about the city of Thessalonica that made it such an important place to plant a church? How does it compare with your city?
4. What was Paul's approach for sharing the gospel? How might you apply his principles?
5. When you preach or teach, do you talk more *about* the Bible than you preach or teach *from* the Bible? How can you do a better job of helping people to see the text?
6. What was the response to Paul's preaching in Thessalonica both positively and negatively? What kind of reaction can you anticipate from those who hear when you faithfully preach the exclusivity of Jesus Christ from the Scriptures?
7. What single characteristic is common to every church? Is this the case in your church?
8. How does adversity reveal the genuineness of one's salvation? How does it affect the genuineness of a church?
9. What do grace and peace mean for your relationship with God? How do they affect your relationship with one another?
10. How are you and your church actively pursuing your calling to advance the gospel?

Living for Today but Longing for Tomorrow

1 THESSALONIANS 1:2-10

Main Idea: The gospel will affect every area of our lives, including our passion for living today and our hope for what is coming tomorrow.

I. **A Genuine Church (1:4-6,9-10)**
   A.   Genuine conversion changes our direction (1:4-6).
   B.   Genuine conversion changes our affection (1:9).
   C.   Genuine conversion changes our reflection (1:10).
II. **A Dynamic Church (1:2-3)**
   A.   A working faith (1:3a)
   B.   A laboring love (1:3b)
   C.   An enduring hope (1:3c)
III. **A Contagious Church (1:8-9)**
   A.   Contagious in our proclamation (1:8)
   B.   Contagious in our passion (1:8-9)

As an athlete, I will always be grateful for the influence that my coaches have had on my life. The life lessons that I learned from them, on and off the practice field, have proven to be invaluable tools in helping me to face life's many challenges. One particular lesson that my coaches taught me was, "little things make big things." My teammates and I were told repeatedly that if we paid careful attention to the little things of life, the big things would take care of themselves. We were thus challenged to be on time for meetings and class, to respect our classmates and professors, to study diligently, to take pride in how organized we kept our lockers, and to perform our practice drills with precision. Our coaches were careful to remind us that our performance during the big game on Saturday would only be as strong as our faithfulness to live with excellence throughout the week.

Mediocrity inspires no one, but those who pursue their lives with passion and excellence challenge and encourage others to do the same. It's no small thing then that Paul begins his letter by thanking God for the genuine commitment of the Thessalonians to the gospel (1:2-3). This church clearly lived for Christ with passion and expectancy. There was nothing mediocre about their faith, their love, or their hope. They were an inspiration to Paul and to the churches of Macedonia and Achaia (1:8-9). But despite the excellence of the Thessalonians' faith, God was ultimately the source behind every good thing that was happening among them. Hiebert makes this point:

> Paul's heart was full of praise because of the good news
> concerning the Thessalonians, but he did not simply
> congratulate them on the success that had been achieved. He
> was well aware that the spiritual results evoking his gratitude
> were due ultimately neither to the preachers nor the converts.
> God Himself was the real cause of it all. To Him belonged
> the thanks for what had been wrought. (Hiebert, *1 and*
> *2 Thessalonians*, 47)

Because God transforms those whom He saves, we should expect that genuine conversion will produce visible results. As we explore this passage more carefully, we will see how Paul expresses gratitude to God for how the gospel has taken root in the hearts of the Thessalonians. He will identify three characteristics of their *authentic faith*: it was genuine, it was dynamic, and it was contagious.

A Genuine Church
1 THESSALONIANS 1:4-6,9-10

After his customary greeting in verse 1, Paul's first words express his joy in hearing a good report from Timothy concerning the status of the church. The months of mental anguish, not knowing what had become of the church, must have been overwhelming. But when the news finally arrived, Paul could rejoice that their faith had proven to be real. If someone had accused them of being genuine followers of Jesus Christ, the evidence to convict them was apparent: they were guilty as charged. Their faith was working, their love was laboring, and their hope was enduring. Their Christianity meant something. Paul could thus say without equivocation that he "knew" their election by God (1:4).

Here is an important theological point: They were not the elect of God because they worked at their faith. **Rather, because they were the elect of God they had a faith that worked.** The distinction is very important. Election is not something that we earn. An earned salvation would destroy the doctrine of grace. However, while election and salvation are not earned, they without doubt produce evidence (Jas 2:14-26). Truly there are no Secret Service agents in God's kingdom. As noted, **genuine conversion produces visible results**. If someone followed us around for a week and observed our lives, would there be enough evidence to convict us of being Christians?

Genuine Conversion Changes Our Direction (1 Thess 1:4-6)

From the moment Paul set foot in the Thessalonian synagogue, his aim was to proclaim the good news. For Paul, there was no good news apart from the gospel, so the heart of his message focused on the Old Testament Scriptures that pointed to a risen Lord Jesus and on his own personal encounter with the Lord (Acts 9:1-9; 17:2). Luke gives a glimpse of Paul's preaching when he writes, "[Paul] reasoned with them from the Scriptures, explaining and showing that the Messiah had to suffer and rise from the dead: 'This Jesus I am proclaiming to you is the Messiah'" (Acts 17:2-3).

While Paul opened the Scriptures and preached Christ to the Thessalonians, the preaching of the good news was only half the equation. For the gospel to take root, God's Spirit must intervene. Concerning this, John MacArthur insightfully notes,

> Faith does not come by merely hearing those words of truth
> . . . [for] if the truth spoken is not accompanied by the power
> of God, it accomplishes nothing. But when empowered by
> God as it enters the prepared soul, the gospel truth saves.
> (MacArthur, *1 and 2 Thessalonians*, 22)

The gospel had come to Thessalonica not in word only but also with great power (1:5). Through the illuminating work of the Holy Spirit they were able to comprehend the gospel, and then by an act of saving faith, they embraced it. When the Holy Spirit opened their eyes to understand the gospel, they recognized its divine origin. This was no ordinary message; it was the Word of God (2:13). Their acknowledgement of the divine source of the message explains why, despite the high cost to their personal welfare, they received it with joy and therefore joined with Paul, Silas, and Timothy in following Jesus (1:6).

Genuine Conversion Changes Our Affection (1 Thess 1:9)

Verse 9 provides a vivid picture of what happens to us when we embrace the gospel: we turn from idols (repentance), turn to God (faith), and turn our lives over to God (service). The Thessalonians did not merely *try on* Jesus to see if He would fit into the wardrobe of their lives. Instead, they *clothed themselves* completely with Him (see Rom 13:14).

Turning from idols is not easy. Idols ostensibly give life security and meaning. We spend our time and money on them. They consume our thinking. They become objects of our worship. Our thoughts are drawn to them and they occupy our dreams. In Timothy Keller's words, "An idol has such a controlling position in your heart that you can spend most of your passion and energy, your emotional and financial resources on it without a second thought" (Keller, *Counterfeit Gods*, 13–14).

How can we break free from something that is deeply rooted in our lives? There is only one way. We have to turn to something better. We have to turn from what is false to what is true and from what is dead to what is living. That is what the Thessalonians did. They turned to the "living and true God" (1:9). They turned from being slaves to lifeless idols to being servants of the living God. God changed their affections.

Of course, such a transformation is the result of genuine conversion. Throughout history, countless numbers of believers have chosen, at great cost to their own personal welfare, to pursue Christ above all else. Writing about early Christian martyrs, MacArthur describes their devotion to Christ:

> Following Jesus Christ was the sum of their entire existence. At the moment when life itself was on the line, nothing else mattered besides identifying themselves with Him. For these faithful believers, the name "Christian" was much more than a religious designation. It defined everything about them, including how they viewed both themselves and the world around them. The label underscored their love for a crucified Messiah along with their willingness to follow Him no matter the cost. It told of the wholesale transformation God had produced in their hearts, and witnessed to the fact that they had been made completely new in Him. They had died to their old way of life, having been born again into the family of God. *Christian* was not simply a title, but an entirely new way of thinking—one that had serious implications for how they lived—and ultimately how they died. (MacArthur, *Slave*, 9)

The transforming work of Christ decisively and completely reoriented the lives of the Thessalonians. So apparent was their break from past pursuits that others took note of this transformation (1:9).

Genuine Conversion Changes Our Reflection (1 Thess 1:10)

One of my best friends once told me that that I should visit a cemetery before making all major life decisions. His rationale was that such an exercise would remind me that life is short and eternity is long. The Thessalonians learned from Paul that **the Christian should view present circumstances in the light of eternal promises**. During Paul's short stay in Thessalonica, he taught the people extensively about the return of Christ (2 Thess 2:5). He clearly wanted them to live their lives in light of the imminent return of the Lord and their promised future with Him. As we will see later, Paul devoted considerable attention to addressing the Thessalonians' lingering questions about eschatological matters. His goal in teaching them about Christ's return was always more pastoral than theological. His purpose was to build within them an expectant hope for the future. He also wanted to reassure them that despite their present persecution, God's "coming wrath" was not something to be feared. Rather, they could be confident and hopeful about their future and pursue their walk with Christ with an expectant anticipation of His return. When everyone else was looking around in confusion, Paul wanted them to be looking up in anticipation. That is the "blessed hope" of the Christian life (Titus 2:13).

A Dynamic Church
1 THESSALONIANS 1:2-3

There are two great independence days in the lives of Christians: the day that you follow Jesus Christ and are set free from the penalty of sin, and the day that you understand the present implications of your salvation. From the moment of a believer's salvation, God begins the process of transformation. As you surrender to God, He transforms your mind and teaches you His will (Rom 12:1-2). As you grasp His will, you begin to understand better His purpose for your life. But you will never understand His purposes for you until you completely surrender your life to Him.

How then does this relate to the present passage? Remember that the letter begins with an expression of Paul's thankfulness (v. 2). Why was he so thankful? The Thessalonians had experienced their independence days. First, they were God's elect and the beneficiaries of His grace and peace (1:1,4). Second, they understood His will and were living out their faith for God's honor and glory.

A Working Faith (1 Thess 1:3a)

God is not as interested in what we do for a living as He is in how we live in the midst of the work He is doing. The Thessalonians had a faith that was working. The visible manifestation of their inward transformation was a faith that was alive. Three times in this passage Paul points to their visible faith as proof of their genuine conversion: "The Lord's message rang out from you," "your faith in God has gone out," and "they themselves report" (1:8-9). They had a faith that showed. Although their active faith was not necessary *for* their salvation, it was most assuredly a testimony *to* their salvation. As he would later teach the Ephesians, God saves for the purpose of fulfilling His purposes through the way we are working (Eph 2:8-9). When God's people grasp this truth their lives are changed and their churches can be transformed.

A Laboring Love (1 Thess 1:3b)

According to Jesus, the disciples' genuine love for one another would send to the world a message that they were His disciples (John 13:35). The Thessalonians had a deep, genuine love for one another. This kind of love was greater than mere sentimentality. Paul emphasizes this point by using the Greek word *kopos* to refer to the manifestation of their love. This word refers to laboring to the point of weariness, sweat, or fatigue (Rienecker and Rogers, *Linguistic Key*, 586). Genuine love is willing to go the distance, even to the point of exhaustion and weariness. It is a love that knows no limits and finds its ultimate source in the love of God (Rom 5:8). This explains why the apostle John implores you and me to "love one another, because love is from God, and everyone who loves has been born of God and knows God" (1 John 4:7). Paul unpacks the essence of love by showing how its absence nullifies even the greatest of Christian virtues:

> *If I speak human or angelic languages but do not have love, I am a sounding gong or a clanging cymbal. If I have the gift of prophecy and*

understand all mysteries and all knowledge, and if I have all faith so that I can move mountains but do not have love, I am nothing. And if I donate all my goods to feed the poor, and if I give my body in order to boast but do not have love, I gain nothing. (1 Cor 13:1-3)

Where there is no love it does not matter what we say, it does not matter what we know, and it does not matter what we do. That is how vital love is to the Christian faith.

An Enduring Hope (1 Thess 1:3c)

Paul commended the Thessalonians for their expectant and patient hope in Christ's appearing from heaven (v. 10). Later in the letter (and in 2 Thessalonians) he will address this theme in much greater detail. The hope that Paul mentions in verse 3 is a hope of endurance and perseverance. The Thessalonians had an unshakable confidence in the Lord regardless of their circumstances. They needed this kind of enduring hope in view of their adversity. As Barclay so aptly puts it, "A man can endure anything as long as he has hope, for then he is walking not to the night, but to the dawn" (Barclay, *Letters*, 218).

Indeed, times were tough for this young church. Satan knew the threat that this church posed to his kingdom, and he was doing everything possible to keep it from succeeding. A successful church plant in this city would open the door for rapid spread of the gospel throughout the Roman Empire. And just as Satan knew the threat of the Thessalonian church, you can be sure that he also knows the threat that all churches pose to his kingdom. He will do everything possible to hinder their success as well. When you declare your allegiance to Jesus Christ, you declare war on hell. When you declare war on hell, hell puts up a fight. If you don't like the sight of blood, you better stay out of the ministry. When I arrived at my first pastorate, I thought that the people would love me if I just loved them and preached the Bible. Less than three months into my ministry I learned otherwise. From lawsuits, false accusations, and personal attacks, I learned quickly that ministry was war. Without the "hope" of my calling, I would not still be in ministry today. This hope, as Leon Morris asserts, "is not a quiet, passive resignation, but an active constancy in the face of difficulties" (Morris, *Epistles of Paul*, 42). You don't curl up in the corner and "hope" that things will get better. You press on with confidence in the living God, the assurance of your salvation, and the certainty of your future in Christ.

A Contagious Church
1 THESSALONIANS 1:8-9

Think for a moment about how many churches you pass every day. What do you know about those churches? I am guessing that all you know about most of them is what you see from the outside. This is most unfortunate because God's plan for the church is not for people on the outside to wonder what's happening on the inside. **His plan for the church is for the people on the inside to take the message to those on the outside. The great commission is not an invitation for outsiders to come and hear but for the church to "go and tell"** (Matt 28:19-20). When Jesus ascended into heaven and the perplexed disciples gazed into the sky, the angel quizzically asked them, "Why do you stand looking up into Heaven?" (Acts 1:11). The implication of these words was a strong message to stop standing around. Jesus is coming back; it's time to get busy. People who grasp what it means to follow Christ are not content to stand around and do nothing. They know that their time is short. They want to make a difference. A contagious church recognizes that there is work to be done, and its people get busy with doing it. The Thessalonians have this kind of contagious enthusiasm.

Contagious in Our Proclamation (1 Thess 1:8)

Though a considerable distance from Athens, Thessalonica was not without its own philosophers and philosophies. To satisfy their religious cravings, the Thessalonians had much from which to choose—whether it be the synagogue, a temple, or an idol. But as Paul makes clear, the gospel was not just one philosophy among many. God was not just another god amid the gods of the Romans. The gospel of Jesus Christ was the "Lord's message" because it came from the one true God. The Thessalonians therefore had not imbibed the musings of some new philosopher. No, they had received a message of divine revelation from God Himself. The power of this message set them free from their sin and from their idols. Their natural response was to live it and to proclaim it. They could not be silent about the message that transformed their lives. All who are in Christ know from personal experience how profoundly life-changing the gospel message is. And we can recall how we longed to experience it from the first time we truly heard it with our hearts. Like the disciples who first witnessed the resurrection of Christ, we know what it is like to have our "hearts ablaze" as the Holy Spirit opens our eyes to understand the Scriptures (Luke 24:32).

Contagious in Our Passion (1 Thess 1:8-9)

Such good news needed to be shared. So from the Thessalonians, "the Lord's message rang out." It thundered forth with great intensity. If the Thessalonians had a church building, people would not be able to pass by and wonder what was going on inside. They could hear it for themselves. The gospel was being preached. Their influence was growing in Thessalonica and the regions beyond. People were talking about their message. Their congregation was not just another irrelevant church on the street corner; they were impacting their world. If you have ever been in a church like this, then you know how contagious its spirit can be. And if you have ever been in a church that is not like this, then you know as well how discouraging its attitude can be.

I can vividly remember my high school football coach taping a clipping from the local newspaper on my locker. A line from the article hit me like a laser beam. It said, "All-conference linebacker Mark Howell was ineffective." What? Of all the things that could have been said, that comment hurt the most. You see, while I may have played in the game that night, my presence on the field made no difference. The truth hurt, but it made a big difference in how I played the rest of the season. Here is the big question: When Jesus looks at how you and I "do church," is it possible that He would say that we are ineffective? We may be singing songs and preaching sermons, but are we really making a difference in our world? Is the "Lord's message" thundering forth from our pulpits to our people?

Conclusion

The greatest danger of any organization is to lose sight of its reason for existence. This is especially true for the church. A number of years ago someone posted on the front door of a Washington, DC area church a sign that read, "Going Out of Business." Not long after the sign was posted someone added these words, "We never really knew what our business was."

Though specific numbers are difficult to come by, conservative estimates suggest that between 3,500 and 4,000 churches will close their doors this year. This means that every week more than 70 churches will hang "going out of business" signs on their doors. Without question, such a trend is troubling and puzzling. After all, if the church is the only human institution that Jesus Himself promised to build and to bless, we should rightly expect it not only to survive but also to thrive.

Despite having access to dozens of helpful books, seminars, and conferences touting the latest church planting and missiological strategies, many pastors continue to struggle in leading their churches to grow. Perhaps we would do well to remember that apart from the gospel and apostolic instruction, the Thessalonian Christians had no materials or seminars from which to glean insight into how they should fulfill their calling. Yet, from Paul's own attestation, this church was a model church among the churches of Macedonia and Achaia (1:7).

What was it about this church that made them such an example? Let's recall three characteristics that made this church exceptional.

They were grounded in their relationship with Jesus. Regardless of its ideal location, innovative strategies, or charismatic leader, a church will never be what God intended for it to be if its people are not passionately in love with Jesus Christ and His glorious gospel. Yes, the church may grow in size and number, but unless it is grounded in the gospel, its people will never grow in the grace and knowledge of Jesus Christ (2 Pet 3:18). Millard Erickson is correct when he asserts,

> Because the gospel has been, is, and will always be the way of salvation, the only way, the church must preserve the gospel at all costs. When the gospel is modified, the vitality of the church is lost. The church dies. (Erickson, *Christian Theology*, 1075)

The young Thessalonian church faced many challenges, but one challenge it never faced was concern about whether or not it would survive. Its future was not in question because its mission was not affected by external circumstances. Instead the Thessalonians were motivated by an internal conviction that Jesus Christ was the Son of God who died to set them free (cf. Rom 8:1-2).

They were passionate about their calling. The presence of the gospel in a person's heart will always be demonstrated by the power of the gospel in a person's life. The gospel is not something that we try on like a new pair of shoes. In fact, we don't "try on" the gospel at all. In a very real sense, when we embrace the gospel, the gospel embraces us. Thus the gospel does more than reform our behavior; it transforms our being.

That is why true followers of Jesus do radical things like faithfully enduring persecution (1:6), boldly sharing the gospel (1:8), and completely walk away from idols (1:9).

They were hopeful about their future. As we will see in the remainder of Paul's letter, this church had its hope firmly fixed on the return of Christ (1:9-10; 2:19-20; 3:13; 4:13-18; 5:23-24). Indeed, the Thessalonian believers provide a fitting illustration for how the believer can live faithfully in the present while looking expectantly at the future. John Stott describes how serving and waiting work together:

> "Serving" and "waiting" go together in the experience of converted people. . . . In Christian terms "serving" is getting busy for Christ on earth, while "waiting" is looking for Christ to come from heaven. Yet these two are not incompatible. On the contrary, each balances the other. On the one hand, however hard we work and serve, there are limits to what we can accomplish. We can only improve society; we cannot perfect it. We shall never build utopia on earth. For that we have to wait for Christ to come. . . . On the other hand, although we must look expectantly for the coming of Christ, we have no liberty to wait in idleness, with arms folded and eyes closed, indifferent to the needs of the world around us. Instead, we must work even while we wait, for we are called to serve the living and true God.
>
> Thus working and waiting go together. In combination they will deliver us both from the presumption which thinks we can do everything and from the pessimism which thinks we can do nothing. (Stott, *Gospel and the End,* 41–42)

Reflect and Discuss

1. Of the three ways in which conversion to Christ changes you, which is most evident in your life?
2. What is the relationship between faith and works in the Christian life?
3. What are some idols to which you cling? How do these idols compete with your loyalty to Christ?
4. Why do so many Christians fail to grasp the significance of what God wants them to do with their lives once they are saved?
5. What does the "work of faith" look like in your life?

6. How can you labor in your love when it comes to your relationship with others in the church? What about those outside of the church?
7. Explain why hope is so important in the Christian life. How does your hope for the future influence how you live today?
8. What was it like the first time that you truly understood the gospel? How did you respond to the message?
9. Why are so many churches ineffective or irrelevant when it comes to impacting their world? What can be done to revitalize them?
10. Are you a contagious Christian? Would others look at your life and be inspired to imitate your devotion to Jesus? How can the faith of the Thessalonians inspire your faith?

Authenticity

1 THESSALONIANS 2:1-12

Main Idea: Authentic Christian leaders will reflect a genuine love for and commitment to the people they have been called to lead.

I. **A Desire to Go the Distance (2:1-2)**
II. **A Commitment to Honor God (2:4,6)**
III. **A Willingness to Be Vulnerable (2:7-12)**
IV. **A Selfless Love for Others (2:3,5)**
V. **A Longing for Another Kingdom (2:12b)**

One evening while having dinner with my family I reached for the pepper grinder only to discover that it was empty. My wife got up from her seat, opened the cabinet and proceeded to refill it. However, instead of using peppercorns she used ground pepper. With a quizzical look on my face I enquired as to the rationale of using ground pepper in a device whose sole reason for existence was to grind pepper. She informed me that her ongoing quest to save money led her to the discovery that peppercorns were much more expensive than ground pepper. She said that she had been refilling the pepper grinder with ground pepper for months and expressed surprise that this was the first time that I had even noticed. You see, I thought that I was getting the real thing, but in reality I was getting a cheap substitute!

Here's a question that every church leader must ask: Are my people getting the real thing from me? When the veneer is stripped away, what do our people really see? Do they see the Wizard of Oz pulling the levers and pushing the buttons of ministry only to discover that all of the activity comes with no reality? Unfortunately, authenticity is a rare trait among leaders.[3] And considering that Jesus was the most authentic person who ever lived, it is unthinkable that any person who claims to

---

[3] A simple web search on "authentic Christianity" will reveal thousands of websites and hundreds of books and articles. It's not limited to Christianity. You'll find information about authentic relationships, authentic marriages, and authentic happiness. Yet, while everyone is talking about authenticity, trying to nail down a universal definition is nearly impossible. It seems as if everyone has his or her own definition. Perhaps even better than a definition is a living example, and Paul's life is just one among many in Scripture.

follow Him would live anything but an authentic life. Whether you look at the life of Jesus, or the lives of Paul, Jeremiah, Amos, or a host of other biblical characters, what you see is what you get. They were real. God expects you and me to be real also. Perhaps no greater example of authenticity and vulnerability can be found than what Paul describes in Philippians 2:

> *Make your own attitude that of Christ Jesus, who, existing in the form of God, did not consider equality with God as something to be used for His own advantage. Instead He emptied Himself by assuming the form of a slave, taking on the likeness of men. And when He had come as a man in His external form, He humbled Himself by becoming obedient to the point of death—even to death on a cross.* (Phil 2:5-8)

Jesus had no personal ambition except to honor His Father. He was even willing to step out of royal glory and into the spotlight of public scrutiny to fulfill the mission for which He came. Regardless of the cost, His agenda was to please His Father.

Such was also the case for the apostle Paul. His life and his ministry were open for inspection, and he was not ashamed of what that inspection would reveal. This truth leaps off of the page in the present passage. Notice how many times Paul challenges the Thessalonians to recall their first-hand experience of how Paul conducted himself among them: "For you yourselves know" (2:1), "as you know" (2:2), "as you know" (2:5), "God is our witness" (2:5), "for you remember" (2:9), "you are witnesses and so is God" (2:10), "as you know" (2:11).

Sometimes there is a great divide between what we think others think about us and what others really think about us. If you truly want to see how authentic your ministry is, then perhaps you would do well to ask the people to whom you minister. Paul provides a fitting example of what it means to be real before your people. Because he had nothing to hide, he was more than willing to allow the facts to speak for themselves. Hiebert makes this point when he writes,

> In refuting these enemy accusations Paul used the method of simply letting the record speak for itself. The facts were still fresh in the memory of the readers. In thus repeatedly asking them to recall what they witnessed, he was letting them judge if the evidence fit in with the charges being made against

them. It was a masterly defense. It proved that the facts needed for the missionaries' vindication were a matter of common knowledge. . . . Such a defense is the best proof of the purity of a preacher's life. (Hiebert, *1 and 2 Thessalonians*, 83)

A Desire to Go the Distance
1 THESSALONIANS 2:1-2

According to John Stott, this passage reveals more about the heart, soul, and emotions of Paul than perhaps any of his other writings. He thus suggests that those who are engaged in full-time ministry will find Paul's words both challenging and encouraging. Stott writes, "No-one who is engaged in any form of pastoral ministry (ordained or lay) can fail to be touched and challenged by what Paul writes here" (Stott, *Gospel and the End*, 45). What Stott points to is Paul's authenticity. He was a man who was willing to go the distance for and with the people he served. The Thessalonians knew this about Paul. And you and I can be sure that our people also know how far we are willing to go for them. You will never lead your church to take any risks for Christ if your people do not first see how committed you are to them and to the gospel that you preach. Clearly a key reason the Thessalonian church was willing to follow Christ despite severe hardship was that they had a pastor who led by example. A simple reading of this passage provides a very personal look at Paul's loyalty to his calling, his churches, and his Savior.

In the face of the many challenges Paul encountered in bringing the gospel to Thessalonica, he wanted these young believers to know that his ministry was not "without result" (literally, "empty or ineffective"). On the contrary, the changed lives of the Thessalonians bore witness to the transforming gospel that Paul brought to them (1:2-3). With passion, courage, and tenacity he and his companions fearlessly preached the gospel to the Thessalonians. There was nothing easy about sharing the gospel in Thessalonica. Paul and his companions "suffered," were "treated outrageously," and faced "great opposition." Yet, despite the hostility, they were "emboldened" by God to share the message courageously.

Courage is a missing ingredient in the lives of many Christians. Because of their fear of personal hardship, they rarely attempt anything bold or risky for Christ. Yet with great risk often comes great reward.

The biblical text is replete with examples of those who were willing to go the distance in pursuing God's calling.

For example, consider the life of Joshua. Upon his anointing as leader of the Israelites, he immediately faced the formidable challenge of crossing a flooded river, conquering an impenetrable city, and leading thousands of helpless people into an unknown land. On top of all of this, he was following in the footsteps of an inimitable leader in Moses. You can only imagine how daunting such a task must have been for an unseasoned leader. Fear could have easily kept him from stepping into a flooded river, marching around an impenetrable city, or speaking God's Word to a stubborn people. But because God called Joshua to go the distance, He exhorted him to fulfill his calling by being "strong and courageous" (Josh 1:6-9). Joshua was emboldened by these words and by God's promise to be with him.

There is also encouragement in looking at the calling of Jeremiah. God informed him that the kings, the people, and even the priests of the land would "fight against" him (Jer 1:19). These are not exactly the most encouraging words to hear about a new calling and assignment. Thus, perhaps sensing his fear, God charges him with these inspiring words: "Do not be afraid of anyone. . . . Do not be intimidated by them" (Jer 1:8,17). This challenge, along with God's promise of ultimate deliverance, gave Jeremiah the desire to go the distance.

Finally, there is the example of the lesser-known prophet Micaiah. When faced with the temptation to compromise God's Word by prophesying only good things concerning Ahab, he fearlessly declared, "As the LORD lives, I will say whatever the LORD says to me" (1 Kgs 22:1-14). Considering that this is the last time we hear from Micaiah in the biblical record, likely those words ultimately sealed his fate (1 Kgs 22:26-28). Micaiah went the distance.

God calls you to have the same kind of commitment to your ministry. To do this you must be willing to accept everything that comes with your calling, including opposition and difficulty. God has not called you to construct half-built towers. He expects you to "calculate the cost" and finish what you start (Luke 14:28). Heed Paul's charge to Timothy: "But as for you, be serious about everything, endure hardship, do the work of an evangelist, *fulfill your ministry*" (2 Tim 4:5; emphasis added).

A Commitment to Honor God
1 THESSALONIANS 2:4,6

W. A. Criswell tells the story of a train master who was responsible for the smooth operation of a busy depot in the heart of a crowded city. A passerby commended him for his obvious display of grace and tact as he juggled his many responsibilities, including answering passenger's queries, giving directions, and maintaining the smooth operation of the depot. "How do you do it?" the passerby asked. "With so many hurried people, disgruntled and angry . . . how do you maintain your composure?" The train master replied, "Why, it is no big deal. I do not have all these people to please. I only have to please just one man." He pointed to an office and to a window on the second floor, and he said, "My master sits in that office, and it is he alone that I have to please" (Criswell, "The Pattern of the Servant of God").

Nothing is more liberating in ministry than to recognize that God is the only One whom you and I must please. Such a conviction not only frees us from the tyranny of people pleasing, but it also emboldens us to speak God's truth with power and conviction. Beale is on target when he asserts,

> In contrast to many today, including some in the church, who gain confidence from the approval ratings of polls, Paul was concerned only about one person's approval—God's. The source of our proclamation should be a heart that is confident before God because God himself knows our heart and that our sole motive is to please him. (Beale, *1–2 Thessalonians*, 67)

Paul wanted the Thessalonians to understand the source of his conviction and boldness. We don't speak "to please men," he writes. We speak to please God "who examines our hearts" (2:4). He was not interested in "glory from people" because God was his "witness" (2:5-6). Paul lived his life for an audience of one.

This conviction has the potential to sober you and to set you free. It is sobering because God "examines our hearts." He knows if you are the real thing or a cheap substitute. He knows the motives behind what you do, and He sees through the excuses of why you do not do what you ought to do. According to Paul, God does not entrust you and me with the gospel if we do not first meet His approval (2:4a). The Greek verb translated "approved" is in the perfect tense, indicating that God's approval is something that began in the past and continues into the present. Thus Paul could preach boldly and courageously, knowing that God's backing and approval was behind the message he proclaimed.

But God not only "approved" you to proclaim the gospel, He also "examines" you as you proclaim the gospel. At the end of verse 4 Paul uses the word "examines" in the present tense to emphasize the ongoing evaluation of God. Stated plainly, God is always looking at your heart. There is not a moment when His eye is not on you (2 Chr 16:9; Prov 15:3; Heb 4:13). Nothing should be more sobering for those entrusted with the gospel than to know that God sees everything. The godly woman Hannah understood this well when she said from her anguished heart, "Do not boast so proudly, or let arrogant words come out of your mouth, for the LORD is a God of knowledge, and *actions are weighed by Him*" (1 Sam 2:3; emphasis added). God does not entrust His gospel to the one whom He does not approve.

That God carefully observes all that we do is not only a cause for reflection, it is also a reason for liberation. Stott drives this home when he says,

> God is a more knowledgeable, impartial and merciful judge that any human being or ecclesiastical court or committee. To be accountable to him is to be delivered from the tyranny of human criticism. (Stott, *Gospel and the End*, 50–51)

How comforting to know that God knows our hearts. Ultimately, what matters most is not what others *think* about you, but what God *knows* about you.

A Willingness to Be Vulnerable
1 THESSALONIANS 2:7-12

Can you think of a more profound way to express your sincere love than by your willingness to share your life with another? One of the greatest joys of my life is getting to share life with my wife and my children. Even on the worst days, I am comforted to know that I am not in this life alone. Whether we laugh together or cry together, we have the joy of getting to experience life together.

Although he had many churches for which he was responsible, Paul treated the Thessalonians as if they were his only church. After spending only a few weeks of ministry with them, they had become precious friends to Paul (v. 8). He had developed a profound love for them and they knew it. In fact, they had become so "dear" to him, that he was more concerned about their needs than he was about his own comfort (v. 9). Though he poured his life into them, he did not expect anything in return. All too often, pastors view their calling with a sense of entitlement. As a preacher and apostle, Paul was entitled to earn his living from the gospel (v. 7; 1 Cor 9:14), but he chose to forfeit this right for the sake of the Thessalonians and for the integrity of his ministry in their city. Thus he did not seek what they could do for him but what he could do for them. This explains why he was so willing to share his life with them. You may choose not to share your heart and life with the people you serve because you expect them to do something for you. **You share your heart and life with those you serve because you endeavor to make their lives better**.

Admittedly, many of us are unwilling to share our lives with our people. Perhaps we have been burned by a past relationship. Or maybe we simply are unwilling to express our vulnerability. But if we desire to connect with those entrusted to our care, then we must be willing to open up and share our lives with them. They need to understand that even their leaders have fears, worries, and struggles. We must never seek to give the impression that we are perfect. One way that we can be real with our people is through the appropriate use of personal illustrations in our preaching and teaching. However, when using personal illustrations you must be careful to share your own shortcomings as well as your victories. It is amazing how people connect with their leaders when they see them as real people who have weaknesses and strengths just as they do. Of course, the life of our Lord is a beautiful example of this vulnerability. The writer of Hebrews explains, "For we do not have a high priest who is unable to sympathize with our weaknesses, but One who has been tested in every way as we are, yet without sin" (Heb 4:15). The only way that Jesus could fully identify with you and me was to come and live among us.

When you begin a relationship with someone, you must be willing to get your hands dirty. Paul speaks of his relationship with the Thessalonians as that of a "father with his own children" (v. 11). You cannot get much more personal than a relationship between a parent and a child. Sometimes your children need your tender words of comfort and encouragement, but other times they need your firm words of warning and correction (v. 12).

Deep and meaningful relationships are at the heart of Christianity. There is no surprise then that Satan's attack in the garden was directed at relationships—our relationship with God and our relationships with one another (Gen 3:1-13). If Satan could persuade Adam and Eve to sneak around behind God's back and steal some fruit from a tree, then perhaps he could persuade you to sneak around behind your spouse's back and cheat on your marriage. Or if he could convince Adam to blame Eve for his disobedience, then perhaps he could also convince us that we are not responsible for our own actions. Satan's approach is to keep us from being real with God, real with each other, and real with ourselves.

Paul and his companions paint a very different picture of how they viewed their relationships. They had nothing to hide from God, and they had nothing to hide from the Thessalonians. Paul makes this clear when he writes, "*You are witnesses, and so is God,* of how devoutly, righteously, and blamelessly we conducted ourselves with you believers" (v. 10; emphasis added). What a powerful statement! In essence Paul is saying, "We have nothing to hide from you and we have nothing to hide from God. Our testimony speaks for itself."

Paul breaks down their lives into three observable areas: devotion, righteousness, and blamelessness.

- They lived "devoutly." That is, they walked with God in such a way that His name, His will, and His kingdom were their first priority (Matt 6:9-10). This commitment is the essence of holiness.
- They lived "righteously." Righteousness points to their conduct. That is, they lived their lives with honesty and integrity, and thus they avoided any appearance of evil.
- They lived "blamelessly." They did not claim to be sinless; they claimed to be blameless. Because they knew that they were targets for their critics, they sought to live their lives above reproach (1 Tim 3:2).

A Selfless Love for Others
1 THESSALONIANS 2:3,5

A cartoon depicting two little sisters rocking on a rocking horse in the family playroom vividly illustrates how many people live their lives. As the two girls rock away, the older looks back at the younger and exclaims, "If one of us would get off this rocking horse, there would be more room for me!" While no one likes a selfish person, all of us are guilty of selfishness at some point in our lives. However, if a relationship with Jesus Christ really does transform people, then one of the first things to go will be our selfishness. What greater display of selfless love can be seen than the sacrifice of Jesus as He died on the cross? Mark captures this selflessness so well when he writes, "The Son of Man did not come to be served, but to *serve*, and to *give* His life—a ransom for many" (Mark 10:45; emphasis added).

God is the ultimate giver. Among many other things, He gives wisdom (1 Kgs 4:29), good gifts (Jas 1:17; Matt 7:11), knowledge (Dan 1:17), gifted leaders to the church (Eph 4:11), and, of course, His greatest gift—Jesus Christ (John 3:16). Children are a reflection of their parents. For that reason, God's children should reflect their Father through their selfless acts of giving.

Paul came to Thessalonica not for what he could get but for what he could give. His motives were pure and his love was selfless. He did not come to Thessalonica to bolster his ego, pad his pockets, or enlist a personal following. He came to bring the free gift of the gospel to the Thessalonians. Yet the city of Thessalonica was full of cult leaders and false teachers who had a very different agenda. Because Paul's message was so countercultural to the spiritual climate of the city, he found himself on the receiving end of slanderous attacks and false accusations. With their empty promises and persuasive speech, the Thessalonian cult leaders and false teachers dangled their bait before the people hoping that they would bite (Matt 7:15; 2 John 1:7; 2 Thess 2:1-3). Their message promised much but delivered little. Many of the people of Thessalonica saw through their religions chicanery and thus knew that these men were in it for the money and not for the people.

As Paul's message began to gain momentum, his critics began to escalate their attacks. Those who opposed his message knew that if they could discredit the messenger, then they could also discredit the message. Though we cannot be certain who these critics were, we do know that they were aggressively seeking to undermine his credibility. Leon Morris suggests that Paul's critics sought to discredit his message by claiming that Paul was just like the rest of the impure, greedy, and unjust false teachers in town (Morris, *Epistles of Paul*, 44).

Paul could not allow such accusations to go unanswered. He replied by denying any intention to "deceive" anyone into receiving his message.

Neither his motives nor the gospel were impure in any way. His goal was not to talk anyone into becoming a follower of Christ. "For we are not like the many who market God's message for profit," he would later tell the Corinthians. "On the contrary, we speak with sincerity in Christ, as from God and before God" (2 Cor 2:17). He wanted the Thessalonians to know that the gospel was not something to be bartered or bought. It was a gift to be received. Paul's concern was not for his own self interest, but the Thessalonians' best interests.

A Longing for Another Kingdom
1 THESSALONIANS 2:12B

In 1836 Thomas R. Taylor penned these profound words:

> I'm but a stranger here, Heaven is my home;
> Earth is a desert drear, Heaven is my home;
> Danger and sorrow stand Round me on every hand;
> Heaven is my fatherland, Heaven is my home. (Taylor, "I'm But a Stranger Here," *The Lutheran Hymnal*)

His words echo the writer of Hebrews when he wrote,

> *These all died in faith without having received the promises, but they saw them from a distance, greeted them, and confessed that* they were foreigners and temporary residents on the earth. *Now those who say such things make it clear that they are seeking a homeland. If they were thinking about where they came from, they would have had an opportunity to return. But* they now desire a better place—a heavenly one. *Therefore God is not ashamed to be called their God, for* He has prepared a city for them. (Heb 11:13-16; emphasis added)

This great host of Old Testament saints reveals a most significant truth about the life of faith—this world is not our home. The person who understands this truth leads a very different kind of life. Paul closes this passage by disclosing his desire for the Thessalonians. Above all, he wanted them to "walk worthy of God." God does not have one standard for us on earth and another standard for those in heaven. His standard is for those who belong to Him to walk in holiness. "So you must be holy because I am holy," declares the Lord (Lev 11:45; cf. 1 Pet 1:15-16). Although we live in an earthly kingdom, we serve a heavenly King. The day is coming when we will enter our heavenly kingdom, behold the glory of our heavenly King, and enjoy living in His presence forever. Until that day arrives, may there be nothing that hinders us from walking in a manner worthy of that wonderful promise. What is the chief end of man? "Man's chief end is to glorify God, and to enjoy him forever" (The Westminster Shorter Catechism, 1647).

Conclusion

In his book *Empowered Leaders: Ten Principles of Christian Leadership*, Hans Finzel makes the following statement:

> Servant leaders must be willing to live with submission on many levels: submission to authority, submission to God the Father, submission to one's spouse, submission to the principles of wise living, and submission to one's obligations. Though conventional wisdom says everyone should submit to their leaders, the real truth is that leaders, to be effective, must learn to submit. (Finzel, *Empowered Leaders*, 40–41)

The Thessalonian Christians knew that Paul was no self-serving leader. He shared his heart with them and rolled up his sleeves and served alongside them. He doubtlessly laughed with them, cried with them, corrected them, and comforted them. He was a pastor to his people, and they knew it. That is why they loved him so dearly (3:6). What a powerful reminder to all who have been called to serve as pastor to God's people. You cannot love your people if you do not spend time with your people. And your people will never fully embrace your leadership if they suspect that you have no desire to spend time with them. To be sure, with authenticity comes vulnerability. But why would any pastor who has nothing to hide be reluctant to share his heart and his life with his people? John Stott is on target when he writes,

> Happy are those Christian leaders today, who hate hypocrisy and love integrity, who have nothing to conceal or be ashamed of, who are well known for who and what they are, and who are able to appeal without fear to God and the public as their witnesses! (Stott, *Gospel and the End*, 47)

In sum, to serve and lead with authenticity requires you to guard diligently two areas of your life: your relationship with God and your motive for ministry. Regardless of what others may say about you, what matters most is what God knows about you. **You will only be as authentic with your people in public as you are in your relationship with God in private**. No pastor or leader can confidently lead his people if he is uncertain that God is leading him. When the inevitable bullets of criticism begin to fly, may you find your refuge in the certainty of your calling and the assurance that God knows the integrity of your heart (2:5).

Reflect and Discuss

1. Why do many people view Christians as phony or fake?
2. How did Paul challenge the Thessalonians to examine the integrity of his life? What did they discover?
3. Do people in your church or small group see you as a leader who is willing to go the distance for Christ? How does your life reflect this kind of commitment?
4. How did Paul go the distance for the Thessalonians?
5. Are you honestly motivated by a desire to please people or to please God? What keeps you from a life of total obedience?
6. Do you share your life with people in your church? What can you do to get to know others better? What can you do to let others get to know you better?
7. What does it mean when Paul says that God "examines" our hearts?
8. How is it liberating to know that God knows everything about your life?
9. What are some ways that pastors can be real in the presence of their people?
10. How did Paul's critics seek to discredit his message?

A Welcome Word

1 THESSALONIANS 2:13-16

Main Idea: God's Word transforms the lives of those who welcome it.

I. **God Speaks (2:13-14).**
   A. The Bible is God's Word.
   B. The Bible is God's Word about Jesus (2:13).
II. **People Respond (2:13).**
   A. We receive the Word intellectually.
   B. We welcome the Word internally.
III. **The Word Transforms (2:14-16).**
   A. The Word transforms our affection (2:14).
   B. The Word transforms our direction (2:14-15).

In his essay "Recent Developments about the Doctrine of Scripture," D. A. Carson warned of the dangers of the diminishing authority of Scripture among evangelicals. Although he penned these words nearly 30 years ago, they are as relevant today as when they were first written. They provide a stern warning to those who claim to hold a high view of Scripture but fail to trust completely in its sufficiency and its authority. Carson writes,

> A high view of Scripture is of little value to us if we do not enthusiastically embrace the Scripture's authority. But today we multiply the means for circumventing or dissipating that authority. I am not here speaking of those who formally deny the Scripture's authority: it is only to be expected that they should avoid the hard sayings and uncomfortable truths. But those of us who uphold the thorough truthfulness of God's Word have no excuse. . . . Even some of us who would never dream of formally disentangling some parts of the Bible from the rest and declaring them less authoritative than other parts can by exegetical ingenuity get the Scriptures to say just about whatever we want—and this we thunder to the age as if it were a prophetic word, when it is little more than the message of the age bounced off Holy Scripture. To our shame, we have

> hungered to be masters of the Word much more than we have
> hungered to be mastered by it. (Carson, *Collected Writings*,
> 106–9)

A diminishing view of scriptural authority in the pulpit invariably affects those sitting in the pews. What a preacher believes about the Bible will determine how he preaches the Bible, and how he preaches the Bible will influence how his church responds to what the Bible says. Thus, to be transformed by Scripture you must trust completely in the authority of Scripture. According to Carson, herein lies the problem in the church. Alarmingly, churches are unaffected by the very truth that they claim to believe. Carson continues:

> The pervasiveness of the problem erupts in the "Christian"
> merchant whose faith has no bearing on the integrity of his or
> her dealings, or in the way material possessions are assessed.
> It is reflected in an accelerating divorce rate in Christian
> homes and among the clergy themselves—with little sense
> of shame and no entailment in their "ministries." It is seen
> in its most pathetic garb when considerable exegetical skill
> goes into proving, say, that the Bible condemns promiscuous
> homosexuality but not homosexuality itself. . . . It finds
> new lease when popular Evangelicals publicly abandon any
> mention of "sin"—allegedly on the ground that the term no
> longer "communicates"—without recognizing that adjacent
> truths (e.g., those dealing with the Fall, the law of God, the
> nature of transgression, the wrath of God, and even the
> gracious atonement itself) undergo telling transformation.
> While I fear that Evangelicalism is heading for another
> severe conflict on the doctrine of Scripture, and while it is
> necessary to face these impending debates with humility
> and courage, what is far more alarming is the diminishing
> authority of the Scriptures in the churches. This is taking
> place not only among those who depreciate the consistent
> truthfulness of Scripture but also (if for different reasons)
> among those who most vociferously defend it. To some extent
> we are all part of the problem; and perhaps we can do most to
> salvage something of value from the growing fragmentation
> by pledging ourselves in repentance and faith to learning
> and obeying God's most holy Word. Then we shall also be

reminded that the challenge to preserve and articulate a fully self-consistent and orthodox doctrine of Scripture cannot be met by intellectual powers alone, but only on our knees and by the power of God. (Carson, *Collected Writings*, 106–9)

The Thessalonian Christians portray the kind of response to God's Word that Carson seeks. When they heard Paul's message, they recognized that he was speaking divine truth, and with their reception of this truth came a willing response to submit to its authority. Paul expresses his gratitude for their reception of his message:

> *This is why we constantly thank God, because when you received the message about God that you heard from us, you welcomed it not as a human message, but as it truly is, the message of God, which also works effectively in you believers.* (2:13)

Wrapped up in this powerful statement are three important truths: God speaks; we must respond to what He says; and His word transforms those who receive it.

God Speaks
1 THESSALONIANS 2:13-14

Today it seems that everyone is looking for a new vision. Football coaches cast a vision for their team's upcoming season. The CEO sets forth a vision for his company's approaching fiscal year. The President lays out a vision for the country in the State of the Union Address. Even a pastor casts the vision for his church. Given all the talk about vision, perhaps an important question is, What is God's vision for His church?

God's vision for His church is not new. In fact, His vision for the church is more than two thousand years old. You don't have to call a meeting or attend a conference to develop a vision for the church. To discover God's vision for His church, you simply need to read Jesus' words in Matthew 16:18. He states, "On this rock I will build My church, and the forces of Hades will not overpower it." God's vision for His church is wrapped up in three truths. First, it is grounded in a confession. Peter's confession that Jesus is the Son of God is the foundation on which the church is built (Matt 16:16). Second, it is backed up by a promise. Jesus promises to "build" His church. Third, it is guaranteed in its success. Not even hell itself can thwart God's ultimate purpose for His church.

The church then is established on Jesus, it is being built by Jesus, and its future is guaranteed because of the work of Jesus. Thus the vision for God's church must be centered on the proclamation of the gospel of Jesus Christ. We don't discover God's vision by "brilliance of speech" or creative "wisdom"; we fulfill His vision by preaching "Jesus Christ and Him crucified" (1 Cor 2:1-5). There should be great hope in this for those of us who lack creativity. God is not interested in how creative you are; He is interested in how faithful you are. And your faithfulness is reflected in the consistent, passionate proclamation of God's Word.

Paul's message in Thessalonica was not creative, but it was powerful. It was not his own, it was God's. When God gives you a word, the only fitting response is to proclaim it. When it's proclaimed, it does its work. Your responsibility is to deliver it just as He gave it to you. John MacArthur said, "the preacher is not a chef; he's a waiter. God doesn't want you to make the meal; He just wants you to deliver it to the table without messing it up" ("Principles"). How true that statement is. God merely calls you to deliver His message. It is up to Him and the power of His Word to "effectively" accomplish its purpose in those who believe.

The Bible Is God's Word

Much as the modern world today, Thessalonica was awash in a sea of religious pluralism. A city with such cultural diversity was sure to be the breeding ground for religious and philosophical speculation. The Thessalonians had doubtlessly seen and heard it all. In fact, in verse 13 Paul must set his message apart from all of the rest by declaring that it was "a message of God" and "a message about God" (2:13). These descriptions imply two truths about Paul's message. First, God was speaking and Paul was His mouthpiece. By the Holy Spirit's inspiration, Paul's message was God's message (2 Pet 1:20-21). Second, Paul's message was not only a message *from* God but it was also a message *about* God. In other words, the God who speaks was making Himself known. And, as the writer of Hebrews made clear, God's ultimate revelation of Himself is through His Son (Heb 1:1-2).

The declaration that "God has spoken" through His Son has serious implications for every human being. C. S. Lewis famously said, "Christianity is a statement which, if false, is of *no* importance, and, if true, of infinite importance. The one thing it cannot be is moderately important" (*God in the Dock*, 101). The writer of Hebrews warns of the serious consequences of ignoring God's message:

We must, therefore, pay even more attention to what we have heard, so that we will not drift away. For if the message spoken through angels was legally binding and every transgression and disobedience received a just punishment, how will we escape if we neglect such a great salvation? (Heb 2:1-3)

Perhaps you can see a little more clearly why Paul was so thankful for the reception of and response to his message by the Thessalonians.

At this point clarification is important. When speaking of God's Word three theological terms are helpful: *revelation, inspiration,* and *illumination.*

Revelation. Simply stated, revelation is God's Word to us. It comes in two forms: general revelation (the created order) and special revelation (the written Word). Both general revelation and special revelation are clearly presented in Psalm 19. Concerning general revelation, David declared, "The heavens declare the glory of God, and the sky proclaims the work of His hands" (Ps 19:1). With reference to special revelation, the psalmist asserts, "The instruction of the Lord is perfect, renewing one's life; the testimony of the Lord is trustworthy, making the inexperienced wise" (Ps 19:7). General revelation declares that there is a God; special revelation tells you how you can know this God. General revelation draws your eyes to the heavens, and special revelation draws your eyes to the Scriptures.

Inspiration. Inspiration and revelation are closely related with a slight distinction. Revelation is God's Word to the biblical authors; inspiration is God's Word from the biblical authors to the written page. Stated another way, revelation addresses the origin of God's truth (God Himself), and inspiration addresses the receiving and recording of God's truth (God through human beings). "All Scripture is inspired by God" (2 Tim 3:16) and thus originates with God Himself. When divinely inspired biblical authors penned their words, they were writing the "God-breathed" Scriptures. The question then is, How can we trust fallible human beings to record infallible truth? The answer lies in God's personal intervention, which came through inspiration. Peter's words are profound: "No prophecy ever came by the will of man; instead, men spoke from God as they were *moved* by the *Holy Spirit*" (2 Pet 1:21; emphasis added). By supernatural means, the Holy Spirit "moved" (lit., "carried along") the biblical writers so that, through their own unique styles of writing, the words they recorded were the exact words of God.

One additional point of clarification must be noted. One can often hear people speaking about receiving a new "revelation" from God. The lyrics of a popular Christian song, for instance, implore God to give us a "revelation" to guide us through life's confusion (cf. Third Day, "Revelation"). While I recognize the intent of the song is to seek God's guidance to navigate life's difficulties, to speak of God giving us a revelation implies that we need God to give us a new word. The fact is God has already given us a word. Jude describes this word for us when he writes, "Although I was eager to write you about the salvation we share, I found it necessary to write and exhort you to contend for *the faith* that was *delivered* to the saints *once for all*" (Jude 3; emphasis added). The definite article preceding "faith" points to an objective body of truth. God Himself delivered this faith to us.

Because he received a revelation from the Lord, Paul could unequivocally say to the Thessalonians that his message was God's message (2:13). God revealed His Word to Paul, and by the Spirit's power he preached that message to them. Later, by the Spirit's inspiration, Paul would write both epistles. Thus, through Paul's Spirit-inspired preaching and writing, God ensured that we have a reliable written record of His Word.

Illumination. The sole criterion for evaluating any new teaching or new idea that comes into the church is not "God told me this," but "What does the Bible say?" George Lawlor makes this point well:

> The Christian faith is unchangeable, which is not to say
> that men and women of every generation do not need to
> find it, experience it, and live it; but it does mean that every
> new doctrine that arises, even though its legitimacy may be
> plausibly asserted, is a false doctrine. All claims to convey some
> additional revelation to that which has been given by God
> in this body of truth are false claims and must be rejected.
> (Lawlor, *Jude*, 45)

To be sure, you must pray for God's guidance and seek His direction (Exod 33:12-16; Ps 24:4-5; Jas 1:5). But your prayers should also be directed toward asking God to enlighten the perception of our minds so that you and I might grasp what He has already revealed in His Word (Eph 1:18-21). God has given to us His Spirit so that we might understand His Word. Without the Spirit's enablement, we will never comprehend God's truth. Jesus said, "When the Spirit of truth comes, He will guide you into all the truth" (John 16:13). Paul drives this point home in 1 Corinthians 2:12: "Now we have not received the spirit of the world, but the Spirit who comes from God, so that we may understand what has been freely given to us by God."

In sum, if we ever desire to know anything about God, then He must not only make Himself known, but He must also open our eyes to see Him. Paul could rejoice in the Thessalonians' reception of the message because He knew that God was at work in their hearts. What an amazing privilege it is for those of us who preach to see firsthand the power of God's Word at work in people's hearts.

The Bible Is God's Word about Jesus (1 Thess 2:13)

The central person and theme of God's revelation is Jesus Christ. His glorious gospel is the "scarlet thread of redemption" that runs throughout the entire Bible.[4] Clearly, Paul did not have a copy of the New Testament to share with the Thessalonians (he was writing it!). So to communicate the gospel message he reasoned, explained, and showed from the Old Testament Scriptures that, as the Messiah, Jesus was God's gift of redemption to a fallen world (Acts 17:1-3). The writer of Hebrews identifies the Bible's central theme when he writes,

> Long ago God spoke to the fathers by the prophets at different times and in different ways. In these last days, He has spoken to us by His Son. . . . [He has made] purification of sins. (Heb 1:1-3)

Now admittedly not every passage of Scripture speaks specifically of Jesus. However the central focus of the Bible is the person and work of Jesus Christ. This has significant implications for preaching the Word. Bryan Chapell shows the importance of seeing the grace of Jesus Christ in every biblical text, including the Old Testament, used by the preacher:

> The question to ask is: "Where is grace evident in the passage?" "How is God revealing His provision for humanity of a rescue that they cannot provide for themselves?" Somewhere that is going to be in the text. God is saying, "I am providing what these people cannot provide for themselves. . . ." And in that sense, a grace principle is being shown that we can say

---

[4] This image comes from a sermon delivered by W. A. Criswell on December 31, 1961.

has its fullest revelation in what Christ has done. Sometimes people fear that this is doing eisegesis, that this is imposing the New Testament on the Old, and I simply reply, "I live on this side of the cross. I know where the story goes." So, for me to say, "Here God is showing the seed of His grace in order for me to understand what the full bloom will be," is okay to do. I can present the revelation of what grace is here, showing that it has its fullest representation in Christ because I know Christ has come. (Robinson, "Q&A with Bryan Chapell on Christ-centered Preaching")

Thus a commitment to expository preaching will also be a commitment to evangelistic preaching. This conclusion is not to suggest that every expository sermon will be evangelistic. It does suggest, however, that every expository sermon will ultimately point people to the Lord Jesus Christ.

People Respond
1 THESSALONIANS 2:13

If the Bible is the Word of God, then we must acknowledge three things: it's true and timeless, it transforms, and it can be trusted. The Bible affirms all three: Concerning its truthfulness, David says that God's law is "perfect" (Ps 19:7). Isaiah declares that it is timeless. Flowers wilt and grass dies, but "the word of our God remains forever" (Isa 40:8). Peter points to its transforming work. He says that we "have been born again—not of perishable seed but of imperishable—through the living and enduring word of God" (1 Pet 1:23). The psalmist says it can be trusted as "a lamp for my feet and a light on my path" (Ps 119:105).

The Thessalonians longed for a word in which they could believe. In their city, talk was abundant and cheap. The empty rhetoric of the cult leaders and false teachers was powerless to transform their hearts. When they heard Paul's message they were drawn to it. They heard it, they understood it, and then they gladly welcomed the Word into their lives.

We Receive the Word Intellectually

They received the Word as not just another human message. The word *received* carries the idea of objective acceptance. When they heard the message, they connected with it intellectually. It made sense.

One of the best ways to deal with objections to the gospel is to preclude them. As wise preachers, you will prepare your messages with your audience in mind. While the text must always shape the message, knowing your audience helps you to explain the passage adequately and illustrate it appropriately. Paul never altered his message, but he did vary his approach in preaching his message.[5] For example, when he was at the synagogue in Antioch he appealed to intellectual Jews by talking *history* (Acts 13:16-21). When he was in the marketplace in Athens he quoted well-known poets by talking *philosophy* (Acts 17:22-31). In the rural "backwoods" of Lystra he pointed around at the world and talked *nature* (Acts 14:15-17). Regardless of where he preached, his aim was to tear down any barriers that would prevent an honest hearing of the gospel.

Luke describes Paul's arrival in Thessalonica: he "reasoned with them from the Scriptures" (Acts 17:2). He dialogued (Gk *dialegomai*) with the Jews about the gospel. Luke does not give specifics about this dialogue, but from what is known about his preaching, you get an idea of his approach. He did not take the "silver bullet" approach where the message only travels in one direction. Paul often began his preaching in the synagogue because it provided fertile ground for an open give-and-take about the gospel. He endeavored to engage people with the message.

We Welcome the Word Internally

Most of us know that there is a difference between hearing something and heeding something. We may know intellectually what we should do, but that knowledge never translates into action. Knowing what to do and not doing it can be dangerous. James even goes as far as to say that "it is a sin for the person who knows to do what is good and doesn't do it" (Jas 4:17). Despite knowing the dangers of not doing the right thing, we may find ourselves repeatedly doing the wrong thing. For instance, we drive and text even though we know the dangers involved. Or we have an extramarital affair, knowing beforehand that sexual immorality destroys marriages and ruins lives. We know from personal experience that receiving the right message is only the first part of the equation; doing something about it is the other part.

---

[5] For a helpful look at Paul's preaching style and approach, see William Barclay, "A Comparison."

The Thessalonians got the message, but then the message got them. They not only received the word, they also "welcomed" the word. The objective message that challenged their thinking also changed their hearts and transformed their living. When you move from an intellectual grasp of the truth to an internal reception of the truth, your life will be radically changed. This happened in Thessalonica. The entire first chapter of 1 Thessalonians paints a vivid picture of how the gospel can transform a people and influence a city. As Hiebert so aptly puts it, "No humanly contrived message can produce such results" (Hiebert, *1 and 2 Thessalonians*, 115).

When you embrace God's Word internally, it "works effectively" in you. It accomplishes its purpose. God's Word has the power to accomplish what no human message could ever do—it can renew one's life (Ps 19:7). However, the best that any man-made system can do is to provide empty promises. The allurements of sin and the deceptiveness of religion invariably lead you down a dead-end street. Many years ago, Dr. R. G. Lee told the story of a young man called the "Chief of the Kangaroo Court." Lee's extensive radio ministry carried his sermons into thousands of homes. As you can imagine, he developed a large following of critics who would regularly send him letters of insult and criticism. Many of the letters were signed by the same individual—"The Chief of the Kangaroo Court." Whoever this individual was, he was not fond of either Dr. Lee or the message he proclaimed. One night Dr. Lee received a telephone call from a local hospital requesting that he come quickly to visit a dying young man who had requested his presence. Inquiring as to who this young man was, the nurse replied, "He told me to tell you that he is the 'Chief of the Kangaroo Court.'" When Dr. Lee arrived in the young man's hospital room, it was apparent that the young man was going to die. Dr. Lee asked him why he requested for him to come. The young man sat up in his hospital bed and exclaimed, "I sent for you because I know you go up and down the land and talk to many young people. And I want you to tell 'em, and tell 'em every chance you get, that the Devil pays only in counterfeit money" (Lee, "Payday Someday").

That story illustrates perfectly the bankruptcy of this world's system, including its philosophies and religious practices. This is why the gospel is so countercultural. It exposes the hypocrisy and emptiness of every man-made attempt to find fulfillment, meaning, and purpose apart from God. We can see now why the Thessalonians were drawn to the gospel. It was so dramatically different from every other message that they had heard. Concerning this, John Phillips writes,

> When Paul preached, the Thessalonians recognized the voice of authority with which he spoke. They heard, recognized, and believed the Word of God. . . . They received it as such without cavil and without question. Nobody had ever spoken to them like that. They had heard the priests of the various pagan religions. They had heard the oracles speak in tongues with the voice of demons. They had heard the rabbis. But Paul, like Jesus, spoke with authority and not as the scribes. When He spoke, they heard, recognized, and understood for the first time in their lives, the Spirit-inspired, God-breathed Word. (Phillips, *Exploring 1 and 2 Thessalonians*, 64)

The Word Transforms
1 THESSALONIANS 2:14-16

Read verse 14 very carefully and allow it to soak in. Paul writes, *"For you, brothers, became* imitators of God's churches in Christ Jesus that are in Judea" (2:14; emphasis added). Did you catch what Paul just said? He said that they *became* imitators of the churches in Judea. Something happened to them. When they followed Christ, their lives changed. No one had to teach them the importance of church membership. They immediately identified with the people of God. This was no small thing. As you will see in what follows, to identify with God's churches in Judea was to identify with their suffering. The Thessalonians were willing to go the distance for Christ, even if it meant persecution, pain, and suffering. The only possible explanation for such a transformation was the power of God at work in them.

The Word Transforms Our Affection (1 Thess 2:14)

Why would Paul commend the Thessalonians for becoming "imitators" of the Judean churches? A little background will help to answer this question. The Judean Christians were the object of intense persecution and suffering. Much of this persecution began as a result of Paul's intense hatred of Christians prior to his conversion (Acts 8:1-3). However, even after Paul was out of the picture, the persecution did not end (Acts 12:1-4). Although there is little insight into the exact extent of the persecution to which Paul referred, we can be certain that it existed. Of course, Jesus warned his disciples that this would come to pass (John 15:18-25). Now that the Thessalonians had declared their loyalty to Jesus, they too had become objects of hatred and persecution. But why would Paul commend them for this? The answer is quite simple: the Thessalonians were willing to suffer for Christ. Jesus changed their affections. Like Paul, they no longer counted their life to be of any value to themselves (Acts 20:24; Phil 3:7-8). Followers of Christ do "not love their lives in the face of death" (Rev 12:11).

A fitting illustration of how Jesus changes our affections is found in chapters 11 and 12 of Luke's Gospel. Jesus had just called out the Pharisees for their hypocrisy. Like stealthy hunters after their prey, the irritated Pharisees had set a trap to catch Him (Luke 11:54). The stakes were high and the intensity was escalating. Sensing the disciples' growing concern for their own safety, Jesus repeatedly tells them not to fear.[6] "Don't fear those who kill the body, and after that can do nothing more," Jesus said. "Indeed the hairs on your head are all counted. Don't be afraid; you are worth more than many sparrows!" (Luke 12:4,7). He then proceeds to tell them that their security is not in their rhetorical ability (Luke 12:11), the amount of money in their wallets (Luke 12:15), how much food is in their pantries, how many clothes are in their closets (Luke 12:22-23), or how much money they have in the bank (Luke 12:33-34). Jesus wants His disciples to recognize that the affections of God's people are strikingly different from those of the Gentile world. Instead of seeking earthly stuff, they should be seeking a heavenly kingdom.

The Word Transforms Our Direction (1 Thess 2:15-16)

Paul did not mince words in his disdain for the Jewish nation's vitriol for Jesus. Compared to the commendation he gave to the Thessalonian Christians, his tone is noticeably different when he describes the Jews as the ones

> who killed both the Lord Jesus and the prophets and persecuted us; they displease God and are hostile to everyone, hindering us from speaking to the Gentiles so that they may be saved. As a result, they are always

---

[6] No less than six times in Luke 12, Jesus tells them not to fear, worry, or be anxious. See vv. 4,7,11,22,29,32.

completing the number of their sins, and wrath has overtaken them at last. (2:15-16)

For him there is no doubt that the Jewish people were ultimately behind the death of Christ (see Luke 23:1-25). Paul's harsh words, however, must be viewed in the larger context of his ultimate view of the Jewish people (see Romans 9–11). On one hand, he knows that their judgment is just (1 Thess 2:16). Yet on the other hand, he longs for their salvation (Rom 10:1). No other nation was exposed to the light of the gospel like the Jewish nation. And still they martyred their prophets and rejected their Messiah. They were guilty of trying to extinguish the "light for revelation to the Gentiles" and to destroy the "glory" of the people of Israel (Luke 2:32).

With great privilege comes great responsibility. The Jewish people were like the person who would rather sit in darkness than investigate the small ray of light peeking through a crack on the other side of the room. Such is the case for all people who reject the gospel. **Whether we have been raised in godly homes, attend a church only once a year, or live in a remote jungle, we are without excuse if we fail to put our trust in Jesus Christ**. The light of the gospel shines brightly, but those who refuse to walk in its light will face their just judgment.

As harsh as Paul's words are in these closing verses, there is still a glimmer of hope. He used to be just like the Jews that he described until the day that he saw the light of the gospel (Acts 9:1-5). Unlike his fellow countrymen, he walked into the light of Christ (Acts 9:6-9). Like the Thessalonians, he welcomed the Word into his life. For him this also was no ordinary word. This was the Word made flesh (John 1:14). What Paul could not do for himself, God did for him. Jesus gave His life to save Paul's life. And He has done the same for you. That is the gospel. "But God proves His own love for us in that while we were still sinners, Christ died for us!" (Rom 5:8).

Conclusion

Surveys show that many Christians who claim to value their Bibles know little about what is in them. Hence, one of the greatest tragedies of the church is the wide divide that exists between what some people say about the Bible being important and how often these individuals actually open and read what their Bibles have to say. The Christian life is not about *accepting* Jesus; it's about *following* Jesus. And following Jesus requires that we submit to a whole new agenda. Thus it is impossible for anyone who claims to follow Him not to be interested in what Scripture teaches. Concerning this, Calvin wisely notes that with the acknowledgement of the divine nature of Scripture comes a readiness to obey:

> For as soon as this persuasion has gained footing, it is impossible but that a feeling of obligation to obey takes possession of our minds. For who would not shudder at the thought of resisting God? Who would not regard contempt of God with detestation? (Calvin, *Commentaries*, 257)

So then, what does it mean to "welcome" the Word? Here I conclude by making two brief observations. First, **we must recognize its origin**. Because the Bible is the Word of God, there is no higher court of appeal than that of Scripture. Thus we must delight in its message, recognize its authority, and proclaim its message. Second, **we must obey its instruction**. Scripture "works effectively" in the lives of those who submit to its authority and follow its instruction (2:13). It's one thing to recognize its divine authority, but it's another thing to acknowledge its sufficiency. If we believe that the Bible is inerrant, then we must also believe that it is totally sufficient to fulfill its purposes.

Reflect and Discuss

1. What is God's vision for His church? How can you better pursue this vision?
2. What is revelation? How is this commonly misunderstood?
3. What is the difference between revelation and inspiration? Why must we be cautious when we speak of seeking revelation or inspiration from God today?
4. How did the Thessalonians respond to the Word of God? Why might people today respond in a similar manner?
5. What is the difference between knowing God's Word intellectually and knowing God's Word internally? Give some examples.
6. How can you build bridges with people when you share the gospel?
7. Name two ways that the Word of God impacts you when you welcome it.
8. What does a church that welcomes the Word of God look like? Does your church look like this?
9. How does Jesus "revalue" your life?
10. How is God's judgment of the Jews just?

You've Got to Love the Church

1 THESSALONIANS 2:17–3:13

Main Idea: God's people must fervently love one another.

I. We Walk Together (2:17-20; 3:8-9).
   A. We share a genuine concern for one another (2:17-20).
   B. We share a mutual admiration for one another (3:6,8-9).
II. We Sacrifice Together (3:1-2a).
   A. We sacrifice our plans for one another (3:1).
   B. We sacrifice our comforts for one another (3:2a).
III. We Suffer Together (3:2b-7).
   A. We hold one another up (3:2b-5).
   B. We pick one another up (3:6-7).
IV. We Pray Together (3:10-13).
   A. We are passionate in our prayers for one another (3:10a).
   B. We are persistent in our prayers for one another (3:10a).
   C. We are purposeful in our prayers for one another (3:10b-13).
      1. Spiritual growth
      2. Open doors
      3. Increasing love
      4. A worthy walk

Most likely you have had the experience of meeting someone who claims to be against "organized religion." As you probe deeper into why this individual has such feelings, you are more than likely to hear him say something negative about the church. Perhaps he had a bad experience with the church in the past, or maybe he simply has no appetite for God. Whatever the case, the church is not for him. For others, attending a church has become a "take it or leave it" proposition. They have no real negative feelings about church, nor do they see church as holding any meaningful place in their lives. They are not against the church and they are not for the church. For them, church is simply a place where they may or may not "go" on Sunday mornings.

God never intended the church to be this way. He did not send His Son to die so that we could attend church once a week. The church was never meant to be a weekly family tradition or just another social affiliation. Jesus did not establish His church so that its congregation could keep the lights on, the piano tuned, the preacher paid and the grass mowed. Deep down many of us know that something is missing in our church. We know that God desires so much more for His people than to sing a few songs, listen to a sermon, and give an offering. As James MacDonald suggests, many Christians are simply discouraged and frustrated by their typical church experience:

> People are deeply dissatisfied with infighting, backbiting, heartbreaking, frustrating church as it exists in the communities and long to stop attending church out of obligation. Too many return to their cars each week unsatisfied, even frustrated or grieved by their church experience only to vote with their feet by doing something different the next weekend. Church shopping quickly becomes just shopping and soon after just sleeping in. Even the most optimistic, persistent churchgoers are forced to agree that we are far from what Jesus had in mind: "I will build my church and the gates of hell shall not prevail against it." (MacDonald, *Vertical Church*, 14)

What then is the purpose of the church? Why does it exist? Fortunately, the biblical writers provide an answer. Jesus established His church so that a forgiven people "without spot or wrinkle" might "shine like stars in the world" (Eph 5:27; Phil 2:15). Peter describes the church in this way:

> *But you are a chosen race, a royal priesthood, a holy nation, a people for His possession, so that you may proclaim the praises of the One who called you out of darkness into His marvelous light.* (1 Pet 2:9)

This description is a far cry from how many people view the church.

In this passage Paul's profound love for the Thessalonian church is clear. He desired nothing more for them than to grow in their love for one another and to mature in their relationship with Christ. Nearly every word in this passage revolves around their love for Jesus, His love for them, and their love for one another. Paul was fully aware of the strategic importance this church played in the advancement of the gospel in Macedonia and to the entire Roman Empire. He knew, however, that they could not do it alone. They needed to do it together—walking together, sacrificing together, suffering together, and praying together.

We Walk Together
1 THESSALONIANS 2:17-20; 3:8-9

Paul's hurried departure from Thessalonica (Acts 17:10; 1 Thess 2:17) must have stirred up a host of emotions in his heart. Traveling by himself to Berea and then later to Athens, Paul's mind was clearly on the Thessalonians. At least four concerns weighed heavily on him. First, knowing that persecution had driven him from the city, he feared that the persecution directed at this young church might be too intense and might lead the people to doubt their faith. Since Satan had repeatedly thwarted his attempts to return to the city, perhaps "the tempter" was also working overtime sowing seeds of fear and doubt among these baby Christians (2:18; 3:5). Second, Paul faced his own doubts about whether he would ever make it back to Thessalonica to see these people again (2:17-18). Third, he also wondered if the Thessalonians were harboring any bitterness or animosity toward him for his hasty departure, perhaps thinking that he had abandoned them (3:6). In addition to these concerns, a fourth likely weighed on Paul more heavily than all the others. He recognized that the moment he left the church, the false teachers would enter the church.[7] Even a cursory reading of chapter 2 shows how passionately Paul sought to contrast his motives and ministry with those of his adversaries (see 2:3-12). He knew that false accusations would come. He was aware that discrediting the messenger could discredit the message.

Paul is giving you a glimpse of his heart. He is revealing his profound love for God's church. While someone else might have easily turned his back on Thessalonica, Paul could not. It was impossible. This was not a journey for the Thessalonians to make alone. It was his also. They were walking together, and Paul wanted them to have that assurance.

We Share a Genuine Concern for One Another (1 Thess 2:17-20)

The pathos of Paul's words is inescapable. He tells the Thessalonians that although he was physically absent in body, his heart remained with

---

[7] The Bible makes explicit the destructive nature of false teaching and false teachers (see Acts 20:29; 2 Pet 2:1-3; 2 Cor 11:13-15).

them. He writes, "But as for us, brothers, after we were forced to leave you for a short time (in person, not in heart), we greatly desired and made every effort to return and see you face to face" (2:17). In 3:1 and then again in 3:5 Paul says that his longing to be with them is so great the he "could no longer stand it." This was more than pastoral concern; it was a deeply rooted love. These words from Paul were not just for a good day. This was the passion in Paul's heart every day. Listen to his words to the Philippians:

> *It is right for me to think this way about all of you, because I have you in my heart, and you are all partners with me in grace, both in my imprisonment and in the defense and establishment of the gospel. For God is my witness, how deeply I miss all of you with the affection of Christ Jesus.* (Phil 1:7-8)

Paul's concern for them was not one-sided. Imagine the joy that Paul must have experienced when he learned that they wanted to be with him as much as he wanted to be with them (3:6). What a picture of the church! Far from a take-it-or-leave-it attitude, this was a church that wanted to be together. There was no mad dash to the parking lot when their worship services were over. What would happen if people in the church began to love each other in this way? What if the people loved each other in such a way that they could look past their petty disagreements and unite around their common passion for the gospel? Admittedly, to be this kind of church requires an investment. When we attend church without any ownership or investment, our tendency is to sit back and play the critic. We are like the father who, upon getting in the car following church services, proceeded to criticize everyone from the pastor to the pianist. Listening intently and recalling his father's contribution to the morning offering, his 10-year-old son exclaimed, "Well you have to admit that it was a pretty good show for a dollar." Neither Paul nor the Thessalonians saw church in this way. Church was far more than a service to attend; the church consisted of God's people doing God's work together.

Paul had more than simply a passing interest in the Thessalonians' spiritual growth. His words express an intimate love for them. He calls them his "hope," "joy," "crown of boasting," and "glory" (2:19-20). The word *crown* refers to the reward given to the winner of a race. It would be similar to the awarding of a gold medal in the Olympic Games. Paul was declaring that the most esteemed prize in his trophy case was the faithful, godly lives of the Thessalonians.

Before moving on, a significant point cannot be overlooked. Two times in these opening chapters Paul spoke of the return of Christ (1:10 and 2:19). This is a theme to which he will turn in much greater detail later in his letters (1 Thess 4:13–5:11; 2 Thess 2:1-12). Jesus' coming was central to Paul's worldview. Even though his stay in Thessalonica was cut short, Paul had apparently spent a considerable amount of time teaching the infant church about Christ's coming (2 Thess 2:5). He wanted them to view their present circumstances in the light of their future hope.[8] This instruction in hope was one way Paul expressed his genuine concern for the Thessalonians. As you read 1 Thessalonians, you see that despite Paul's instruction, they still had many questions and concerns about Jesus' return. Yet, even in their confusion, the imminent return of Christ served to remind them of three significant truths:

- Jesus would come to meet His Church face to face.
- All believers would give an account of their lives to God. Therefore, how they lived really did matter.
- God would ultimately judge this world according to His perfect justice and righteousness.

These truths were not only important to the early church; they also have significant implications for how you and I live today. Notice three ways that the promise of His coming should impact us.

We do not have to allow the troubles of life to discourage us. Christ will one day remove us from our troubles and take us to be with Him (John 14:1-3). We may not be able to ignore the things that we experience in this life, but we do not have to focus on them (2 Cor 4:18). Like the Thessalonians, we must fix our eyes eagerly toward heaven to wait for God's Son. If He is able to rescue us from the "coming wrath," then surely He is able to deliver us from life's tribulations (1:10). Every day should be met with the expectation and anticipation that this might just be the day of His coming.

We will be accountable to Him when He comes. Concerning this, Jesus offers these sobering words:

---

[8] How you respond to what happens to you and around you is filtered through the lens of your worldview. As a Christian you interpret your world through the lens of the Bible. That is why Paul could repeatedly face hardship and still maintain a hopeful outlook. He knew that a sovereign God was overseeing every detail of his life. For a helpful resource on the importance of a Christian worldview, see Moreland and Craig, *Philosophical Foundations.*

Then the kingdom of heaven will be like 10 virgins who took their lamps and went out to meet the groom. Five of them were foolish and five were sensible. When the foolish took their lamps, they didn't take olive oil with them. But the sensible ones took oil in their flasks with their lamps. Since the groom was delayed, they all became drowsy and fell asleep.

In the middle of the night there was a shout: "Here's the groom! Come out to meet him."

Then all those virgins got up and trimmed their lamps. But the foolish ones said to the sensible ones, "Give us some of your oil, because our lamps are going out."

The sensible ones answered, "No, there won't be enough for us and for you. Go instead to those who sell, and buy oil for yourselves."

When they had gone to buy some, the groom arrived. Then those who were ready went in with him to the wedding banquet, and the door was shut.

Later the rest of the virgins also came and said, "Master, master, open up for us!"

But he replied, "I assure you: I do not know you!"

Therefore be alert, because you don't know either the day or the hour. (Matt 25:1-13)

His imminent return is not meant to be a doctrine to confuse us but a promise that motivates us. When He comes we will be accountable for what we did with Jesus and how we lived for Jesus. Paul's words of encouragement should call us to action repeatedly:

But you brothers, are not in the dark, for this day to overtake you like a thief. . . . We do not belong to the night or the darkness. So then, we must not sleep, like the rest, but we must stay awake and be serious. (1 Thess 5:4-6)

We don't have to right every wrong that is done to us because we have the promise that God will exercise His righteous judgment at Christ's coming. God is more than capable to balance the books. Peter's words are a reminder that all human beings will "give an account to the One who stands ready to judge the living and the dead" (1 Pet 4:5). And we must not forget what Paul told the Thessalonians about God's righteous judgment: "It is righteous for God to repay with affliction those who afflict you and to reward with rest you who are afflicted, along with us" (2 Thess 1:6). So until that day we can confidently entrust ourselves to "the One who judges justly" (1 Pet 2:23). Instead of looking for the day when we finally get revenge, we should be longing for the day when God judges in righteousness.

We Share a Mutual Admiration for One Another (1 Thess 3:6,8-9)

The Thessalonians were indebted to Paul, Silas, and Timothy. After all, these men imparted to them the gospel of Christ and the investment of their own lives. What person would not hold in high esteem someone who loved him enough to share his life with him? But we also must not miss the fact that Paul held the Thessalonians in high esteem. It's true. The great apostle exclaims, "Now we *live*, if you stand firm in the Lord" (3:8; emphasis added). If that statement is not striking enough, he says two verses later that he prays night and day "to see you face to face" (3:10). Did you catch the significance of those statements? Paul was telling the Thessalonians that he needed them! What could they possibly give him? The answer is joy. One of Paul's greatest joys was to be around people who passionately love Jesus. The greatest gift that this church could give to him was for them to continue to cherish Christ above all else. What pastor would not desire this for his people?

Some of God's greatest saints sit in the churches. They may never write books, preach crusades, or offer invocations at prestigious events, but they faithfully and consistently walk with Jesus Christ. Their presence in the churches raises an important question for church leaders: is their admiration for their people as great as their people's admiration for them? Paul recognized the value and worth of people. Most significantly, he recognized that he needed others as much as they needed him. People were not stepping stones for him to get where he wanted to go. He loved the people to whom he preached, and he longed to be with them. You can see his admiration for others in the opening of his letter to the Romans. "For I want very much to see you," Paul wrote, "[so that we can] be mutually encouraged by each other's faith, both yours and mine" (Rom 1:11-12). The apostle wanted to be with the people so that they could encourage him. The man of God longed to be with the people of God. This is truly following in the footsteps of Jesus:

> But He said to them, "The kings of the Gentiles dominate them, and those who have authority over them are called 'Benefactors.' But it must not be like that among you. On the contrary, whoever is greatest among you must become like the youngest, and whoever leads, like the one serving." (Luke 22:25-26)

You can't serve your people if you don't love your people, and you can't love your people if you don't spend time with them. The true evidence of love is longing to be with the ones you love. Imagine telling your spouse, child, or parent that you love them but have no interest in spending time with them. That is unthinkable.

We Sacrifice Together
1 THESSALONIANS 3:1-2A

A little background will enable us to keep these verses in perspective. Here Paul is sharing some autobiographical insights. Remember that his joyful response to the Thessalonians' spiritual condition (1:2-10) came only after Timothy had returned from the city with a full report. Up until Paul sent Timothy back to Thessalonica, he had no way of knowing their spiritual state. When Paul writes 3:1-2 he is giving a look into his heart during the immediate days and weeks after his departure from Thessalonica. He shows what he was experiencing after his departure.

When Paul, Silas, and Timothy left Thessalonica, they made their way to Berea. Their initial reception in Berea was most favorable. Luke describes the Bereans as "more open-minded than those in Thessalonica, since they welcomed the message with eagerness" (Acts 17:11). Just as in the city of Thessalonica, many Bereans responded to the gospel. The spread of the good news, however, once again presented Paul and his companions with a big problem. An angry mob of Jews from Thessalonica had come to Berea (Acts 17:13). Hence, Paul fled the city leaving Silas and Timothy behind to continue the work. The new plan was for Paul to travel to Athens and for Silas and Timothy to meet him there later.

We Sacrifice Our Plans for One Another (1 Thess 3:1)

Step back and consider what must have occupied Paul's thinking as he pressed on with his work. The mob that came to Berea doubtlessly reminded him of the difficult plight of the Thessalonian Christians. Without his companions by his side, he was now alone both on his journey and with his thoughts. He simply could not get the Thessalonians off of his mind. Even after arriving in Athens, Paul's heart was still in Thessalonica. The eager anticipation of what God was going to do in Athens did not erase his memories of what God was doing in Thessalonica. When Timothy finally arrived in Athens, he discovered that Paul had different plans for him. Let's allow Paul to tell the rest of the story:

> *When we could no longer stand it, we thought it was better to be left alone in Athens. And we sent Timothy, our brother and God's coworker in the gospel of Christ, to strengthen and encourage you concerning your faith, so that no one will be shaken by these persecutions.* (3:1-3)

Paul's plan to send Timothy back to Thessalonica was no small thing. Simply put, he had his plate full in Athens. The city was a philosopher's playground. It was also home to more than 30,000 different gods. This was a university town, with more than its fair share of Christianity's critics. If ever Paul needed reinforcements on the battlefield, it was here. Yet Paul was willing to engage the enemy alone if it meant that he could somehow learn the fate of the Thessalonian church. Timothy was sent to "strengthen and encourage" them (3:2). The Greek word translated "encourage" means to "call alongside." Paul sent Timothy for the purpose of cheering them on. He was willing to adjust his plans to accomplish God's plans. That's what believers do. They recognize that God is working in a thousand ways that they cannot see. **You and I often become so wrapped up in our world that we miss out on what God is doing in His world**. We might justify keeping our "Timothy" by our side by claiming how much more we could accomplish together. Yet underlying this justification might very well be our reluctance to walk the streets alone. Setting aside our own comforts and ambition is often easier said than done. Paul had the bigger picture in mind. He was able to balance his desire to advance the gospel with his understanding that the work of the gospel was much bigger than his personal ambitions.

We Sacrifice Our Comforts for One Another (1 Thess 3:2a)

The experience of traveling to distant lands and the joy of meeting new people is one of life's greatest joys. To engage unreached people groups with the gospel is indeed a high calling. But anyone who has traveled to a third-world country learns very quickly that "we're not in Kansas anymore." You will eat different food, learn new languages, adapt to unusual customs, and adjust to different bathrooms! Sacrifice is what it is all about.

In 1858 Scottish missionary John G. Paton and his wife sailed for the New Hebrides Islands in the South Pacific (now called Vanuatu). Against the advice of many who saw this endeavor as a suicide mission,

Paton and his wife left their families, their friends, and the comforts of home for a strange and distant land. Their consuming passion was to share the gospel of Jesus Christ with the native peoples, among whom were thousands of barbaric cannibals. Three months after arriving in the islands, his wife died. One week later his infant son also died. Paton eventually remarried and after a short time away, returned to the Islands with his new bride. Together, they spent the next 41 years faithfully sharing the love of Jesus. Today more than 80 percent of the inhabitants of Vanuatu identify themselves as Christian in large part due to the sacrifices of Paton. An incident early in his life gives us some insight into the convictions of this man. Before leaving for the New Hebrides, Paton was warned by one of his fellow Scotsmen that the cannibals would almost certainly eat him. His reply is classic:

> Mr. Dickson, you are advanced in years now, and your own prospect is soon to be laid in the grave, there to be eaten by worms; I confess to you, that if I can but live and die serving and honouring the Lord Jesus, it will make no difference to me whether I am eaten by Cannibals or by worms; and in the Great Day my resurrection body will arise as fair as yours in the likeness of our risen Redeemer. (Paton, *Missionary to the New Hebrides*, 56)

The rewards awaiting you in heaven always trump the sacrifices made while here on earth. As God told Samuel, "To obey is better than sacrifice" (1 Sam 15:22).

For Paul then, sacrificing the companionship of Timothy in Athens was a small price to pay for the sake of the Thessalonians. If they were being "shaken" by persecutions, then perhaps Timothy could encourage them (3:3). Paul's willingness to sacrifice for the sake of the church is expressed clearly in 2 Corinthians 11:23-28. An incessant stream of trials constantly flowed into his life. He knew the pressures of life and the pressures of ministry. From the hands of evil men to natural phenomena and physical maladies, every new day seemed to bring some new obstacle. Yet despite all of his personal pressures, Paul was still willing to carry the burdens of God's people. His comforts were secondary to those of the church. How many of you would be willing to make this kind of sacrifice? What an amazing leader and pastor Paul was!

We Suffer Together
1 THESSALONIANS 3:2B-7

New Christians quickly realize that even though their sins are forgiven, their problems seldom go away. Far from living a life free from problems, followers of Jesus Christ experience a whole new set of problems. Added to the struggles of living in a fallen world is the ever-present reality of persecution. New believers must prepare for the inevitable casualties of war. Peter knew this well when he warned,

> *Don't be surprised when the fiery ordeal comes among you to test you as if something unusual were happening to you. Instead, rejoice as you share in the sufferings of the Messiah, so that you may also rejoice with great joy at the revelation of His glory.* (1 Pet 4:12-13)

Peter was no stranger to persecution. He had a front row seat to the persecution directed at his Lord. He saw how Jesus responded, and he remembered what Jesus said about persecution:

> *If the world hates you, understand that it hated Me before it hated you. If you were of the world, the world would love you as its own. However, because you are not of the world, but I have chosen you out of it, the world hates you. Remember the word I spoke to you: "A slave is not greater than his master." If they persecuted Me, they will also persecute you.* (John 15:18-20)

Persecution, hardship, and difficulty are expectations for the Christian; they were never meant to be exceptions for the Christian. So the real question is not, *Will* I face trouble? But, How will I respond *when* I face trouble? In one of the very first letters written to the church, James gave us some helpful advice: "Consider it a great joy, my brothers, whenever you experience various trials, knowing that the testing of your faith produces endurance" (Jas 1:2-3). We should respond to trial and hardship like the sage who lived on a tiny island in the Pacific. When asked by the residents how they should prepare for a rapidly approaching tidal wave, he replied, "We would all do well to learn how to live underwater." We can't expect to avoid it; we should prepare to endure it. Paul gives us two valuable ways that the church can endure persecution: we hold one another up, and we pick one another up.

We Hold One Another Up (1 Thess 3:2b-5)

Paul never pulled his punches. He was not like the false teachers who promised much and delivered little. He wanted the Thessalonians to know what Christianity was and what Christianity was not. He never promised them that it would be easy. In fact, he reminds them that he delivered his message with no "intent to deceive" (2:3). During his short stay in Thessalonica, his teaching about the reality of persecution was straightforward and direct. "For you yourselves know," he reminded them (3:3). And, "When we were with you we told you" that persecution would come (3:4). As Ray Comfort puts it, Jesus is not a something that we put on to make our journey more comfortable. He's not a "life enhancer." He is a "life rescuer" ("Tips for a Biblical Altar Call"). He definitely makes our lives richer, better, and more meaningful. But far greater than all of these temporary benefits, He gives us eternal benefits like forgiveness of sin and an eternal dwelling place with God. Although life is indeed better with Jesus, that life will not necessarily be easier with Jesus. If church leaders love those whom they lead, then they will prepare them for every eventuality of the faith, including persecution, suffering, and pain. In his insightful book on the subject of God and pain, Phillip Yancey makes a startling statement about how some Christians view pain: "Christians would probably admit that pain was God's mistake. He should have worked a little harder and invented a better way of coping with the world's dangers" (Yancey, *Where Is God?*, 23). By contrast, Paul wanted the Thessalonians to know that pain was not their enemy. As we know, he was speaking from personal experience. Countless Christians have found solace in these comforting words:

> But He said to me, "My grace is sufficient for you, for power is perfected in weakness." Therefore, I will most gladly boast all the more about my weaknesses, so that Christ's power may reside in me. So I take pleasure in weaknesses, insults, catastrophes, persecutions, and in pressures, because of Christ. For when I am weak, then I am strong. (2 Cor 12:9-10)

The more that you grow in your relationship with Christ, the more you grow to appreciate the depth of these words.

Paul knew that following Christ meant something. He also knew that following Christ would not be easy. A formidable foe stood ready to oppose God's work in Thessalonica. The real foe, however, was not an angry mob. The real foe was "the tempter," or Satan (3:5). Paul did his best to prepare this infant congregation for Satan's attack. His instruction clearly echoed what he taught the Ephesians (Eph 6:10-17). In his later instruction to the Thessalonians he will encourage them to "Put the armor of faith and love on [your] chests, and put on a helmet of the hope of salvation" (1 Thess 5:8). A prepared soldier is never surprised when the enemy attacks. Paul sought to prepare them the best he could, but it was now up to the Thessalonians to stand their ground. Although he desperately wanted to be there to strengthen and encourage them in this fight, Satan "hindered" his attempts to return to Thessalonica (2:18). They were now on their own until Timothy could return to strengthen and encourage them.

A vibrant church posed a significant threat to Satan's stronghold in Thessalonica. Paul knew this before he arrived. Satan's strategy was "to steal and to kill and to destroy" (John 10:10). If he could steal the Thessalonians' joy he could also destroy their work. But his ultimate goal was to steer people away from God's saving gospel. Death is his ultimate goal. Today, Satan's strategy may manifest itself in many ways, but its purpose is always the same. If he can't render the church inoperative, he will work tirelessly to make the church ineffective. If an attack from without proves futile, he will attempt to destroy it from within. It is no coincidence that petty church disagreements often grow into giant church problems. Unwittingly, church members zealous for their particular cause may think that they are defending their church when in reality they are destroying it. To quote the esteemed philosopher Pogo Possum, "We have met the enemy, and he is us!" When internal wars distract the church, it never advances in its external mission. Think about a church that is experiencing internal conflict. Are lives being changed, or are lives being destroyed? Are people on the outside talking more about the conflict in the church, or are they marveling at the gospel message that is coming out of the church? "The tempter" is going to work tirelessly to destroy God's work. Paul never underestimated his enemy. He warned the Thessalonians in advance that Satan was looking for any opening to destroy this infant congregation. The church needed to be prepared (1 Pet 5:8).

We Pick One Another Up (1 Thess 3:6-7)

No Christian is immune from discouragement. Even when prepared for the reality of Satan's attack, we still have moments when our fears and doubts get the best of us. Paul also experienced moments of doubt. He never attempted to hide his feelings from the church. In fact, through-out his letter he openly shares his doubts with them. At least three are implicit within the letter:

- Were false teachers causing the Thessalonians to question his motives (2:3-8)?
- Did the Thessalonians now believe that his sole purpose in visiting them was for personal gain (2:9-11)?
- Had Satan sown seeds of doubt concerning their salvation (3:5)?

We may be saved by grace alone through faith alone, but God never intended for us to live life alone. Nowhere is this truth more important than when dealing with doubts and discouragement. If you recall the seasons of your life when you were the most discouraged, more than likely these were times when you were alone. It may not be that you were isolated from the presence of people, but you may have been insulated from sharing your heart with them. Human beings are quite adept at keeping things inside. When you and I learn to be real with one another we often discover that we are not alone in our discouragement. This may sound strange, but sometimes it is simply encouraging to know that you are not the only one who is discouraged. Try to name one great bib-lical saint who did not struggle with some type of pain, disappointment, doubt, or discouragement. You might have a difficult time naming one. Don't believe the lie that life will be easy. Also, don't lose hope when you struggle with life's ambiguities. Nowhere does the Bible teach that to be used by God you have to have life figured out. In reality, for God to use you, you first must admit that you don't have life figured out.

A classic illustration from Peter's life is helpful. Peter had been fish-ing all night with little to show for his efforts. While Peter was putting his gear away for the day, Jesus gets into his boat and begins to teach the crowd. Perhaps sensing Peter's frustration at his lackluster night of fishing, Jesus gave Peter a tip as to where to find the fish. Peter let down his nets into the water just as Jesus suggested, and he landed the biggest catch of his life. While he was filling the boat with fish, conviction filled Peter's heart. In a moment that changed his life forever, Peter fell on his knees in the pile of fish and called out to Jesus, "Go away from me, because I am a sinful man, Lord!" Jesus' response to Peter came as a result of Peter's response to Jesus. "From now on," Jesus exclaimed, "you will be catching people!" (Luke 5:1-10). Peter saw God in his boat that day. When you see God for who He is, you will see yourself for who you really are. But when you confess to God who you really are, God makes you into the person He wants you to be.

We are encouraged when we read in Scripture that even Peter struggled with his self-confidence. After he admitted his weakness and submitted to Jesus, God was able to use him in a mighty way. It is heartening to learn that we are not the only people who don't have life totally figured out and that God has not given up on us. Using the same approach to encourage the Thessalonians, Paul admitted to them that he was struggling with questions and apprehensions.

Paul was willing to be vulnerable by sharing his fears and doubts with this infant church. And just as he proved to be an encouragement to them through the message that he sent with Timothy, they proved to be an encouragement to Paul by the report that Timothy brought back to him. Timothy's news was most encouraging. Paul no longer had any reason to doubt. Timothy's report provided the answers Paul was seeking. The report dispelled his doubts in three ways: First, far from dismissing Paul and his companions as just another bunch of false teachers, the Thessalonians had "good memories" of them (3:6). Paul could rest assured that his name and his reputation were intact. Second, Paul learned that they wanted to see him as much as he wanted to see them (3:6). This is hardly the response of a church that has lost confidence in its founder and leader. Finally, neither distress, persecution, nor the craftiness of "the tempter" could dissuade this church from keeping the faith (3:7). Paul had prepared them for the battle and they were advancing. The sunshine of certainty had broken the clouds of doubt that obscured Paul's vision.

In this give-and-take between Paul and the Thessalonians, both were encouraged. This models how fellowship and vulnerability work in the church: we share our doubts and discouragement, and we pick one another up.

We Pray Together
1 THESSALONIANS 3:10-13

The apostle Paul was one of the most transparent men who ever lived. To read his letters is to see into his life. He willingly shares his doubts, hopes, concerns, joys, sorrows, and weaknesses. But of all the things that Paul shares about himself, perhaps the most profound is his prayer life.

Through reading his prayers, you can see Paul in a light that reveals his heart for God and his heart for people. In these closing verses of chapter 3 Paul shows how you and I ought to pray for one another, what our petitions ought to be when we pray for one another, and the reason we pray for one another.

We Are Passionate in Our Prayers for One Another (1 Thess 3:10a)

Paul last saw Timothy in Athens. From Athens he sent Timothy back to Thessalonica. After an extended time apart, Timothy has now rejoined Paul in Corinth. With the fresh news of Timothy's report, Paul pens 1 Thessalonians. The Thessalonians were more than just another church to Paul. He loved them dearly. This is most evident in how he prayed for them. "We pray very earnestly night and day," Paul wrote. The emphasis here is not so much on what time of the day he prayed but on how fervently he prayed. E. M. Bounds speaks of this kind of passionate praying:

> The praying which makes a prayerful ministry is not a little
> praying put in as we put flavor to give it a pleasant smack,
> but the praying must be in the body, and form the blood and
> bones. Prayer is no petty duty, put into a corner; no piecemeal
> performance made out of the fragments of time which have
> been snatched from business and other engagements of life;
> but it means that the best of our time, the heart of our time
> and strength must be given. (Bounds, *Power Through Prayer*, 39)

Paul's fervency in prayer was much different from that of many Christians. When we end our prayers with the generic phrase, "Bless our church," what are we really asking God? Are we asking with a sense of desire or fervency for God to give us the specific thing for which we pray? When children want something from a parent, you will hear no ambiguity in their request. They let their parents know what they want and how badly they want it. Given the lack of fervency and specificity in some prayers, no wonder many of them go unanswered.

We Are Persistent in Our Prayers for One Another (1 Thess 3:10a)

Paul not only prayed fervently (night and day), he also prayed "earnestly." The use of the adverb *earnestly* points to the intensity or focus of his prayers. His specific choice of the Greek word for "pray" emphasizes the need or wish behind the request. In this case the persistence of Paul's prayer revolved around his desire for God to "direct" his way to them

(3:11; see also 2:18). He did not rattle off a perfunctory list of people for God to "bless" or a vague list of things for God to do. As we will see in 3:11-13, Paul's prayers were specific, persistent, and focused. Jesus taught that healthy prayer life is to be marked by how persistently we pray (Luke 11:8-10; 18:1-8) and how specifically we pray (Matt 6:9-13; Luke 11:11-13).

We Are Purposeful in Our Prayers for One Another (1 Thess 3:10b-13)

The first three chapters of 1 Thessalonians form Paul's lengthy and purposeful introduction. The heart or meat of the letter does not begin until chapters 4 and 5. Up to this point, Paul has rejoiced in the Thessalonians' spiritual growth (1:2-10), defended his motives in ministry (2:1-12), thanked God for the faithfulness of this infant congregation (2:13-16), and reassured them of his love (2:17–3:9). He now is ready to tackle some of the most significant theological themes of the Christian life. But before diving in (and he does so quickly in chapter 4), Paul pauses to pray for them. In the simplest of prayers, he offers four profound requests.

Spiritual growth. Paul wanted desperately "to complete" what was lacking in their faith (3:10b). As he saw it, his work in Thessalonica was incomplete. This was not to suggest that Paul somehow thought that the church was spiritually anemic. He knew that love for Christ was evident and their faith was vibrant and growing. However, they were still an infant church with much to learn. He desired for them to be spiritually strong. His prayer expresses a fervent request that God would enable them to mature. Paul knew that their faith must be grounded on God's truth. Questions still remained about the Lord's return (4:13–5:11), spiritual leadership (5:12-13), interpersonal relationships (5:14-15), and spiritual disciplines (5:16-22). He will address these themes as the letter progresses. But Paul knew that they were "lacking in [their] faith" and needed God's wisdom to face the many challenges confronting them. He was a pastor who yearned for the spiritual growth of his people (cf. Col 1:9-10). However, Paul was not content merely to pray for them, he wanted to see them, to teach them, and to encourage them.

Open doors. We can plan and prepare for ministry but ultimately we are dependent on God to open and close doors. Paul knew that if he were going to return to Thessalonica, God would have to make it happen (3:11). Only God Himself could make the impossible possible. Though Satan placed roadblocks in Paul's path (2:18), it did not deter him from repeatedly asking God to make a way. An important lesson here must not be overlooked. We must trust God implicitly to do what is in His best interest and not ours. We are not architects for *our* kingdom; we are ambassadors for *His* kingdom. Kicking in doors that God is unwilling to open will only lead to disaster. Ask Moses what it cost him to kick in a door at Meribah (Num 20:2-13). When God puts a pathway in front of us, His expectation is that we stay on it no matter how enticing the other pathways may appear (Josh 1:7-8). Our journeys are all different. Let God's plan be your plan. Don't let that keep you from praying for Him to open doors, but make a commitment that you will stay behind the doors that He keeps closed and walk confidently through the doors that He opens (2 Cor 10:12-13).

Increasing love. Jesus said to His disciples, "By this all people will know that you are My disciples, if you have love for one another" (John 13:35). The Thessalonians were working hard at loving one another (1:3). However, you never reach a point in your spiritual journey where your love stops growing (1 Cor 13:8,13). As you grow in your relationship with Christ, you will also be growing in your love for one another. Paul emphasizes this by praying, "May the Lord cause you to *increase* and *overflow* with love for one another and for everyone, just as we also do for you" (1 Thess 3:12; emphasis added).

Charles Swindoll identifies at least four ways that we can express love to others:

- Listen to others, including those who hold viewpoints with which you disagree.
- Demonstrate grace by looking past people's "faults" to see their strengths.
- Recognize the value and dignity of other human beings, regardless of their ethnicity, socioeconomic class, or background.
- Show God's love by selflessly serving and sacrificing for others. (*Contagious Christianity*, 40)

A worthy walk. The challenges of living out the faith in a city like Thessalonica were great. Much as in the world today, the Thessalonians were faced with constant pressure to conform to the culture around them. However, Christians must view their world in a different way. The culture says if you want to get along, then you must go along, but God has a much different perspective. Paul told the Romans not to be "conformed" to this world (Rom 12:2). John put it this way: "Do not love the world or the things that belong to the world. If anyone loves the world, love for the Father is not in him" (1 John 2:15). If the Thessalonians were going to "walk worthy of the Lord" (Col 1:10), then they were going to need help. To this end, Paul prayed that God would establish their "hearts blameless in holiness before our God" (1 Thess 3:13). What he has in mind here is not the *process* of *becoming* holy, but a *standing* because they *were* holy (Morris, *Epistles of Paul,* 71). In other words, he prayed that they would live in the light of their holiness. Thus, this assurance of their standing before God at the "coming of our Lord Jesus" was to be their motivation for faithful living. Instead of fearing His coming, they could look expectantly for it. Paul will have much more to say about this in chapters 4 and 5. By recognizing their standing in Christ and by anticipating His coming, Paul desired that they would excel still more in their walk with Christ.

Conclusion

To be in Jesus Christ is to be a part of His church. Indeed, the concept of a believer not affiliating with God's people is foreign to the New Testament (cf. 1 Cor 12:13-16). A genuine love for Jesus produces a profound love for the church, and you cannot love God's church if you do not love God's people. That's why Paul could speak so affectionately about the Thessalonian believers. They genuinely loved one another. This love was evident in several ways.

They recognized that they were on the journey together. The mutual love between Paul and the Thessalonians should serve as a reminder to us that you and I genuinely need one another. Imagine what would happen if Christians spent as much time praying for one another as they did posturing to see who will control the church. God has called His people to be partners, not competitors.

They saw a greater purpose in their suffering. Most of us would view suffering as a bad thing. Paul, however, found much encouragement by the Thessalonians' endurance and perseverance in the face of their suffering. As in 2 Thessalonians 1:5, God often uses the sufferings of His people to prepare them for their future glory. Thus, despite his affliction, Paul speaks of being comforted by the faithful endurance of the Thessalonians. And there is little doubt that the feeling was mutual for the Thessalonians.

They prayed for one another's continued spiritual growth. Far from the superficial prayer "God bless them," Paul instead prayed for the Thessalonians to grow in love for one another and in holiness before

God. He further prayed that their faith would persevere until the coming of Christ. As Fee notes,

> Only the Lord himself can strengthen them in their inner being for the two ways necessary to be prepared for his coming: "blameless" with regard to their outward, visible conduct toward each other and the world; and "in holiness" with regard to their relationship with God and Christ. (Fee, *First and Second Letters*, 133)

What would happen in churches if God's people would pray for one another according to this pattern?

Reflect and Discuss

1. How did Paul continue to view the Thessalonian church after his abrupt removal from the city?
2. How does Paul's love for the Thessalonians speak to pastors as they seek to lead their churches?
3. What is the context of 1 Thessalonians 2:17–3:5? What does this tell you about the heart of Paul?
4. What sacrifices did Paul make for the Thessalonians? How does this challenge you today?
5. What implications does the doctrine of Christ's return have for the church? How does it provide both hope and a warning?
6. How can a pastor prepare his church for the reality of persecution?
7. How does Satan seek to destroy the work of God's church? What steps can we take to counter his strategy?
8. How should Christians respond to the ever-present reality of discouragement?
9. What does Paul teach you about prayer in this passage? How would your spiritual health benefit from modeling your prayer life on Paul's?
10. How should Christians pray for one another? What are four specific petitions that you should make for one another?

The Priority of Purity

1 THESSALONIANS 4:1-8

Main Idea: Because God has called us to holiness, we must flee from any form of sexual impurity.

I. **Our Walk Must Be Our Priority (4:1-2).**
   A. Commit to know what God says.
   B. Commit to do what God commands.
II. **God's Will Must Be Our Guide (4:3-7).**
   A. Avoid impurity (4:3-5,7).
   B. Respect others (4:6a).
   C. Assume responsibility (4:6b).
III. **God's Approval Must Be Our Passion (4:8).**
   A. Our loyalty is to the Father (4:8a).
   B. Our power is by the Spirit (4:8b).

After a lengthy introduction (1:1–3:13), Paul is now ready to get to the main point of his letter. He has praised them for their faithfulness, defended his motives, shared his gratitude for their love of Scripture, and expressed His personal love for them. The tone of the introduction is positive and upbeat. If you read back through the first three chapters you will find no words of correction or rebuke. This is quite remarkable considering the relative status of the Thessalonian believers as young in the faith. Though many of Paul's churches brought him sorrow and grief (e.g., Corinth and Galatia), the Thessalonian church was a source of encouragement and joy.

Timothy's time in Thessalonica proved to be refreshing both for the Thessalonians and for Paul. The Thessalonians were strengthened by his visit, and Paul was relieved to hear of their faithfulness (3:6-8). Timothy's visit revealed some issues with which the Thessalonians were struggling. At the end of chapter 3, Paul therefore prayed for their spiritual growth and for God to open a door for him to see them again (3:10-13). But until he could return, he wanted to leave them with some final exhortations in his letter. His primary intention was to clear up some of the issues that Timothy had told him about and to "complete" what was lacking in their faith (3:10).

Paul transitions into the heart of his letter by providing the Thessalonians with a series of exhortations. Some of these exhortations receive merely a cursory mention while others receive a more detailed explanation. Reading through them, you clearly get the sense that this is not the first time that the Thessalonians have heard these things. In fact, you know that they have heard them before by Paul's statements, "as you have received" and "for you know" (4:1-2). Paul's instruction to the Thessalonians was grounded in God's truth. His commitment to a Scripture-saturated ministry should serve as a challenge to every pastor. In his brief time with them he exposed them to some profound theological truths. This spiritual maturity is remarkable because this church was only a few weeks old at the time. I do not know too many pastors who would be willing to teach an infant church (or even a mature church) about the return of Christ (4:13-18), the Day of the Lord (5:1-11), and the "man of lawlessness" (2 Thess 2:1-12). Yet Paul was a master at putting the theological cookies on the bottom shelf so that everyone could reach them. Pastors who shy away from taking their congregations deep in scriptural truth abdicate their God-ordained responsibility and deprive their people of essential spiritual nourishment (1 Pet 2:2). To "complete what is lacking" in the faith of our churches has less to do with establishing new programs and so much more to do with faithfully proclaiming God's truth.

One final word is necessary before we turn our attention to the first of these exhortations. Already you can observe in Paul's letter that for him Christianity means something. Implicit in his teaching is his conviction that an external transformation is the evidence of an internal regeneration. Stated another way, it's one thing to say that you are saved, but the proof of your salvation will be revealed by the way you live (Jas 2:14-17). This, of course, is one of the main reasons for Paul's rejoicing over Timothy's report. The Thessalonians' conduct pointed to the genuineness of their faith (1:9). As Paul begins the second half of his letter, he will return to this theme repeatedly.

Thus Paul turns his attention toward the Thessalonians' continued spiritual growth. In essence, he is challenging them to continue building their lives on a theological foundation. God's truth touches every key on the keyboard of your life. When you allow God to speak into your life, your life will be different. Peter makes this clear:

Therefore, with your minds ready for action, be serious and set your hope completely on the grace to be brought to you at the revelation of Jesus Christ. As obedient children, do not be conformed to the desires of your former ignorance. But as the One who called you is holy, you also are to be holy in all your conduct; for it is written, Be holy, because I am holy.

And if you address as Father the One who judges impartially based on each one's work, you are to conduct yourselves in fear during the time of your temporary residence. For you know that you were redeemed from your empty way of life inherited from the fathers, not with perishable things like silver or gold, but with the precious blood of Christ, like that of a lamb without defect or blemish. (1 Pet 1:13-19)

A genuine faith makes a difference in how we live. Paul shows how this translates into specific areas of life. Not surprisingly, the first area that he addresses is sexual purity. The gross immorality of Thessalonica was doubtlessly on his mind. Nothing destroys relationships, deepens shame, and destroys witness like sexual impurity, which has no place in the life of the redeemed. Paul addresses three truths that will enable us to avoid such destructive influences: our walk must be our priority, God's will must be our guide, and God's approval must be our passion.

Our Walk Must Be Our Priority
1 THESSALONIANS 4:1-2

The 1991 hit comedy film *City Slickers* chronicles the lives of three middle-aged men who, in an attempt to "find themselves," set off on a cattle drive across the Wild West. Their chaperone for the trip is a mysterious and seasoned cowboy named Curley (played by Jack Palance). In a powerful scene from the movie, Mitch (played by Billy Crystal) has a private conversation with Curley. During the course of the conversation, Mitch tells Curley how complicated and confusing his life has become. Curley looks Mitch straight in the eye and says, "You city slickers are all alike. You spend fifty weeks out of your year putting knots in your rope and expect to come out here and in two weeks get them out."

That scene illustrates a powerful truth: the easiest way to get the knots out of your rope is to avoid getting knots in your rope in the first place. While that might be a firm grasp of the obvious, consider how many people you know, if given a chance to live life over again, would make some very different choices.

Arguably one of Satan's most effective methods for destroying lives and ruining relationships is sexual sin. This world is sex-saturated. Every day we are exposed to a myriad of alluring enticements that make up the sexual culture. It is no accident that pornography is a fifty-billion-dollar industry. Sex sells, and a lot of people are buying it.

The parallels between Paul's day and the modern era are striking. From prostitution on the streets to prostitution in the temples, if you wanted sex in Thessalonica you could have it. And from websites to video chat rooms, if you want sex on your street, you can have it, too. None of this comes without a great price. In his insightful book *Finally Free*, Heath Lambert describes the destructive nature of sexual sin, specifically as it relates to pornography. Concerning those who have succumbed to its alluring enticement, Lambert writes,

> Pornography has now chewed them up and spit them out. At the beginning of the journey, watching people commit acts of sexual immorality seemed fun, intriguing, comforting, and exhilarating. Now, the sin has bitten back hard. Their hearts are weighed down with guilt, their relationships are strained, their view of sex is corrupted, and their Christian witness is marred. (Lambert, *Finally Free*, 19)

Paul knew that sexual sin would destroy the lives and ruin the testimony of these young believers. Like any good coach, he knew that the best defense is often a good offense. To achieve victory over sexual sin, they needed to go back to the fundamentals—their personal walk with God. Sexual sin, like any other type of sin, ultimately finds its roots in our unwillingness to do what God says. In Romans 12:1 are these familiar words: "Therefore, brothers, by the mercies of God, I urge you to present your bodies as a living sacrifice, holy and pleasing to God; this is your spiritual worship." Do you see how "mercies," "sacrifice," and "worship" are related? The only fitting response (worship) to God's gift of grace (mercies) is your willingness to surrender completely to Him (sacrifice). Every act of sin and disobedience can ultimately be traced back to your unwillingness to surrender to God by obeying His Word.

Commit to Know What God Says

Like a house anchored to a stone foundation, a personal faith built on Scripture will not wash away when tested, crumble when shaken, or collapse when threatened. When the Thessalonians welcomed God's Word, their foundation was laid (2:13). And the cornerstone of this foundation was their commitment to and relationship with Jesus Christ (1 Cor 3:11). Paul knew that victory over sexual sin would only be possible if they continued to build on this foundation.

Building on this foundation, however, would not come by trying harder; it would only be possible by digging deeper. Paul wrote, "You know what commands we gave you through the Lord Jesus" (4:2). Paul reminds them of the specific biblical commands he had taught them while he was with them. There is an important principle that we must not miss. When you teach biblical truth you must not only tell people what the Bible says, but you must also show them where in the Bible that truth is found. Preachers are often very good at *stating* the truth, but they often fail when it comes to *showing* where they found that truth. When the world is falling apart, your first response should not be to recall what the preacher said; your first response should be to remember what God said. This is no small thing. Think about the prophet Jeremiah as he walked brokenhearted amid the destruction of a once great Jerusalem. He describes his feelings of brokenness, loneliness, affliction, and pain. But something happens to him that changes his outlook. You can see it in his words: "Yet *I call this to mind* and therefore I have hope: Because of the LORD's faithful love we do not perish" (Lam 3:21-22; emphasis added). What did Jeremiah call to mind? He remembered God's promises. His mind was drawn back to God's truth. When you view your life through the lens of God's truth, it dramatically changes how you interpret your circumstances.

Another fitting illustration of this is found in Nehemiah 8 when Ezra the priest read from the Book of the Law in the presence of the people. He, along with a host of other priests, "translated" and "gave the meaning" so that the people would know what the Law said and how they should respond to it (Neh 8:7-8). Nehemiah wrote that upon hearing the law, the people had a great celebration "because they had understood the words that were explained to them" (Neh 8:12). The very next morning the people assembled once again "to study the words of the law" (Neh 8:13). As the rest of the book of Nehemiah unfolds, the people began to respond enthusiastically to what they had learned. God's Word had powerfully impacted them in such a way that it dramatically transformed their lives.

A faithful pastor will forever be imploring his congregation to seek the truth. Not simply the truth *about* Scripture but the truth *of* Scripture.

This is no small task in a world that is accustomed to quick fixes and shortcuts. Many of us would rather read books about the Bible that offer quick and helpful fixes to life's problems than to mine the depths of Scripture itself, which has the power to renew one's life (Ps 19:7). Small group leaders often ask me for suggestions about which book their group might consider using for their next study. I never cease to be amazed at their lackluster response when I suggest that they consider the Bible! To "walk and please God" (1 Thess 4:1) means that you will see His truth as "more desirable than gold . . . and sweeter than honey, which comes from the honeycomb" (Ps 19:10).

Commit to Do What God Commands

Knowing the truth is one thing; doing it is another. The Thessalonians were taught by one of the greatest preachers who ever lived. Their spiritual depth was as deep as it was wide. Their spiritual growth, however, was contingent on more than just having a breadth of theological knowledge. They had to determine that they were going to continue to pursue God. In essence, Paul tells them, "You started the race well, now keep running." "You have the foundation in place, now keep building on it." Quite plainly he says, "Take your spiritual devotion to another level." As he put it, "Do so even more" (4:1). To put it another way, let your walk with God spill over into every area of your life. In a sense this statement, together with the call to sanctification in verse 3, will form the basis for every other exhortation that Paul gives in the remainder of the letter.

Following Christ is not a sprint to the finish line; it is a marathon that requires commitment, tenacity, and discipline. You don't enter this race to try it out; you enter this race to finish. You burn your bridges. You turn away from your past. You don't look back, and you can't go back. Like Peter, you look to Jesus and say, "Lord there is nowhere else for me to go. 'You are the only One who has the words of eternal life'" (see John 6:68).

Paul would later give Timothy the same challenge that he gave the Thessalonians. He shared three analogies that would help both Timothy and us to understand the level of commitment required for pursuing Christ (2 Tim 2:3-7): .

- *The good soldier.* A soldier is dedicated above all else to please his commanding officer. His personal preferences become secondary to that of his superior. In the same way, we surrender our agenda for Christ's agenda. We are no longer our own; we belong completely to Him (see also 1 Cor 6:19-20).

- *The disciplined athlete.* An athlete knows the rules before the game begins. If he cannot accept them then he does not compete. The rules are not viewed as burdensome but as necessary for the fairness of the competition. Likewise, we "calculate the cost" of following Christ before entering His race, and since Jesus sets the rules for the race, we only enter if we are willing to follow them completely. We are willing to do what is necessary so as not to be disqualified from the race.
- *The hardworking farmer.* The farmer painstakingly tills the soil and plants the seed. He does this not simply to produce a crop, but to reap a harvest. The farmer knows that there will be no harvest if there is no diligent labor. As Christians, we diligently work the field where God places us, knowing that if we desire to reap a harvest, we must continue to plant some seeds.

In sum, King David's words capture Paul's desire for the Thessalonians: "As a deer longs for streams of water, so I long for You, God" (Ps 42:1). That encapsulates what kind of commitment we must have if we desire to pursue God.

God's Will Must Be Our Guide
1 THESSALONIANS 4:3-7

To achieve victory over sexual sin we obviously need some help. Paul provides this help by giving the necessary motivation: "For this is *God's will,* your sanctification" (4:3; emphasis added). If we aim to please God, then we first must know what pleases Him. God does not leave us with any question as to how He feels about sexual sin. Paul makes this clear to the Thessalonians: "For this is God's will, your sanctification: that you abstain from sexual immorality" (4:3). "Stay completely away from it," he asserts. The thought here is similar to that of his admonition to Timothy when he commanded him to "flee from youthful passions" (2 Tim 2:22). If we keep in mind the context of 1 Thessalonians, we will recognize that what Paul says here has serious implications for the young Thessalonian Christians.

Thessalonica was a sex-saturated city. Much like the world today, the Greco-Roman world viewed sex as simply another biological function like eating or drinking. When you were hungry you ate and when you were thirsty you drank. In the same way, when you craved sex, you had sex. No restrictions. No guilt. It was simply accepted, and it was readily available if you desired it. The Thessalonians were immersed in this culture, and doubtlessly some of those who followed Christ were former participants in this culture.

Consider parenthetically that the transforming power of the gospel is why its message is such "good news." No person stands outside of the reach of God's amazing grace. From former prostitutes and thieves to the sexually perverse and alcoholics, the power of the gospel can transform them all. At my church, we are constantly reminding one another that we are real people in a real world who have been transformed by a real God. I call my congregation's attention repeatedly to 1 Cor 6:11. After listing all of the heinous sins that keep people from heaven, Paul looked squarely at the Corinthians and said, "And some of you used to be like this. But you were washed, you were sanctified, you were justified in the name of the Lord Jesus Christ and by the Spirit of our God" (1 Cor 6:11).

That Paul begins his discussion about sanctification by addressing the issue of sexual conduct is therefore no accident. He fully recognized that for those who were saved from this culture and for those who lived within this culture, the temptation to succumb to sexual sin was great. He arms them with the necessary motivation to achieve victory— God's will.

What pastor has not been asked by someone in his congregation, "How can I know God's will?" Contrary to the mistaken notions of many, God's will is not hidden and mysterious—it's not like you have decipher some code to "find" it. Throughout the Scriptures you read specific statements that reveal God's will for you. Here are just a few:

- It is God's will that you be saved (1 Tim 2:4).
- It is God's will that you live transformed lives (Rom 12:2).
- It is God's will that you have a good testimony to those outside of the church (1 Pet 2:13-15).
- It is God's will that you suffer for living righteous lives (1 Pet 3:17-18).
- It is God's will that you be Spirit-filled (Eph 5:18).
- It is God's will that you be thankful (1 Thess 5:18).

For the Thessalonians, turning "to God from idols" (1:9) now meant that they were going to live according to a new set of standards. Instead of acquiescing to their culture, God desired for them to transcend it. To do this they needed to know His expectations about their sexuality. His will was not something that had to be discovered; it was something that had only to be obeyed. Paul shows them three ways in which they must obey His will.

Avoid Impurity (1 Thess 4:3-5,7)

God's desire for us is that we would make Him our greatest desire. Paul wrote, "For this is God's will, your sanctification" (4:3). The word "sanctification" occurs three times in this passage (4:3,4,7). The word means to be "set apart" or "dedicated" to God. The idea is literally that of holiness. Sanctification is both a standing and a process. On one hand, when you come to Christ, He transfers you into a new kingdom. You now stand redeemed and forgiven. You are not partially redeemed; you are fully redeemed (Col 1:13-14). You instantly have a new standing with God. On the other hand, however, you still live in a fallen world in unredeemed flesh. While you are saved from the penalty of sin, the power of sin is an ever-present reality with which you still must wrestle. In this sense, sanctification is the ongoing process whereby you grow in holiness. As Paul's prayers for the Thessalonians in 3:13 and 5:23 show, the process of sanctification will continue until their final glorification at His coming.

Sanctification touches every area of a person's life. In fact, Paul will address several specific areas in the coming verses. But given the setting in the city of Thessalonica, he begins with the subject of sexual purity. The command is simple and direct: "Abstain from sexual immorality" (4:3). No excuses. No "what ifs." Stay away from it. Now remember that Paul has been preparing them for this. "You already love God and you love His truth," he reminded them. "Now it's time to take your commitment to another level and run away from any form of sexual impurity." His point is total abstinence.

"Sexual immorality" refers to any form of illicit sexual behavior outside of what is prescribed by God in His Word. This encompasses both the actions of the body and the thoughts of the heart (Matt 5:28). Sex according to God finds its perfect fulfillment only in the marriage relationship between a man and woman (Heb 13:4). Since sex was God's idea (Gen 1:28), it follows that you should not deviate from the parameters that He has established concerning it. Christianity had come to Thessalonica, but the city had not yet come to Christ. The Thessalonian believers had a new King and were anticipating a new kingdom, but until they could enter that kingdom, God called them to "shine as stars in the world" in their city (Phil 2:15). To live in this manner would require a decisive break from old patterns of thinking and living.

Abstaining from sexual sin involves the ability to "control" your "body" (4:4). Debate persists as to what exactly Paul had in mind in this verse.[9] The word translated "body" literally means "vessel." Paul was clearly using this word metaphorically, but the question is, How? Some commentators have opted to translate the word as "wife."[10] In this sense, Paul would be telling the Thessalonians that God's design for sexual fulfillment is within the marital relationship. Contrary to the "anything goes" philosophy in Thessalonica and the destruction of marital fidelity that came with it, these new believers were instructed to be faithful to their wives.

Other commentators see Paul's metaphor differently. Some follow the translators of the HCSB and conclude that Paul is using the word "vessel" as a metaphor for "body." Viewed in this way, Paul is telling the Thessalonians that abstinence from sexual sin is tied directly to how well they control their bodies. Chuck Swindoll illustrates this well:

> Abstaining begins with "possessing" our own vessels, that is, knowing our own bodies—how our sex drives function, what weakens our self-control, and what strengthens it. Possessing our bodies involves admitting temptations we can't handle and avoiding those enticing situations. Certain conversations with coworkers may lure us, and friendly touches may be too personal—avoid those situations. Some films, books, or magazines may ignite lustful passions, and some settings may provide opportunities for compromise—stay away from them. No one remains pure by accident. (Swindoll, *Contagious Christianity*, 49)

Thus, pleasing God means saying "no" to the flesh. Simply stated, we must control our bodies and not allow our bodies to control us. We must therefore "put on the Lord Jesus Christ, and make no plans to satisfy the fleshly desires" (Rom 13:14).

---

[9] For a helpful look at the varying ways in which one can interpret Paul's use of the word "vessel," see G. K. Beale, *1 and 2 Thessalonians*, The IVP New Testament Commentary Series (Downers Grove: InterVarsity, 2003), 116–20.

[10] See 1 Peter 3:7 where Peter refers to the wife as the "weaker vessel."

Wherever people land on how they interpret verse 4, the focus of the text remains clear: God has a standard for sex, and any deviation from that standard falls outside of His will. Failure to meet God's standard has serious consequences, both for the believer (Heb 11:5-6) and for the unbeliever (1 Cor 6:9-10). He expects that our bodies and our marriages be set apart to him "in sanctification and honor" (4:4). To drive this home, Paul paints a stark contrast between the believer and the unbeliever. Those who "don't know God" (Gentiles) exercise "lustful desires" to satisfy their sexual appetites (4:5), but those who "walk to please God" pursue purity and holiness (4:1,7; see also Rom 6:13).

Respect Others (1 Thess 4:6a)

Sexual sin is a transgression not only against the holiness of God but also against the dignity of other people. God establishes boundaries for your life. His boundary for sexual impurity must not be crossed (4:3). His boundary for how we view others should also be respected. To be sexually impure therefore is basically to tell God that we don't care what He says and to tell others that we don't care who they are. As Paul might describe it, when we commit sexual sin, we disobey God's will and we disregard our brother's personhood.

Most people never think of sexual sin in this way. Even a "harmless" consensual sexual encounter with another person is an offence against that other person. Concerning this, John Phillips offers a stern word: "God has written 'No Trespassing' over every man or woman who is not one's own wife or husband. . . . He has also posted the warning 'Trespassers will be prosecuted'" (Phillips, *Exploring 1 and 2 Thessalonians*, 103). When we commit sexual sin with another person we cross a boundary that God never intended to be crossed. We are taking from someone something that does not belong to us. In essence we are really saying to the other person, "I do not care about you." Often we hear one person say to another, "If you really love me, you will have sex with me." The truth is that if that person really loved the one with whom he wanted to have sex, they would not have sex at all. The only time that God removes the "No Trespassing" signs are when a man and woman are married.

Outside of marriage, the "No Trespassing" sign applies to both parties. A sexual encounter never involves just one person sinning; two people are sinning. **Sexual sin is saying to God, "I don't care if I sin against**

You, and I also don't care if I cause this other person to sin against You."
Jesus has strong words for those who cause others to sin:

> But whoever causes the downfall of one of these little ones who
> believe in Me—it would be better for him if a heavy millstone were
> hung around his neck and he were drowned in the depths of the sea!
> (Matt 18:6-7)

Assume Responsibility (1 Thess 4:6b)

Why is Paul sharing this with the Thessalonians? After all, he praised
them for turning away from idols to serve God (1:9). Surely this must
have included their turning away from the idol of sexual immorality. He
also rejoiced that they "welcomed" God's Word into their lives (2:13).
Wouldn't this imply that they also welcomed God's instructions about
sexual purity? He even encouraged them to keep up their passion for
God (4:3). Doesn't a passion for God imply a hatred for sin?

Why was this subject so important to Paul? He gives us a straightforward answer: "The Lord is an avenger of all these offenses" (4:6b).
Stated plainly, God takes sexual sin very seriously. The Bible has much
to say on this subject. Consider the following passages:

> Marriage must be respected by all, and the marriage bed kept
> undefiled, because God will judge immoral people and adulterers.
> (Heb 13:4)

> But sexual immorality and any impurity or greed should not even be
> heard of among you, as is proper for saints. (Eph 5:3)

> Therefore, put to death what belongs to your worldly nature: sexual
> immorality, impurity, lust, evil desire, and greed, which is idolatry.
> Because of these, God's wrath comes on the disobedient. (Col 3:5-6)

> Don't you know that your bodies are a part of Christ's body? So
> should I take a part of Christ's body and make it part of a prostitute?
> Absolutely not! Don't you know that anyone joined to a prostitute is
> one body with her? For Scripture says, The two will become one flesh.
> But anyone joined to the Lord is one spirit with Him.
>
> Run from sexual immorality! "Every sin a person can commit is
> outside the body." On the contrary, the person who is sexually immoral
> sins against his own body. Don't you know that your body is a
> sanctuary of the Holy Spirit who is in you, whom you have from God?

You are not your own, for you were bought at a price. Therefore glorify God in your body. (1 Cor 6:15-20)

The Thessalonians needed to hear that they were accountable for their actions, even those things done in secret. Crossing God's boundaries has consequences because the Lord is the "avenger of all." He will hold accountable all who transgress His moral laws (Heb 4:13).

God's Approval Must Be Our Passion
1 THESSALONIANS 4:8

The closing verse of this passage brings Paul's teaching on sexual purity to a fitting conclusion. In this final verse Paul issues a solemn warning: "Therefore, the person who rejects this does not reject man, but God, who also gives you His Holy Spirit" (4:8). The "this" to which he refers is God's call to a life of purity and sanctification, specifically as it relates to sexual purity (4:7). Interestingly, he begins his discussion with an exhortation to please God and ends with a warning about rejecting God (4:1,8). Pleasing God means living a pure life. Rejecting God means living an impure life. It's not complicated. Jesus said, "If you love Me, you will keep My commands" (John 14:15). Likewise He also said, "The one who doesn't love Me will not keep My words" (John 14:24).

Our Loyalty Is to the Father (1 Thess 4:8a)

In verse 8 Paul draws a line in the sand. On one side of the line is obedience and on the other side is disobedience. If we cross the line, we reject both God and His Spirit within us (4:8). However, the opposite response brings about very different results. To acknowledge the boundaries that God has established means that we desire to acknowledge the God who established those boundaries. In so doing, we honor God and His indwelling Spirit. This concluding verse brings us full circle back to our relationship with God. Everything in your Christian life rests on this relationship, including your response to sexual temptation. Our motivation to obey God comes not only from the benefits of obedience but also from our commitment to acknowledge God for who He is. Concerning this, Jeremiah declares that if we boast about anything, we should boast in the reality of understanding and knowing God Himself (Jer 9:23-24). Paul echoed this same sentiment when he said, "So the one who boasts must boast in the Lord" (2 Cor 10:17). One of the primary ways that we boast in God is by keeping His commandments (1 John 2:3). When we know God, we not only do what He says, we also delight in what He says (1 John 5:3). The psalmist writes,

> *How happy is the man*
> *who does not follow the advice of the wicked*
> *or take the path of sinners*
> *or join a group of mockers!*
> *Instead,* his delight is in the LORD's instruction. (Ps 1:1-2; emphasis added)

When the disciples asked Jesus how they should pray. Jesus taught them to begin their prayers by finding their delight in God (Matt 6:9-10). He gave them (and us) three ways to do this:

- *Remember God's name.* He is our Father. He has adopted us into His family through Jesus Christ. As His children, we reflect Him in everything, from what we think to what we say and what we do. We exist to bring honor to His great Name.
- *Seek God's kingdom.* As citizens of His kingdom our priorities are different from those of the "Gentiles" (1 Thess 4:5; cf. Matt 6:32). From how we invest our time to how we spend our money, every decision we make is filtered through kingdom lenses. Before you do anything, one of your first questions should be, How will this activity advance His kingdom?
- *Do His will.* We gladly surrender our will to do His will. Since He created us (Ps 139), He knows what is best for us. Our passion then is to know and to do His will. Our lives no longer revolve around what *we think*; they now revolve around what *God says*.

You and I live in a culture where people reject God without giving Him a second thought. God has called us to be different. Our Christianity really does matter, and how we live matters to God. The Gentiles pursue their "lustful desires" for the pleasure of the moment, but those who follow Christ pursue God for the promise of lasting fulfillment. The writer of Hebrews tells us that Moses made the choice to pursue God. He considered it worthwhile

> *to suffer with the people of God rather than to enjoy the short-lived*
> *pleasure of sin. For he considered the reproach because of the Messiah*
> *to be greater than the treasures of Egypt, since his attention was on the*
> *reward.* (Heb 11:25-26)

Our Power Is by the Spirit (1 Thess 4:8b)

In 1 Thessalonians 4:1-8 Paul specifically mentions all three Persons of the Trinity: God (4:1,3,5,7,8), Jesus (4:1-2), and the Holy Spirit (4:8). By referring to the Trinity, Paul shows how all three Persons of the Godhead are actively involved in our sanctification.[11] Clearly, God sees our holiness as a priority. A quick look back at these verses gives keen insight into how this works. First, God establishes the pattern for our lives by revealing His will and holding us accountable for how we respond to it (4:3,6). Second, Jesus Christ provides our only access to knowing and pleasing God (4:1). Only by entering into a relationship with Christ can we fully grasp the significance of God's commandments (4:3). Third, God gives His Holy Spirit to us (4:8). The Spirit then empowers us to live a holy life. Allowing impurity to invade our lives would be in direct opposition to the work of the Holy Spirit (4:8).

Before moving on, consider a final observation about Paul's reference to the "Holy Spirit" (4:8b). Paul states that the person who "rejects" a life committed to sexual purity "does not reject man, but God, *who also gives you His Holy Spirit*" (4:8; emphasis added). The implication here is that to reject God's commandments is to reject the Spirit of God. This statement raises an important question: Why did Paul include this passing reference to the Holy Spirit? To answer this question we must first understand how God's Spirit is at work in us. When you are saved, God "seals" you with His Spirit. The Holy Spirit is God's earnest money contract. God gives you His Spirit as a guarantee of your future in God's presence forever (2 Cor 1:22; Eph 1:13-14). But God's Spirit is not just a promise for your future; His Spirit empowers you to live today. The Spirit takes up permanent residence in your life. He makes your heart His home (John 14:15-26; Rom 8:9). God gives you all of His Spirit (1 Cor 12:13). You, however, have not yet yielded all of yourself to Him. This is why God commands you to "be filled by the Spirit" (Eph 5:18). As you yield to the Spirit, He dramatically changes you (Eph 5:19–6:9). He changes you in a number of ways:

- He enables you to know God's truth (1 Cor 2:10-13).
- He helps you in your weaknesses (Rom 8:26).

---

[11] For a more detailed exposition of Paul's trinitarian theology, see Eph 1:1-14, where he specifically outlines the work of the Trinity in salvation.

- He confirms your salvation (1 John 3:24; 4:13).
- He points you to Jesus (John 15:26-27).
- He convicts you of sin (John 16:8).
- He helps you to pray (Rom 8:27).
- He helps you to have victory over sin (Gal 5:16).

Keeping in mind the Spirit's work, turn your attention back to Paul's reference to the Holy Spirit in 1 Thessalonians 4:8. Remember the context that surrounds this verse. Paul is entreating the Thessalonians to "abstain from sexual immorality" because God has called them to a life of purity and holiness (4:3). As we have just seen, God gives you His Spirit to indwell you and to empower you to live the kind of life that He requires. The Holy Spirit's presence then does two very important things: First, He ensures your legitimacy as His children and guarantees your future with Him. Second, He powerfully works in you to bring about your holiness. Thus when we "reject" God's commandments, we are rejecting the very Holy Spirit who empowers us to keep those commandments. That is why the Bible teaches that believers can "stifle" (1 Thess 5:19) and "grieve" (Eph 4:30) the Holy Spirit.

Conclusion

The inescapable conclusion of this passage is that a decision to follow Jesus Christ does not mark the end of our journey—it is only the beginning. God did not save us to sit in a church pew, to listen to sermons, or to put money in an offering plate. While these are good things, they do not account for the sum total of our salvation. When we follow Christ, we commit to pursue Him with our entire being, including our bodies. Nothing that we have truly belongs to us; and nothing should be more important to us than following Him. Through the work of His Spirit, God is transforming us from who we are into who He wants us to be. Our holiness is His priority. Along our journey the road ahead is riddled with many pitfalls to our holiness. Satan wants nothing more than to keep us right where we are. He wants us to be comfortable with our church membership, complacent in our walk with God, and callous in our view of sexual purity. We must recognize these dangers. We dare not ask what the minimum requirement is for being a Christian; we pursue God with an ever-increasing zeal. We ought not see how close to God's moral line we can walk before we get too close; we stay as far away from the line as possible. Unlike those who have no regard for God, we use our passions not to satisfy our cravings but to please our God.

Reflect and Discuss

1. What is required of a person who desires to "walk and please God" (4:1)? How are one's head, heart, and hands included?

2. In the context of this passage, explain why it is important both to *know* what God says and to *do* what He says.

3. If we say we don't know God's exact will in a particular situation, is that most often a legitimate excuse or an attempt at self-justification? Explain your answer.

4. How would you explain the doctrine of "sanctification" in a youth Sunday school class?

5. Why did Paul begin this series of exhortations with the topic of sexual immorality?

6. What does Paul mean by "abstain"? How can you practice this today? Be specific.

7. How does sexual promiscuity "transgress against and defraud" another human being?

8. Do you think telling people that God is the "avenger" of those who commit sexual sin is an effective tool for evangelizing nonbelievers? Is it effective for encouraging the sanctification of believers? Why?

9. What should your real motivation be for keeping the commandments of God?

10. In view of the role of the Holy Spirit within us, what are the disadvantages and pitfalls of rejecting God and His Spirit?

Love Matters

1 THESSALONIANS 4:9-12

Main Idea: A genuine love for others is reflected by how you live and work.

I. **You Love Each Other Genuinely (4:9-10).**
    A. Your love shows (4:9).
    B. Your love goes (4:10a).
    C. Your love grows (4:10b).
II. **You Do Your Work Diligently (4:11).**
    A. You lead a quiet life (4:11a).
    B. You mind your own business (4:11b).
    C. You work with your hands (4:11c).
III. **You Live Your Life Purposefully (4:12).**
    A. You make a difference in your world (4:12a).
    B. You don't take advantage of others (4:12b).

Most likely you have had the unfortunate experience of saying something that you regretted. I can vividly recall one experience where I wish I had kept my words to myself. One evening while attending college, a few friends and I had a little too much time on our hands. While out looking for something fun to do, we noticed that a business down the street had just installed a beautiful engraved wooden sign in its front yard. Upon closer inspection, it just so happened that one of our friends had a last name that was identical to the name of the business. Without even thinking, we took the sign and excitingly presented this gift to our friend. Our reasoning was that it would look better on his wall than it did in front of the business.

A few weeks later I received a call from my head football coach informing me that two detectives from the local police department had visited him that afternoon. They had a warrant for our arrest. As it "just so happened" that we saw the sign in the lawn that night, it also "just so happened" that a campus security guard saw that sign hanging on my friend's wall. Being a true friend, when confronted by the security guard He turned us in! Our coach told us that he convinced the detectives to give us a chance to return the sign and to ask the owner of the business to drop all charges.

Without delay, and fearing the worst, we went to meet the owner. To say that this person was unhappy would be an understatement. Nevertheless, we sat at her desk and pleaded our case while praying silently for our acquittal. The owner looked us squarely in the eyes and asked, "Why should I let you guys off the hook?" Without thinking I replied, "Because we are Christians." Wrong answer. She looked at me and said sternly, "Well, if you guys were really Christians you would not have stolen my sign in the first place." Ouch! Fortunately for us, and despite my stupidity, she dropped the charges. I guess she thought that the look of embarrassment on my face was punishment enough. What a lesson learned in so many ways.

It's one thing to say that you are a Christian; it's another thing to prove you are a Christian by the way you live. As Paul penned the final two chapters of his epistle, he directed his instruction toward the behavior of the Thessalonians. He aimed at their behavior not so that they would be *good* but so that they would be *godly*. His will for believers is nothing less than their complete sanctification (4:3). In fact, God takes the matter of your holiness so seriously that He leaves no room for you to misunderstand His expectations: "You are to be holy to Me because I, Yahweh, am holy, and I have set you apart from the nations to be Mine" (Lev 20:26).

Because God is committed to our holiness, He will chip away at any imperfection and remove every impediment that keeps us from looking like Him. God is like the stone sculptor who, when asked how he could create such a beautiful masterpiece from an ugly piece of granite, replied, "I simply begin with an image in mind and chip away at everything that does not look like that image until the masterpiece remains." That vividly describes the process of sanctification. God's ultimate goal for believers is that they will reflect the image and likeness of God. Thus, as Millard Erickson writes, through the process of sanctification,

> one's moral condition is brought into conformity with one's legal status before God. It is a continuation of what was begun in regeneration, when a newness of life was conferred upon and instilled within the believer. (Erickson, *Christian Theology*, 980)

Erickson is saying that what God did internally at salvation, He continues to do externally through sanctification. Through the ongoing work of sanctification, God's glory is reflected in the life of a believer. Thus the only reliable physical evidence of a redeemed heart is a transformed life. Paul illustrated this vividly when he wrote,

> *Do everything without grumbling and arguing, so that you may be blameless and pure, children of God who are faultless in a crooked and perverted generation, among whom* you shine like stars in the world. (Phil 2:14; emphasis added)

Through a series of succinct exhortations, Paul sets his sights on the ongoing process of sanctification in the Thessalonian Christians. After tackling the issue of sexual purity (4:1-8), he now turns his attention to the matter of love. Covering the space of only four verses, his discussion is direct and to the point. Yet each verse carries with it significant implications for Christian living. Paul sees the matter of love as so basic to being a Christian that he states, "About brotherly love: You don't need me to write you because you yourselves are taught by God to love one another" (4:9).

You Love Each Other Genuinely
1 THESSALONIANS 4:9-10

How you respond to God's Word will directly influence how you love other people. Paul therefore reminds the Thessalonians that they are "taught by God" to love one another (4:9). Grasping this truth will affect how we relate to all people, including those who seem unlovable. Sadly, however, Christians often spend more time quarreling than they do loving one another. The world often displays a more profound love for its own than God's people do for their own. Church fights and church splits have become all too commonplace in the modern culture. The song "They Will Know We are Christians by Our Love" could very well be renamed "They Will Know We are Christians by Our Fights." Although the Thessalonian church did not have internal conflict, Paul nonetheless challenges them to love one another "even more" (4:10). When God's people have a genuine love for one another it will be reflected in three ways: it will be obvious, it will know no limits, and it will continue to grow.

Your Love Shows (1 Thess 4:9)

Let's focus on the phrase, "You yourselves are *taught by God* to love one another" (4:9; emphasis added). This unusual expression is used only here in the New Testament and conveys the idea of an innate knowledge made available by the indwelling presence of the Holy Spirit. With the Spirit as their teacher, Paul saw no urgent need to give them any further instruction. As Marshall explains,

> Exhortation is not needed because the readers have experienced an inward, divine compulsion to love one another. In other words, Paul ascribes their growth in love (1:3) to the sanctifying power of the Spirit (cf. 4:8). (Marshall, *1 and 2 Thessalonians*, 115)

In reality, God is the only One fully qualified to teach on the subject of love, because love would not exist without Him. He is its author. He is its commentator, because you would not know how to love without His instruction. So then, God not only teaches you about love, but He also teaches you how to love. Therefore, to begin any discussion on the subject of love, the logical starting point must be with God Himself. Just as we lack the ability to "abstain" from sexual sin without the Spirit's empowerment, we also lack the ability to love others without God's help. Without God's "divine power" we would never have the capacity to share in God's "divine nature" (2 Pet 1:3-4).

How then does this work in a Christian's life? When the new birth occurs, you receive God's Spirit. At that moment an exchange takes place: "old things" are replaced with "new things" (2 Cor 5:17). One of the new things that you receive is God's love. Paul tells us in Romans 5:5 that "God's love has been poured out in our hearts through the Holy Spirit who was given to us." Our capacity to love others does not come by trying harder; it comes by yielding to God's Spirit. When you yield to the Holy Spirit, He gives you the capacity to love others. Consider, for example, Paul's instruction to the Ephesian church concerning healthy relationships between a husband and wife, child and parent, and slave and master. It is no coincidence that he prefaces the entire discussion by emphasizing the importance of being "filled by the Spirit" (Eph 5:18–6:9). When we struggle with the ability to love others, the real question we should ask is, Does God's Spirit dwell in us? John writes,

We know that we have passed from death to life because we love our brothers. . . .

This is how we have come to know love: He laid down His life for us. We should also lay down our life for our brothers. If anyone has this world's goods and sees his brother in need but closes his eyes to his need—how can God's love abide in him?

Little children, we must not love with word or speech, but with truth and action. This is how we will know we belong to the truth. (1 John 3:14,16-19)

Paul challenged the Corinthians, "Test yourselves to see if you are in the faith" (2 Cor 13:5). Our capacity to love others will reveal much about our hearts since genuine love is a reflection of God's presence in us.

Let's consider for a moment how the presence or absence of love impacts our churches. When we think of the ingredients of healthy churches, we often identify such things as biblical preaching, evangelistic zeal, doctrinal fidelity, and dynamic worship. Yet many of us have doubtless had the experience of visiting a church where the preaching was solid, the music was uplifting, and the doctrine was sound, but we still left with a feeling that something was missing. Perhaps we were sensing a lack of genuine love? When love is absent from the church, something is seriously wrong. Sometimes we can observe this by how late people arrive and how quickly they exit when the service has ended. Or we might sense a feeling of aloofness or superficiality among the people. Whatever the case, we just know when love is absent.

By contrast, where there is a genuine "brotherly love" in a church, our experience is altogether different. Jesus said, "By this all people will know that you are My disciples, if you have love for one another" (John 13:35). Paul prayed for the Philippians' love to "keep on growing" (Phil 1:9), and he thanked God that the Colossians' hearts were "joined together in love" (Col 2:2). When love is present in a church, the people are real with one another, the singing is joyful and the fellowship is sweet (Eph 5:19-20; Col 3:16-17). Love is not something that can be faked. Words can't make up for it, knowledge can't do it, and even genuine acts of kindness fall short where love is absent (1 Cor 13:1-3). Genuine love flows directly from a genuine relationship with God. A church might have all the necessary ingredients to *do church*, but if it lacks love, it is not *being the church*. We cannot expect the people on the outside to come in if the people on the inside do not love each other in such a way that their faith shines out.

The Thessalonians' love for one another was deeply rooted in their relationship with God. Because God had given them His Holy Spirit, they now had the capacity to love like they never had before. Their love for one another was a reflection of their new nature. Warren Wiersbe's insight about the "new nature" of a Christian is good:

> Fish do not attend classes to learn how to swim. . . . And birds by nature put out their wings and flap them in order to fly. It is nature that determines action . . . because a Christian has God's nature (2 Peter 1:4), he loves, because "God is love" (1 John 4:8). (Weirsbe, *Be Ready*, 177)

Your Love Goes (1 Thess 4:10a)

The Thessalonians' love went beyond their city; it extended "toward all the brothers in the entire region of Macedonia" (4:10). What a marvelous statement! Their love for the other churches literally went the distance. We have already observed this in chapter 1 where Paul commends them for their "labor of love." Such a passionate commitment to love others was paying off because it moved outside of the walls of their fellowship and into Macedonia and the regions beyond (1:3,8). The newly established churches in Philippi (Acts 16:12-40) and Berea (Acts 17:10-14) were reaping the benefits of the Thessalonians' love.

What a powerful truth to grasp! Our love for *our* church is not enough; we must love *God's* church. This distinction is important. Today, many churches are fighting for their very survival. Declining memberships, internal conflicts, and a transitioning world outside their doors have led many churches to circle the wagons. Struggling to sustain their own existence, the last thing in importance for many of these churches is what is happening in God's extended kingdom. But God is at work in the world.

The local church was never intended by God to be an island in its community or the "Lone Ranger" in God's work. God has called believers to do His work together. We are not in competition. One of the true tests of our love for others is our ability to rejoice when God chooses to bless others more than He blesses us. For example, can we rejoice when the church down the street is experiencing revival and our church is not? Do we thank God for the people who are coming to Christ in another church even though a group of people left our church to start it? How about when social media is abuzz with testimonies of God's power at work in others—are we jealous that He's not doing the same in us?

God's love in us enables us to love others the way that God loves us—unconditionally. When we willfully withhold our love from others, especially those who belong to God's church, we rob others of the love they deserve, and we rob ourselves of the joy that comes from loving others. Since Jesus is building His church, we can be sure that He is at work in many churches, including those in other countries. While we may never get to go to these countries or attend these churches, God has given us the privilege of showing our love by praying, encouraging, and giving. Perhaps the greatest thing you can do in your church is to ask God continually how you can extend your love outside the walls of your church.

This truth hit home a few months ago when I received an envelope in the mail containing dozens of handwritten notes from members of another local church. The cover letter attached to these notes informed me that the membership of this small, aging congregation wanted to make a difference in God's kingdom. Because most of the members were advanced in years, they believed that their biggest impact could come by praying for and writing notes to local pastors. As I read the notes, not only was my heart encouraged, but I was also reminded that we are all in this journey together. Instead of circling its wagons and fighting for survival, this church decided to extend its love beyond its walls.

Your Love Grows (1 Thess 4:10b)

What further encouragement can be given to a church that was already excelling in its love for one another? Paul continues, "we encourage you, brothers, to do so even more" (4:10b). We might recall that he also gave them a similar command in 4:1 where he challenged them to grow "even more" in their relationship with God. In both cases his challenge is the same: "You are pursuing God, but you should pursue Him even more." And, "You are loving one another; now love one another even more."

Loving others is not an item to be checked off of our daily "to do" list. It's not like you say, "Okay, I loved my spouse today. Now I can move on." Or, "I just finished showing love to my friend today. I'll be back to do it again tomorrow." Loving others is an ongoing activity—it is a pursuit. Because we are progressing continuously in our personal sanctification, our love will always be growing. Paul uses the present tense of the verb *love* to express the idea of continual action. Thus loving others is not a task we complete—it is an ongoing activity and a lifelong pursuit. *The Message* paraphrase of 1 Thessalonians 4:9-10 captures this idea well:

> *Regarding life together and getting along with each other, you don't need me to tell you what to do. You're God-taught in these matters. Just love one another! You're already good at it; your friends all over the province of Macedonia are the evidence. Keep it up; get better and better at it.* (Emphasis in original)

Paul commended them for the breadth of their love (toward all the brothers) and challenged them to increase the depth of their love (do so even more).

Jesus provided a poignant example of selfless love on the night He gathered His disciples in the upper room. In a selfless act of service and humility He methodically washed their feet, including those of Judas. His display of love was a living illustration of the selfless love He expected His followers to show one another (John 13:1-17). However, we will never entirely grasp the full force of His lesson until we first understand His motivation. What prompted this display of love by Jesus? John says that Jesus loved His disciples "to the end" (John 13:1). His love for them knew no limits. It had no boundaries. His love for them was both deep and wide.

The same motivation is necessary for us to love others in the way that God commands. Our love must also have no limits or boundaries. It may be easy to love the "Macedonians" when we think they deserve it, but what about when they do something that offends us? Sure, it's easy to love people in your church when they agree with your ideas and go along with your plans, but what happens when they question your ideas and resist your plans? We can never take a break from loving others, even when we think they don't deserve it. We cannot obey God's command to love one another "even more" if we selectively choose whom we will and will not love.

You Do Your Work Diligently
1 THESSALONIANS 4:11

Many Christians compartmentalize their faith. With their Christianity neatly tucked away in their back pocket, backpack, or purse, they head off to work, school, or their daily activities. While they may see their

Christianity as a *part* of their lives, they fail to acknowledge it as the *heart* of their lives. Unfortunately, many Christians never see the direct link between their faith and their daily activities. Their thinking may go something like this: employment is for working, school is for learning, leisure is for playing, and church is for Sunday. By viewing life in this way they miss the whole point of their faith. As Paul put it, Jesus is not a part of your life; Jesus *is* your life (Col 3:4). By acknowledging this truth, you will no longer see Jesus as a part of your workday—you will see Him as the One who sets the agenda for how you work. You will no longer see Him as a part of your school day—you will see Him as the One who sets the agenda for how you study. You will no longer see Him as a part of your daily schedule—you will see Him as the One who sets the agenda for how you schedule your days.

The Thessalonians loved those inside the church, but they also needed to love those outside the church. One of the simplest ways in which they could demonstrate their love and respect for others was by working diligently at their jobs. We would do well to remember that how we work at our jobs says much about how we view our faith (Col 3:23-24). That Paul saw the need to address the irresponsible behavior of some of the Thessalonians clearly indicates that their poor testimony was adversely affecting the ministry of the church and the integrity of the gospel (4:11-12). Bruce makes this point well:

> Non-Christians must be given no pretext for thinking that Christians were unprofitable members of society. The church could not discharge its ministry of witness and reconciliation in the world unless its members adorned the gospel with their lives as well as their lips. (Bruce, *1 and 2 Thessalonians*, 93)

To understand what prompted Paul to address this situation, we need to understand some important background information. During his initial visit to Thessalonica, Paul gave the people specific details about the Lord's return (5:2; 2 Thess 2:5). In light of his instruction, the church was eagerly anticipating the day when Jesus would return for His church (1:10). Convinced that Christ's return was imminent, some in the fellowship had apparently decided to quit their jobs. For them, working was pointless since any material possessions or wealth would be left behind. Their idleness was creating tension within the church and reflecting a poor testimony outside the church (2 Thess 3:6-13). With too much time on their hands, these misguided and irresponsible busybodies were intruding into everyone's affairs. Further, because they no longer had any income, they were forced to sponge off of others to meet their basic necessities (2 Thess 3:10-11). We can see very clearly how these lazy, inconsiderate believers would be a drain on their friends, former employers, and fellow church members.

Paul most likely had these irresponsible believers in mind when he wrote this portion of the letter. If so, he was sternly reminding the church that how they live and work reflects on the faith they profess. The promise of the Lord's return should have motivated the Thessalonians to work faithfully. Instead, many of these misguided believers were viewing their jobs apathetically. Knowing that when Jesus comes we will give an account for how we lived should provide sufficient incentive for us to pursue any task with passion and excellence (2 Cor 5:10).

You Lead a Quiet Life (1 Thess 4:11a)

Commentators are divided in how they interpret Paul's admonition to "seek to lead a quiet life" (4:11a). Some see this as a direct injunction against the irresponsible Thessalonians who were unnecessarily burdening others. Others believe Paul is encouraging the whole community of believers to live restful, quiet lives free from anger, conflict, or hostility. While either view would fit the context well, Paul appears to be addressing the entire fellowship. The Greek word translated "seek to lead" means to "strive after" or "be zealous for" and conveys the idea of ambition. The word translated "quiet" refers more to a state of being than to an absence of words. It appears likely that in light of their expectation of Christ's return, Paul exhorts them to strive to live faithfully, quietly, and restfully.

In this generation, ambition is rarely directed at restfulness. Most often it is directed toward the relentless pursuit of some goal, achievement, or status. Yet God's view of ambition is so different. Christians must make it their ambition to live in such a way that they project a "quiet" confidence in the God they serve. Christians live such a drastically different life from that of the rest of the world. Paul reminds his readers of this as he brings Christianity down to workplaces, schools, and neighborhoods. Just as God wills for us to be sexually pure (4:3), He also desires for us to live for Christ in such a way that our love for Him and our quiet confidence in Him will be a witness to the world around us (4:12).

While Paul's admonition may have been clear, some of the Thessalonians had clearly not taken it to heart. Quitting jobs and taking advantage of others was not how God expected them to live. An eager anticipation for the return of Christ was admirable, but failing to live faithfully until He returned was not. Such a lifestyle did not take seriously their calling to "walk properly in the presence of outsiders" (4:12). **The Thessalonians needed a firm reminder that the gospel is only as believable as the changed lives of those who proclaim it. Paul was attempting to bring their Christianity back to earth where it belonged.**

When this powerful truth comes to bear on our lives, it has serious implications. Instead of taking advantage of others, we will choose to trust God to supply our needs. Instead of cutting corners at work, we will do our work diligently as unto the Lord. Instead of fretting about every little thing, we will choose to present our requests to God. If Christianity means something in your church, then it will also mean something in your world. We therefore make it our ambition to do our work quietly and faithfully. Little things will not bother us because we understand the big picture (Matt 6:31-33). We show love to a watching world by displaying a quiet confidence in God. We don't quit our jobs and withdraw from the world. We don't take advantage of others. Instead, we confidently take our faith on vacation, to work, and to school. We aspire to "lead a tranquil and quiet life in all godliness and dignity" (1 Tim 2:2).

You Mind Your Own Business (1 Thess 4:11b)

The natural result of leading a quiet life is "to mind your own business" (4:11b). A person who minds his own business has little time to meddle in the affairs of others (2 Thess 3:11-12). Paul clearly has in mind those who had quit their jobs in anticipation of Christ's return. With too much time on their hands they were needlessly interjecting themselves into the business of others. Nothing is more disruptive to the unity of a church than a nosy individual who desires to know every detail of another person's life, and few things present a more distorted view of the Christian faith than a group of Christians who make it their business to get in everyone else's business.

Unfortunately, this is the picture that many people have of the "typical" church. They see it as a group of self-righteous, nosy people who have nothing better to do than to sit around and talk about what everyone else is doing. Of course, this is not what the church is or what the church does. Paul illustrates how you should conduct yourself with one simple statement: Mind your own business! We are not like the world. The sordid details of other people's lives and the latest tidbits of gossip do not concern us. Our life is a stewardship entrusted to us by God. One day we will be required to give an account of how well we managed it. The promise of Christ's return does not give us a reason to be lazy; it gives us a reason to get busy. Jesus had strong words for the "lazy" servant who did not faithfully invest the talents that his master gave him (Matt 25:14-30). The dividends that you get from your investments are God's business—but how you invest your life is your business. For this reason, Christians should be the hardest working and most conscientious people in their schools, on their athletic fields, in their workplaces, and in their neighborhoods (1 Cor 10:31; Eph 5:15-16; 6:6-8; Col 3:23-24; Titus 2:7-8).

You Work with Your Hands (1 Thess 4:11c)

Work enables us to live with dignity and purpose (Gen 1:28; 2:15; 3:23; Ps 8:4-8). Paul's challenge to "work with your own hands" (4:11c) is a powerful reminder that the Christian faith is a practical faith. It goes far beyond what happens in a church building at 11 a.m. on Sunday; it affects your life from 9 to 5 on Monday through Friday. Our faith goes to work with us.

Paul's reference to working with your hands may be an indication that many of the new Thessalonian believers had working class jobs, which required manual labor. Also, quite possibly many of them were subjected to slave labor. Perhaps these Christian slaves now thought that they were freed from the tyranny of their work. Greek culture frowned upon any type of manual labor. Only slaves were fit to perform certain jobs. Hard work, toil, and sweat were viewed as demeaning and undignified. In his book *Every Good Endeavor*, Timothy Keller offers some insight on the Greek view of work:

> Work was a barrier to the highest kind of life. Work made it impossible to rise above the earthbound humdrum of life into the realm of philosophy, the domain of the gods. The Greeks understood that life in the world required work, but they believed that not all work was created equal. Work that used the mind rather than the body was nobler, less beastly. The highest form of work was the most cognitive and the least manual. (Keller, *Every Good Endeavor*, 71)

God's view of work is very different. Far from shirking our responsibility to work, we honor Him by working diligently with your "own hands"

(4:11c). Hard work is not a demeaning exercise; it is a means by which God sustains our lives (2 Thess 3:10).

God raises the bar when it comes to how we live and work. Nothing about our lives is insignificant. Everything we do sends a message to the world about what we believe about God (4:3,12). From our words to our work, we are accountable to God for how we live. If our faith is real on Sunday at church, then it will be just as real on Monday in the office. The most tangible way that we can express love to others is passionately to live out our faith in the world. We do this by not being a nuisance to those within the church; and by being serious about how faithfully we live our lives outside of the church.

You Live Your Life Purposefully
1 THESSALONIANS 4:12

Paul sums up this entire passage by stating why his instruction is so important. Whatever you do, he admonished, be careful to "walk properly in the presence of outsiders and not be dependent on anyone" (4:12). In this verse Paul makes two significant statements: God never intended for the church to be isolated from its world, and God never intended for His church to be dependent on the world.

You Make a Difference in Your World (1 Thess 4:12a)

God established His church to be more than buildings dotting the landscapes of towns, cities, and countrysides. In fact, God never intended for His church to be a building at all. To be sure, church buildings are important and necessary, but Jesus did not die on the cross so that we could build buildings. He died on the cross to redeem a people. Peter describes the purpose of His redeemed people:

> But you are a chosen race, a royal priesthood, a holy nation, a people for His possession, so that you may proclaim the praises of the One who called you out of darkness into His marvelous light. (1 Pet 2:9)

He has called out a people to make a difference in His world by proclaiming His praises. While no Christian would disagree with that statement, not every believer understands how this is supposed to happen.

The Bible gives us two specific ways that we do this. First, we preach the gospel. God has chosen to use "the foolishness of the message preached" to make known His amazing redemptive provision of the cross (1 Cor 1:21). So central is preaching to God's redemptive plan that Paul rhetorically asks the Romans, "and how can they hear without a preacher?" (Rom 10:14). The implication is obvious: it is impossible to hear the gospel unless someone preaches it. A few verses later he makes that point clear by saying, "Faith comes from what is heard" (Rom 10:17). For the church to impact its world, the gospel must be heard; for the gospel to be heard, preaching must be central (Matt 28:18-20; Luke 24:46-47; Acts 1:8; 8:4; Eph 3:7-9). Even a cursory reading of the book of Acts reveals that this was a priority for the early church. **Preaching was not simply one means by which God established His church; preaching was the primary means by which God established His church.** His plan has not changed today.

However, while the preaching of the gospel is primary, it is not the only means by which the church witnesses to the world. The changed lives of those within the church also paint a picture of the gospel. Peter made this clear when he wrote,

> *Conduct yourselves honorably among the Gentiles, so that in a case where they speak against you as those who do what is evil, they will, by observing your good works, glorify God on the day of visitation.* (1 Pet 2:12)

To be clear, Peter is not saying that a silent witness is a substitute for preaching, but he is saying that the world judges the validity of your words by the conduct of your life. Paul is making this point to the Thessalonians: the message that we preach and the life that we live are inseparable.

You Don't Take Advantage of Others (1 Thess 4:12b)

Paul's concluding instruction, to "not be dependent on anyone" (4:12), fittingly sums up this section. A church that is a drain *on* its city is not going to make a positive impact *in* its city. As Marshall puts it, Christians should

> avoid bringing themselves into disrepute by failing to live up to the accepted standards of the society in which they live. . . . Christians must aim not to be dependent on anybody, especially those outside the church who will take a poor view of them if their religion makes them a public nuisance and burden. (Marshall, *1 and 2 Thessalonians*, 117)

Lazy, non-working, unproductive, and inconsiderate Christians who depend on others to meet their needs will be doing little to meet the needs of others. Paul's corrective to this kind of lifestyle is straightforward: love each other genuinely, do your work diligently, and live your life purposefully.

Conclusion

Ron Hutchcraft tells the story of meeting a woman from his church. Upon greeting her, he asked, "What do you do for a living?" With a huge grin she replied, "Pastor, I'm a disciple of Jesus Christ—cleverly disguised as a machine operator!" That woman clearly understood that her faith meant something. She got it. Paul did not want the Thessalonians to forget that their faith really mattered. He taught them that their Christianity should show up in the most basic aspects of their lives—including their relationships and their jobs. The profound truth of salvation was imminently practical. Heaven could veritably touch earth through their faith. God did not save them to sit around and wait for heaven. Yes, heaven was their home, but their city was their mission field.

The same is true for us. If we are looking for a practical way that we can take the gospel to our "unreached people group" at work, school, or in our neighborhood, the place to begin is with Paul's practical teaching. We have to live out externally what Jesus has done for us internally. In other words, we've got to live out our faith. Here is how we can do this.

Love others genuinely (4:9-10). God is so passionate that you and I love one another that He not only commands us to do it, but He also empowers us to do it. We will never love others the way we should until we first love God for who He is. Concentrate then on the depth of your walk with Him, and watch how He increases the breadth of your love for others. Yield your will to the Spirit's will. Your heart is His home. Be filled with His Spirit by filling your life with His truth (Col 3:1-2). Don't allow sinful habits to "stifle" His sanctifying work in you (1 Thess 5:19; Eph 4:30). That would only serve to inhibit your ability to love others. Since your heart belongs to Him, allow Him to rearrange things the way He sees fit. Perhaps there will even be a thing or two that He will discard. When He does this, you might discover that the big things that really bother you about other people really aren't that big at all. The envy that keeps you from loving your coworker or the bitterness that prevents you from forgiving your spouse will be replaced by a love you never thought possible. It's not because you are trying harder; it's because you are yielding to God's Spirit.

Do your work diligently (4:11). Let us do our work for the approval of God and we will be freed from the tyranny of seeking the approval of others. Remember that how you work matters to God. Trust Him to meet your needs, but work diligently. Wisely invest the talents that He has given you. Do your job with a quiet and restful spirit. Use your hands to reflect a deeper motivation for your work than that of merely earning a paycheck. Don't spend your time worrying about what everyone else is doing. Focus instead on pleasing the Father in the exact place where He has placed you (2 Cor 10:13-15). Don't give a half-hearted effort or cut corners. Give God your all by giving your all to your job. When He is ready to move you, let Him open the doors, but until that day be diligent in how you work.

Live your life purposefully (4:12). We should ask God to make us sensitive to how we live "in the presence of outsiders." Your life is a platform from which you share the gospel. The foundation of that platform is your credibility as a Christian. A genuine love coupled with a diligent work ethic will create open doors for you to share with others what Christ has done for you. Paul demonstrated how your life and lips intersect when you share the gospel. Listen again to his words: "We cared so much for you that we were pleased to share with you not only the gospel of God *but also* our own lives" (1 Thess 2:8; emphasis added). Living out your faith involves more than just loving others or working hard; it means giving your life to love and serve others for the purpose of proclaiming His glorious gospel.

Reflect and Discuss

1. What is the value of teachers and preachers giving Christians practical ways they can show love to one another? Why is such teaching often not successful?

2. How does the indwelling presence of the Holy Spirit enable you to love others?

3. Given Paul's commendation of the Thessalonians' love for one another, why does he tell them to love one another even more? What are some ways in which you can practice this?

4. How can you tell if the members of a church genuinely love one another? What happens when love is absent?

5. Based on this passage, give some examples of how Paul connects the *faith* of the Christian with the *life* of the Christian?

6. What does leading a "quiet life" mean? How does this apply to your life and work?

7. Why did some of the Thessalonian believers quit their jobs? What effect did this have on their church and their witness?

8. What does Paul mean by "mind your own business"?

9. Give some specific examples of how Christians can work with their hands in such a way that their work points to Christ.

10. What are some practical ways that you can apply Paul's instruction in this passage to your work, school, or leisure activities?

Hope Is Not Wishful Thinking

1 THESSALONIANS 4:13-18

Main Idea: God's promises about tomorrow give us hope for how we face today.

I. **A Fundamental Question: What Happens to Christians Who Die (4:13)?**
    A. Death is a certainty (4:13).
    B. Ignorance creates confusion (4:13).

II. **A Foundational Truth: Our Faith Is Backed Up by Fact (4:14-15).**
    A. We have a forgiven past: Jesus died (4:14a).
    B. We have a verifiable faith: the resurrection (4:14b).
    C. We have a trustworthy guide: the Scriptures (4:15).

III. **A Future Promise: The Lord Is Coming (4:16-17a).**
    A. The certainty of His coming (4:16)
    B. The suddenness of His coming (4:16)
        1. Christ's return will bring a reunion.
        2. Christ's return will bring relief.
    C. The timing of His coming
    D. The specifics of His coming (4:16-17a)

IV. **A Fitting Conclusion: Our Hope Is Secure (4:17b-18).**
    A. We have assurance about tomorrow (4:17b).
    B. We have hope for our lives today (4:18).

The present text is one of the most well-known passages in 1 Thessalonians, and perhaps even in the Bible. This passage stirs up the curiosity of even the most casual readers of Scripture, primarily because of Paul's reference to the "snatching away" or "rapture" of the church. Indeed, the topic of the rapture has served as the story line for dozens of books and movies and has also been the topic of much speculation, debate, and fanaticism through the centuries. One pastor has rightly observed, "If you want to get a crowd at your church, then just open your Bible and start talking about the rapture." The truth is that many people are more fascinated by the mysterious nature of the rapture than they are interested in knowing its implications for their lives and for human history.

Human beings have an insatiable curiosity about the future. From horoscopes and stock speculators, to the *Farmer's Almanac* and Nostradamus, we want to know what the future holds—from the size of our 401(k) when we retire to what the weather will be like this winter. Of course, there's a bit of irony in all of this. Although human beings take great pride in their intellectual acumen and technological achievements, when it comes to knowing the future, every human being must claim ignorance. Thus, despite your best prognostications, if you desire to know anything about the future, you are going to need help. Fortunately, God's Word provides you with the help you need. Indeed, the Bible paints such a vivid picture of the future that it leaves no doubt as to God's ultimate plan for human history, including the ultimate fate of every person who has ever lived.

This uncertainty about the future was a pressing issue for the Thessalonians. After visiting Thessalonica, Timothy brought back word to Paul that the Thessalonians were struggling with how to reconcile their understanding about the return of Christ with the recent deaths of some fellow believers. They feared that those who died prior to Christ's return would somehow miss out on the great gathering of God's people that would occur at the end of human history. To make matters worse, false teachers were adding to their confusion by circulating a letter, purportedly from Paul, suggesting that the day of the Lord's judgment had already come (2 Thess 2:1-2). Considering their ongoing suffering and persecution, some of these young believers were convinced that they had missed the rapture and were now experiencing the Day of the Lord. Despite their reception of God's truth (1 Thess 2:13) and their spiritual growth (3:6), the church was shaken and confused.

Paul will address their confusion in two specific ways. First, he will remind them of truths that they already know and firmly believe. Second, he will further expand on truths that he previously introduced by applying them to their current confusion. Thus, on the one hand, he will point them back to the historical fact of the cross and the resurrection; on the other hand, he will point them forward to the promise of the glorious return of Christ. In other words, Paul teaches them to look back and be grateful for what Jesus has done and to look ahead and be hopeful for what Jesus is going to do. Sensing their anxiety, Paul will seek to quell their doubts by unveiling one of the greatest promises of the Christian faith—the return of Christ for His church.

Before we carefully examine his teaching about this great event, perhaps a general observation about the passage will be helpful. Notice how Paul begins by addressing the Thessalonians' confusion. He writes, "We do not want you to be *uninformed*, brothers, concerning those who are asleep, so that you will not *grieve* like the rest, who have *no hope*" (4:13; emphasis added). Paul clearly reveals that their grief and hopelessness was the direct result of their failure to understand death from God's perspective. **Theological ignorance invariably leads to confusion, worry, and frustration**. Think of all the sleepless nights and restless days we can avoid if only we learn to view every circumstance through the lenses of God's Word.

Fortunately, however, the passage ends on a much better note than it begins. When we jump ahead to verse 18, the picture is much more hopeful. Paul concludes with this admonition: "Therefore *encourage* one another *with these words*" (4:18; emphasis added). Do you see the connection between their encouragement and the exposition of God's Word? The passage begins with confusion, hopelessness, and grief but ends with understanding and encouragement. Clearly, the "revelation from the Lord" in verses 14-17 was sufficient to address their most profound confusion. In a very practical sense, Paul has provided an illustration of the power of expository preaching.

You can also see a similar illustration in Jesus' incognito encounter with two confused disciples on the road to Emmaus (Luke 24:13-35). Like the Thessalonians, these men failed to view their circumstances through a biblical perspective. As a result of their ignorance, they were discouraged (v. 17), confused (vv. 19-20), and hopeless (vv. 21-24). After Jesus confronted them with the Scriptures (vv. 25-27), their perspective was dramatically transformed. Their personal, first-hand testimony of the transforming nature of Scripture is powerful: "Weren't our *hearts ablaze* within us while He was talking with us on the road and *explaining the Scriptures* to us?" (v. 32; emphasis added). Only Scripture can transform a heart in this way. No wonder David could exclaim,

> The instruction of the LORD is perfect,
> renewing one's life;
> the testimony of the LORD is trustworthy,
> making the inexperienced wise.

> *The precepts of the LORD are right,*
> *making the heart glad;*
> *the command of the LORD is radiant,*
> *making the eyes light up.* (Ps 19:7-8)

One final word is necessary. Paul's instruction is more pastoral than it is theological. His concern is to give pastoral exhortation to a grieving church, and not to provide detailed theological explanation about future events. In this regard, this text will not answer every question about future events. In some ways, more questions will be raised than will be answered. But Paul's exhortation includes some magnificent insights concerning the future hope of every believer at Christ's return, including some that we learn only in this passage. As we work through this text, we cannot miss his point: God's promises about tomorrow enable us to live a hopeful life today.

A Fundamental Question: What Happens to Christians Who Die?
1 THESSALONIANS 4:13

The centerpiece of Paul's instruction to the Thessalonians concerned the imminent return of Christ (1:10; 2:19; 3:13; 4:14-17; 5:23; 2 Thess 1:7; 2:5,8). The context of both letters reveals the Thessalonians' belief that Christ would come in their lifetime. This conviction had positive and negative impacts on their church. Positively, the promise of His imminent return brought them strength to persevere in trials and gave them courage to endure persecution (1:10; 3:13; 5:9,23). Negatively, the expectation of His imminent return provided some with an excuse to quit their jobs and cease doing any meaningful activity while waiting for His arrival (4:11-12; 5:14; 2 Thess 3:6-12).

Without question, the return of Christ was anything but an afterthought for the Thessalonians; it was their preoccupation. For this they were to be commended. Apart from the lazy believers who refused to work, the majority of the Thessalonians were serving faithfully and living expectantly. In fact, this is exactly what Jesus taught His disciples to do. The promise that His return could come at any moment was intended to create a sense of expectancy, urgency, and obligation for the church to be busy with things that mattered. In Matthew's Gospel Jesus gave four parables to teach His disciples about His coming (24:42-44,45-51;

25:1-13,14-30). In each case His point was inescapable: be prepared and be busy. In the final chapter of the book of Revelation Jesus Himself drives this truth home in three separate verses by warning that He is coming quickly (22:7,12,20). The promise of Jesus' coming then is a reason to be hopeful and a call to be fruitful.

The Thessalonian believers eagerly worked and patiently waited for the Lord's return. But Jesus was not coming as quickly as they expected, and their trials and persecution were continuing. To make matters worse, some of their fellow church members were dying. Questions flooded their minds: Would those who died miss out on this glorious gathering? What about their bodies? If their souls are in heaven, will their bodies forever remain in the grave? These questions weighed so heavily on the Thessalonians that their hope had given way to grief (4:13).

Death Is a Certainty (1 Thess 4:13)

Three times in this passage Paul refers to Christians who "sleep" (4:13,14,15). He is using the word *sleep* as a euphemism for death. Paul recognizes the source of the Thessalonians grief and confusion. His primary focus is to address the question that was weighing so heavily on the Thessalonians' minds: What happens to Christians who die prior to the return of Christ?

We cannot overlook the significance of Paul's use of the word *sleep* to describe death. There is a reason the biblical authors, including Jesus, describe believers who die as being asleep (Matt 9:24; 27:52; Mark 5:39; John 11:11-14; Acts 7:60; 1 Cor 15:6,18,20,51). Sleep is never final; it is always temporary. Paul uses the word *sleep* to refer specifically to the physical body. When believers die, their bodies sleep. Paul is not referring to "soul sleep." The concept of soul sleep is completely foreign to Scripture. On the contrary, the Bible explicitly affirms the eternal consciousness of every person. In other words, there will never be a time when a person ceases to exist or ceases to be conscious of his existence. This is true for both the believer and the non-believer. For example, when Christians die their bodies go into the grave but their spirits go directly into the presence of God (2 Cor 5:8). By contrast, when non-Christians die their bodies go into the grave but their spirits go immediately to hell (Luke 16:22-23). Nowhere does the Bible teach that a person ever loses a conscious awareness of where he is or what is happening to him after he dies. Hence, at death your existence does not end. Your physical body goes to sleep, but your spirit continues to exist.

One day your body will be united with your spirit in a glorified form (1 John 3:2). So, for now your body sleeps until God awakens it at the resurrection (1 Cor 15:51-52). For the Christian, death has no final word. Leon Morris states this well:

> For Christians death is no longer that adversary whom no person can resist, that tyrant who brings all worthwhile existence to a horribly final end. Death has been overcome by the risen Lord, and that has transformed the whole situation for those who are in Him. (Morris, *First and Second*, 136)

Paul wanted the Thessalonians to understand that those who die suffer no defeat and experience no loss. Their bodies may be asleep in the grave, but a day of awakening is coming! The Thessalonian Christians therefore had every reason to be hopeful and optimistic (1 Cor 15:54-57).

Ignorance Creates Confusion (1 Thess 4:13)

As settled as the Thessalonians were about other doctrinal issues, surprisingly they were confused when thinking about the Lord's return. Their confusion was evidenced in two ways. First, some of the Thessalonians were guilty of extremism. Their overzealous reaction to the Lord's return was creating conflict with each other and sending the wrong message to a watching world. Convinced that Christ was on His way, some deadbeat members of the fellowship had apparently quit their jobs and were depending on others to meet their needs (2 Thess 3:11-12). As you can imagine, such irresponsible conduct bred frustration within the church. Perhaps even more troubling, however, was the poor testimony these Christians were conveying to a lost city. **I think that it is safe to say that excessive eschatological fanaticism does more to drive people away from Christ than it does to draw people to Him.**

A second way that we can see the Thessalonians' confusion is by their willingness to believe misinformation. Whether from a false prophet on the outside or a misguided teacher on the inside, the Thessalonians were building their end-times theology on speculation rather than Scripture (2 Thess 2:1-3). The end result is confusion and ignorance.

To balance their extremism on one hand and to clear up their misinformation on the other, they needed to hear from God. Paul was not content to add more speculation to their lives. He knew that the Thessalonians didn't need more questions; they needed answers. And the place to go to find these answers was God's revelation.

A Foundational Truth: Our Faith Is Backed Up by Fact
1 THESSALONIANS 4:14-15

Anyone familiar with the art of rhetoric has heard of Socratic reasoning. The principle underlying the Socratic method proposes the use of a series of questions in order to expose weaknesses and contradictions in your opponent's thinking. The goal of such an exercise is twofold: to help your opponent arrive at a particular conclusion and to create for your opponent an awareness of his limits of knowledge. Good teachers recognize that one of the best ways to help students learn is to begin where they are and build from there. The goal is to lead them on a journey of self-discovery to arrive at the proper conclusion.

Paul was a master teacher. He would begin where the audience was and build from there. His goal was to take the people from where they were to where they needed to be. To clear up the Thessalonians' confusion and to answer their questions, Paul was going to begin with what they already knew was true—the historicity of the Christian faith.

We Have a Forgiven Past: Jesus Died (1 Thess 4:14a)

Paul begins by reminding the Thessalonians of the most significant truth of the Christian faith: "We believe that Jesus died and rose again." We might ask why Paul would begin an eschatological discussion by speaking about the resurrection. His rationale is fairly easy to discern. The Thessalonians' confusion was the direct result of a lack of theological understanding and perspective. Their ignorance led to their grief and sorrow. Paul's aim is to use logical reasoning to help them discover that their excessive grief is unnecessary and unwarranted. The place for him to begin such a discussion was the resurrection. Christianity is a historical faith. It is not some whimsical religious belief that is detached from the real world. It is rooted in verifiable history. It's not simply a faith; it's a reasonable faith. It is on the foundations of this reasonable faith that the future hope of every Christian rests.

So, Paul takes them back to the fundamentals of their faith—the death and resurrection of Jesus Christ. He is laying a foundation on which he will build his teaching about the destiny of the "dead in Christ." The statement "Since we believe that Jesus died" is the cornerstone of this foundation (1 Cor 15:1-3). Without the death of Christ, Christianity crumbles. Paul therefore begins here. By referring to the death of Christ, he confronts the Thessalonians with a number of powerful truths:

- Jesus Christ was not some mythological god amidst the pantheon of Greek gods. He actually existed in human history. Christianity is built on a historical Jesus (1 John 1:1-4).
- By His death, Jesus accomplished something for us that we could not accomplish for ourselves (2 Cor 5:21; 1 Pet 2:24).
- His death transforms our death into sleep. He died "once for all" so that all who look to Him would not have to experience death (Rom 6:10; Heb 9:28; 1 Pet 3:18).
- By means of His death, we are delivered from God's wrath and delivered into God's kingdom (1 Thess 1:10; 5:9-10).

The Thessalonians needed to be reminded of the very truth that transformed their lives. Grief was a normal emotion as they thought about their dead loved ones, but to sorrow like those who did not have hope was to forget the very purpose for which Jesus came.

Such a reminder is important for every generation. Have you noticed that the further you get from your conversion experience with Christ, the less you tend to think about it? It is not unimportant to you, but you simply move on to bigger and better things. We must never lose the wonder of what Christ has done for us. Without His sacrifice we have no standing. Nothing in our lives is "bigger and better" than what Christ has done for us. Like Paul, may it be your desire to know nothing "except Jesus Christ and Him crucified" (1 Cor 2:2).

We Have a Verifiable Faith: The Resurrection (1 Thess 4:14b)

Paul shifts the discussion from Jesus' death to His resurrection. His reasoning goes like this: That Jesus died is essential, but that He was raised from the dead is imperative. A dead Jesus does nothing to bring Christians hope. Paul therefore reminds them of a transforming truth: the death of Christ *purchased* their redemption, but the resurrection of Christ *proves* their redemption. This is the amazing way that God works. He backs up His promises with proof. To be sure, God's promises are true regardless of the proof that He chooses to provide. After all, because He is God, He can be fully trusted. David declared that God's way is "perfect" and His Word is "pure" (2 Sam 22:31). His Word can withstand scrutiny. He is always true to His Word and He always keeps His Word (Ps 119:140).

However, God does far more than to share His promises; He fulfills His promises. This truth is illustrated throughout Scripture. When some friends went to great extremes to bring a paralyzed man to Jesus (Mark 2:1-11), Jesus' immediate reaction to their passionate faith was to say to the man, "Son, your sins are forgiven." Hearing Jesus' words, the scribes accused Him of blasphemy for claiming to have the ability to forgive sin. Sensing their contempt, Jesus told the man to get up and walk. His response is classic. Ignoring the scribes, He said to the man, "So you may know that the Son of Man has authority on earth to forgive sins . . . I tell you: get up, pick up your mat, and go home" (Mark 2:10-11). By healing the man's physical problem, Jesus proved that He was more than able to deal with his spiritual problem. Proof was not necessary to procure the man's forgiveness. He was forgiven because Jesus declared Him forgiven. But Jesus chose to back up His promise with proof. Again, this is how God works. He not only tells us that He loves us, He proves He loves us. "But God *proves* His own love for us in that while we were still sinners, *Christ died* for us!" (Rom 5:8; emphasis added).

Paul thus points to the historical fact of the resurrection as proof that God will also resurrect every believer who dies. He wants the Thessalonians to see that such a promise is not based on wishful thinking but is instead built on the foundation of a fact. Since God was faithful to raise Jesus from the dead, the same promise holds true for those who love Him. Paul is imploring the Thessalonians to look back at what they know. They know that Jesus is not in the tomb. They know that the resurrection is not an abstract theological concept; it is a historical fact and a life-transforming truth. Paul is saying to them, "If you want to know what God thinks about your loved ones who have died, look no further than the resurrection!" Every Christian can and should live with the hope of this promise. As Paul would later write to the Corinthians, "We know that the One who raised the Lord Jesus will raise us also with Jesus and present us with you" (2 Cor 4:14). The resurrection of Jesus is our assurance that God keeps His Word. The death of a fellow believer may bring grief for a moment, but the resurrection of Christ guarantees our hope for eternity. As Jesus said, "Because I live, you will live too" (John 14:19).

Despite Paul's assurances about the resurrection, questions still lingered concerning the future fate of the bodies of their deceased loved ones. The Thessalonians clearly understood the implications of saving faith. They knew that to be "out of the body" was to be "at home with the Lord" (2 Cor 5:8). The issue for them was not about where their loved ones were. The issue was how the return of Christ fit into all of this. Since believers were dying before He returned, questions about bodies in the grave were creating much confusion. Paul comforts them by helping them to see what will happen to their loved ones' bodies when Christ does come. He states that "in the same way" that God raised up Christ from the grave, He will "bring with Him those who have fallen asleep through Jesus" (4:14b). Those dearly loved friends who have died will not miss out when Christ comes for His church. God did not allow Jesus' body to remain in the grave, and He will not allow their loved ones' bodies to remain in the grave either. What greater hope could we have as followers of Christ than to know that one day "we will always be with the Lord" (4:17)?

We Have a Trustworthy Guide: The Scriptures (1 Thess 4:15a)

Paul encouraged the Thessalonians to anchor their hope in the work of the cross and the certainty of the resurrection (4:14) by looking back at God's activity in the past. He is now going to encourage them to anchor their hope in the future based on the promise of God's activity in the future. Interestingly, he begins by saying, "For we say this to you by a revelation from the Lord." Commentators are divided about the specific source of this "revelation." Some suggest that Paul may have in mind a specific word from Jesus concerning the future (perhaps not recorded in the Gospels). Others contend that he may be referring to special insight concerning future events given to Him by God Himself. Though any guess is only speculation, we can be certain that God intended for us to have a reliable written record of these things (2 Tim 3:16-17; 2 Pet 1:20-21). The confusion in Thessalonica rested on misinformation and false teaching. Paul wanted them to understand that his teaching was not simply another opinion to consider. He wanted them to know that He was speaking for God.

A Future Promise: The Lord Is Coming
1 THESSALONIANS 4:16-17A

This section focuses on one of the most discussed and debated passages in the Bible. The focus of this debate is centered on Paul's reference to the snatching away or rapture of the church (4:17). Admittedly, the word "rapture" does not appear in the passage. The word comes from the Latin translation of the Greek word that Paul used to describe the church as being "caught up" in the clouds. The word means "to seize or snatch away." It implies a sudden, violent event. While the exact term *rapture* is not used in this passage, one must not miss the unmistakable fact that the promise of Jesus' sudden return for His church is presented here. Throughout history there have been many ways that interpreters have sought to understand this text.[12] Before exploring the text more carefully, we must note again that the meaning of the text is not in question. The passage portrays one of the most significant events in the history of God's church: the "Day" when Jesus gathers His church to be with Him. Regardless of where commentators land in their various interpretations of this text, the hope and comfort offered by it must not be missed. If the element of encouragement is in any way removed, the entire text loses its meaning. There is no element of encouragement in this passage if the promise of the rapture is not central.

The debate surrounding this passage is focused on many different issues that spill over into other passages of Scripture. Paul did not write this text with the purpose of providing his readers with a comprehensive eschatological overview of the Bible. So we cannot walk away from this passage expecting to have answers for every question about the end times. We can identify, however, several truths that this passage emphatically teaches:

- Jesus is coming again.
- He is coming for His church.
- The "dead in Christ" will not miss this event.
- When He comes, there will be a glorious reunion with Christ.
- The expectation of this event is to be a reason for encouragement.

Having put forth what we do know from this text, there are also several questions that this text raises:

- Will Jesus return before or after the Day of the Lord?
- When He comes, will the church go with Him to heaven or will He come with the church to the earth?
- Does Christ's return happen in two stages: the rapture and the second coming?

---

[12] Though many variations exist, this text has been viewed in primarily three ways historically: (1) pretribulation, that is, the rapture of believers occurs before the tribulation/Day of the Lord; (2) midtribulation, that is, the rapture occurs at the mid-way point of the tribulation period; and (3) posttribulation, that is, the rapture occurs after the tribulation/Day of the Lord and is synonymous with the second coming of Jesus. For a helpful overview of these positions, see Gundry, *Three Views on the Rapture.*

Clearly, the most effective way to answer these questions is to start with what is known and then allow the context to lead you to the answers. Note facts that we can glean from this passage.

The Certainty of His Coming (1 Thess 4:16)

Without question the Bible teaches that Jesus is coming again. For instance, 23 of the 27 books in the New Testament state that He is coming. One out of every 30 verses in the New Testament either speaks directly of His coming or of the end times surrounding His coming. For every biblical reference to Jesus' first coming there are eight that point to His return. Clearly the biblical writers did not want their readers to miss this truth. From the perspective of the biblical authors, Jesus' coming was never intended to be a subject for speculation; it was always intended to be a reason for anticipation and motivation. Such an awareness of Christ's imminent return is vividly portrayed in the Thessalonian letters. In the Greek of this passage, he refers to Christ's return as the *parousia* (4:15). The word points to the arrival of an important person or dignitary. The Thessalonians were to be watching, waiting, and expecting the day when Christ Himself would come for them.

The Suddenness of His Coming (1 Thess 4:16)

Paul introduces the subject of the Lord's return with these simple words: "For the Lord Himself will descend from heaven with a shout, with the archangel's voice, and with the trumpet of God." No advance warning, no heads-up, and no notice given. With a shout, a voice, and a trumpet, the Lord will come. Paul makes this same point to the Corinthians when he writes,

> *We will not all fall asleep, but we will all be changed,* in a moment, in the blink of an eye, *at the last trumpet. For the trumpet will sound, and the dead will be raised incorruptible, and we will be changed.* (1 Cor 15:51-52; emphasis added)

Scriptural support for the imminent return of Christ is not lacking (Phil 3:20; Col 3:4; Jas 5:8; Rev 3:3). The resounding message of the New Testament is that Christ could come at any moment. Consider Paul's words to Titus: "We wait for the blessed hope and appearing of the glory of our great God and Savior, Jesus Christ" (Titus 2:13).

The promise of Christ's coming is to be a source of encouragement for God's people. In this passage Paul reveals two reasons why Christians should be hopeful as they anticipate this event: Christ's return will bring a reunion, and Christ's return will bring relief. Let's examine each of these more closely.

Christ's return will bring a reunion. When Jesus comes for His church, at least three reunions will occur. First, the bodies of the dead in Christ will be reunited with their spirits (1 Cor 15:23,52-54). We know that when believers die, their bodies go in the grave but their spirits go to be with the Lord (2 Cor 5:8; Phil 1:23). When Christ comes, He will gloriously reunite body with spirit. Second, those who are alive when Christ returns will be united with Him (1 John 3:2). Finally, in one magnificent gathering, both those who were alive at Christ's coming and those who were dead will be reunited in the presence of the Lord. Paul is saying that grief over the loss of loved ones need not lead to hopelessness. The grave is not the end. Death is not final. Just as you have the absolute assurance that you will see Jesus one day, so too you have the same assurance that you will see your loved ones again. This promise of a coming reunion should give every believer a present hope.

Christ's return will bring relief. The truth of Christ's coming brings more than just the hope of a reunion; it also brings the promise of deliverance. Life was difficult for the Christians in Thessalonica. Their faith in Christ resulted in severe persecution and intense hardship (1:6; 2:14-15; 3:3-4; 2 Thess 1:4-6). Christ's return would bring them the relief they longed for. Even the presence of severe hardship and intense suffering could not steal their joy or diminish their hope. They could live with the anticipation of that day when Christ would judge their enemies and deliver them from their suffering (2 Thess 2:6-8).

The Timing of His Coming

Despite Paul's assurances, the Thessalonians were still concerned about their future. Their desire to know more details about the coming "Day of the Lord" (5:1-2) gives some insight into their concerns. Apparently, false teachers were claiming that the Day of the Lord had already arrived (2 Thess 2:1-3). We can imagine how unsettling this news must have been. After all, they were anticipating that Jesus would come in their lifetime to deliver them from wrath and judgment. Yet, from their limited perspective, their present circumstances were painting a very different picture. With their loved ones dying and the presence of persecution and trials increasing, some in the fellowship had become convinced that they somehow missed Jesus' return. This led them to the conclusion that perhaps the false teachers were correct and the Day of the Lord had already arrived.[13]

The reasons for Paul's mention at the beginning of this passage of their ignorance now becomes more clear (v. 13). For whatever reason, the Thessalonians had chosen to interpret their circumstances and to build their future on false teaching and speculation rather than on the truth. Yet Paul had taught them much more about Christ's return than you and I have available to us (2 Thess 1:5). Perhaps this gives us a better idea as to why Paul expressed concern over their ignorance. The Thessalonians should have known better than to worry about their deceased loved ones or the coming Day of the Lord.

As you look carefully at the context of Paul's instruction here and also in the larger context of the Thessalonian letters, seemingly he taught them to anticipate Christ's return (the rapture) before the Day of the Lord.[14] There is little doubt that the Thessalonians were eagerly looking for Christ's return. However, there is little indication that they ever expected to experience the Day of the Lord. In fact, given the Thessalonians' concern about being caught in the Day of the Lord, you may safely conclude that they were fully anticipating not being around for it. There is no doubt that Paul taught them about the Day of the Lord. Yet there is no suggestion that he ever sought to prepare them to be in it. Rather, his intention was to give them sufficient truth to clarify their confusion about it. The implication is Paul knew that the church would be gone because Jesus was coming to rapture the church out of the world before this day would come (John 14:1-3). The focus of the passage is encouragement. Just as Paul sought to comfort the Thessalonians about their departed loved ones, so also he attempted to reassure them about their future. If he knew that believers would be

---

[13] The "Day of the Lord" does not represent a literal 24-hour period. Rather, it more generally refers to an extended time of God's wrath and judgment, also known as the "Great Tribulation" (Matt 24:21; Dan 12:1). Paul will elaborate further on the concept of the "Day of the Lord" in 1 Thess 5:1-11 and 2 Thess 2:1-12.

[14] How we wish that Paul were more specific concerning the exact timing of the rapture! While we may have good reason to suggest a particular view, we must admit that many able Bible scholars and commentators hold differing views. Leon Morris expresses the thoughts of many when he writes, "There are many things that we would like to know, but the Bible was not written to satisfy our curiosity. Rather, it is intended to help us in our Christian lives, and for that the important thing is to be ready when the Lord comes" (Morris, *First and Second*, 142).

alive at the time of the Day of the Lord, he would have most certainly sought to prepare them for such a time.

To be sure, although their persecutions were real, they were not indisputable signs of God's wrath. As Paul told them, "For God did not appoint us to wrath, but to obtain salvation through our Lord Jesus Christ" (5:9). In His letters to the seven churches, Jesus makes a similar promise to the church of Philadelphia: "I will also keep you from the hour of testing that is going to come over the whole world" (Rev 3:10). The Thessalonians could anticipate Christ's coming because He would remove His church from the terrible judgment that was to come. They were eagerly waiting for Jesus who would "rescue" them from the "coming wrath" (1 Thess 1:10). What an encouraging promise for the church—a reunion with the ones we love and a rescue from the wrath to come.

The Specifics of His Coming (1 Thess 4:16-17)

Whenever the subject of Christ's return is discussed, the conversation invariably turns to signs and dates. The Thessalonians were not unlike you and me in many ways. They, too, wanted to know when Christ would come. After all, if they somehow missed His return, as the false teachers purported, then they needed to know all they could about the "times and the seasons" (5:1). Paul reminded them that they had all the information they needed. Their concern should not be the date when Jesus will come. Their concern should be how faithfully they are living until He comes. The emphasis is not on the *when* of His coming, but on the *how* of His coming. Stated another way, since we know that He is coming, how are we living in light of His coming (Rev 22:8-12)?

While Paul did not give them specific insight into the date of His return, he did provide them with a specific sequence of events that will occur when Christ returns. First, he says, "the Lord Himself will descend from heaven" (4:16). What stronger word of encouragement could be offered to a Christian? Paul says that the "Lord Himself" will come to gather His people. He left heaven the first time to come to earth for us, but He will leave heaven again to take believers from earth to be with Him. Jesus offered these words of hope and comfort to His disciples:

> *Your heart must not be troubled. Believe in God; believe also in Me. In My Father's house are many dwelling places; if not, I would have told you. I am going away to prepare a place for you. If I go away and*

*prepare a place for you, I will come back and receive you to Myself, so
that where I am you may be also.* (John 14:1-3)

Could you think of a better antidote for a troubled heart than to know
that Jesus Himself will come and take you to be with Him? Jesus will
fulfill this promise when He comes for His church.

Second, Christ's return will be initiated by three specific calls: "a
shout," "the archangel's voice," and "the trumpet of God" (4:16). To
know why Paul chooses each of these terms is difficult. However, the
thought that Paul wishes to communicate by using them is not difficult
to discern. The shout, the voice, and the trumpet will be God's inescapable call to His people that Jesus is coming. This call will be loud
enough to reach both those who are alive and those whose bodies are in
the grave (John 11:43).

A third event that will occur at Jesus' return concerns the order
in which the church will be caught up to be with Him. Paul says, "The
dead in Christ will rise first. Then we who are still alive will be caught up
together with them" (4:16-17). This passage underscores the purpose
for which Paul writes. He is reassuring the church that those who die
will not miss Christ's return. To drive this point home, he says that they
will in fact, "rise first." Death did not separate them from the Lord, and
it will not separate them from the Lord's return (Rom 8:38).

The final event that Paul mentions is when the church is "caught
up together" to be with Christ (4:17). Those "dead in Christ" and those
alive in Christ will be gathered together to be with Him. It will be the
most impressive family reunion in history. Paul adds some detail by stating where this reunion will take place—"in the clouds." His reference
to the clouds is another way to emphasize that this majestic gathering
will take place in Christ's presence (Exod 16:10; Ps 104:3; Dan 7:13;
Acts 1:9). But the cloud reference also points to his statement that we
will "meet the Lord in the air" (4:17). No specific indication is given
as to where God's people go following this reunion. However, the logical reading of the passage suggests that they go to be with the Lord in
heaven (John 14:1-3). There is no reason to believe that Paul has in
mind a return to the earth. Why would He gather His people "in the
air" only to bring them back to earth? He will return to earth one day.
When He does return, He will not be coming for His church; He will be
coming with His church (Rev 21:1-4).

What an amazing picture Paul paints in this text! With an economy
of words, he provides a description of one of the most significant events

in human history—an event reserved only for those who have put their hope in Christ alone. Jesus Himself will come to gather His church (past and present) together, and the church will assemble in the clouds to "meet the Lord in the air."

A Fitting Conclusion: Our Hope Is Secure
1 THESSALONIANS 4:17B-18

As noted above, Paul's description of Jesus' coming is brief, leaving us with many questions—perhaps even more questions than the text answers. In working through this text, we must be careful not to miss the point of the passage. Paul's concern here is pastoral and not eschatological. we may wish that he had divulged more details, but that was clearly never his intention. Fortunately, however, by a "revelation from the Lord" (v. 15) he does open our eyes to some transforming truths. These truths are meant to encourage and not to confuse. Paul's aim was to provide answers and not to create more questions. To make this clear, he ends his discussion with two promises.

We Have Assurance about Tomorrow (1 Thess 4:17b)

We live in a world where there are few guarantees. Most of us would admit that the only certainty about life is its uncertainty. John Lennon even wrote a song about life's uncertainties. In a memorable line from that song he says, "Life is what happens to you while you're busy making other plans" ("Beautiful Boy [Darling Boy]," 1981). James said it much better when he wrote,

> Come now, you who say, "Today or tomorrow we will travel to such and such a city and spend a year there and do business and make a profit." You don't even know what tomorrow will bring—what your life will be! For you are like smoke that appears for a little while, then vanishes. (Jas 4:13-14)

The Thessalonians' uncertainty about their future and the fate of their dead friends had undermined the Thessalonians' hope and robbed them of joy. They needed assurance and they needed it quickly. What greater assurance could Paul have given them about their future than to assert, "and so we will always be with the Lord" (4:17b)? Their questions and uncertainties about the future are swallowed up in that word, *always*. Those who die in Christ are with Him now, they will be with Him when He comes, and they will be with Him always. The same guarantee is offered to those who are alive. One can find no greater assurance than to hear that the Lord Himself wants nothing more than for His children to always be with Him.

We Have Hope for Our Lives Today (1 Thess 4:18)

Verse 18 presents a striking contrast with where the passage began. What begins with ignorance, grief, and hopelessness ends with comfort. Only God could take the deepest of human sorrows and in only six verses transform them into hope. That is exactly what this passage is about—hope. Death does not have the final word. The false teachers do not have the final word. Human speculation does not have the final word. Into the darkness of our confusion, God shines the light of His truth. God's truth can transform ignorance into understanding, grief into joy, and hopelessness into assurance.

Conclusion

A few years ago while visiting a small Argentinian town in the foothills of the Andes Mountains, I was awestruck by the surrounding beauty of the landscape. From nearly every vantage point in town I could see the towering peaks off in the distance. Curious, I asked a local shop owner if he ever tired of seeing the majestic mountains in the distance. I will never forget his reply: "I hardly even notice them." How could it be possible for one to be surrounded by the majesty of the Andes Mountains and yet miss their beauty? I suppose it's not difficult for someone who sees it every day.

Jesus made a promise to you and me. He told us that he would come back one day and take us to be with Him. This promise towers over us from every conceivable vantage point of our lives. If we look up and see it, we will find hope. It will always be there. We cannot forget Jesus' words, "If not, I would have told you" (John 14:2). He did tell us. Yet I wonder how often we fail to look up and see what He said. It's no wonder that we struggle to find peace today and we worry about life tomorrow. When we ignore His promises, that's exactly what we should expect, but if we truly want comfort, then we have to look up. We have to see His truth towering over us. Jesus is coming. He is coming soon. He is coming for His church. We as believers will always be with the Lord.

Reflect and Discuss

1. How would you state the main point of this passage in a sentence?
2. Why were the Thessalonians experiencing sorrow and grief? What are some examples today where ignorance of biblical doctrine creates confusion and grief?
3. What are the two foundational doctrines of the faith that Paul calls to remembrance? Why?
4. What argument does Paul use to convince the Thessalonians that their loved ones will not miss Christ's return? How does this give us hope today?
5. What do you think Paul meant by a "revelation from the Lord"?
6. Explain the reunions that will take place at Christ's coming. How do these reunions reverse the curse of Genesis 3?
7. How will the rapture deliver a believer from the "coming wrath"?
8. Explain how this passage is more pastoral than eschatological. What questions remain?
9. How should you live in light of Christ's imminent return? Give some specific examples.
10. Explain the contrast between verse 13 and verse 18. What did Paul discuss in verses 14-17 that would enable the Thessalonians to move from sorrow to hope?

Judgment Day

1 THESSALONIANS 5:1-11

Main Idea: God's message about future events must influence how we live in our present circumstances.

I. **God's Judgment Is Declared (5:1-3).**
   A. A solemn warning (5:1-2)
   B. An indifferent response (5:3a)
   C. A sobering result (5:3b)
II. **God's People Respond (5:4-8).**
   A. They walk in the light (5:4-5).
   B. They live with purpose (5:6-8).
      1. They live their lives soberly.
      2. They take their faith seriously.
III. **God's Deliverance Comes (5:9-11).**
   A. They are delivered from wrath (5:9a).
   B. They are delivered from sin (5:9b-10).
   C. They are delivered from discouragement (5:11).

Most people are notoriously lazy. Because of an inclination to slothfulness, you must build accountability through a variety of means and methods. For example, many of us have scales in our bathrooms because we recognize that the only true way to be accountable for our weekly eating habits is to have an objective means for measuring our caloric intake. Teachers also recognize the value of accountability. Fully aware of the human tendency to choose play over study, teachers keep their students motivated by administering quizzes and tests. While most students would gladly welcome a test-free world, they admit that tests serve as proper motivation for them to study and learn. **Indeed, the promise of a coming evaluation always serves as the best means for a present motivation**.

A number of years ago, the Hollywood movie *The Truman Show* hit the big screen. It featured a man named Truman Burbank whose life, unknown to him, was a manufactured reality television show. The show was broadcast daily to millions of viewers. Everywhere Truman went and everything he did were available for the world to see. While most of us would grimace at the thought of being subjected to such scrutiny, we would do well to remember that our lives are being broadcast to an even greater audience. We are confronted with this reality in Revelation.

> *Then I saw a great white throne and One seated on it. Earth and heaven fled from His presence, and no place was found for them. I also saw the dead, the great and the small, standing before the throne, and books were opened. Another book was opened, which is the book of life, and the dead were judged according to their works by what was written in the books.*
>
> *Then the sea gave up its dead, and Death and Hades gave up their dead; all were judged according to their works. Death and Hades were thrown into the lake of fire. This is the second death, the lake of fire. And anyone not found written in the book of life was thrown into the lake of fire.* (Rev 20:11-15)

This passage draws attention to two different sets of books—the book (singular) and the books (plural). The subject matter contained within each of these proves to be significant by providing the basis for either your salvation or your damnation. John's point could not be clearer: In God's "books" one can find a complete record of all human sin, including every wicked deed, every impure thought, and every evil intention. Nothing we do escapes the attention of an omniscient God. At the final judgment, the content of the books will provide the evidence necessary for a just verdict of judgment. To be acquitted, your name must be found in "the book of life." And the only way that your name can be inscribed in that book is by trusting in Christ alone for salvation (Isa 43:25; 2 Cor 5:19; Eph 2:1-5). However, those whose names are not written in the book of life will be judged according to what is recorded in their "books."

We are foolish if we think that God is not keeping a detailed record of our lives. Concerning this, the writer of Hebrews issues a stern warning: "No creature is hidden from Him, but all things are naked and exposed to the eyes of Him to whom we must give an account" (Heb 4:13). But as foolish as it is to think that God does not see our actions, it is even more foolish to think that He will not hold us accountable for them. While there may be a momentary delay in the balancing of God's books, that delay will not last forever. Luke says that God has "*set a day* when He is going to judge the world in righteousness by the Man He has appointed" (Acts 17:31; emphasis added).

While human beings may choose to ignore the reality of judgment, they can do little to delay it or even to soften its severity. **The only way to survive God's judgment is to avoid it altogether, and the only way to avoid it is by the deliverance that only Jesus can bring**. Paul says, "For God did not appoint us to wrath, but to obtain salvation through our Lord Jesus Christ" (5:9). The good news is that God's wrath can be avoided.

During Paul's brief stay in Thessalonica, he taught the church about a coming day of judgment. Yet, despite his teaching, the Thessalonians were still puzzled about many of the details. They had three basic questions: What happens to Christians who die prior to the Lord's return? Was it possible that they had somehow missed the Lord's return and were now living in the Day of the Lord? What would be the signs indicating that the end of the age had come? He answered the first question in 4:13-18 by informing them that they would see their dead loved ones again. Paul addresses their other two questions both in this text and in 2 Thessalonians.

Paul begins chapter 5 by making a notable transition in subject matter. To make this transition, he uses the Greek phrase translated "about" or "concerning." In his writings, Paul often uses this phrase to indicate a shift from one subject to another (e.g., 1 Cor 7:1,25; 8:1; 12:1; 16:1,12). Here, he uses the phrase to transition in his discussion from the rapture (4:13-18) to the Day of the Lord (5:1-11). Paul does not combine the two discussions. Had he done so, we might conclude that the rapture is somehow to be included in the events surrounding the Day of the Lord. However, rather than tying these events together, he appears to separate them purposely into two distinct events. This separation, of course, raises the question of the timing of the rapture: Will it occur before, after, or in the middle of the Day of the Lord? Although the text does not give conclusive evidence, which would merit dogmatism in how we answer, the context appears to indicate that Jesus will remove His church *prior* to the Day of the Lord. Here are four reasons for such a conclusion:

- As noted, Paul chooses to address the rapture and the Day of the Lord separately. It is not coincidental that the rapture discussion precedes the Day of the Lord discussion. The natural reading of the text implies that the Day of the Lord would follow the rapture of the church.

- One cannot read both texts without seeing Paul's emphasis on imminence—that Jesus could return at any moment.
  Imminence suggests that the next event on God's timetable
  for history is Christ's return. However, if the Day of the Lord
  precedes His return then imminence is watered down because
  one could simply count the remaining days of tribulation
  until Christ finally returns. Paige Patterson's insight concerning imminence is significant. He suggests that placing Christ's
  return after the Day of Lord not only eliminates the possibility
  of the imminent return of Christ, but also has the unfortunate
  result of rendering Jesus mistaken when He said that no one
  knew the time of Christ's return (Patterson, *Revelation*, 43).
- Paul's point in both 4:13-18 and 5:1-11 is to encourage the
  Thessalonians. What could be more encouraging for a discouraged church than to know that they are not appointed to wrath
  (5:9)? To be sure, this includes deliverance from the wrath of
  eternal damnation, but given the context, Paul more likely has
  in mind the wrath of the Day of the Lord. Jesus offered a very
  similar word of encouragement to the church at Philadelphia
  when He said, "Because you have kept My command to endure,
  I will also keep you from the hour of testing that is going to
  come over the whole earth to test those who live on the earth"
  (Rev 3:10).
- In 1 Thessalonians 5:4-11 Paul paints a sharp contrast between
  those who walk in the day and those who walk in the dark.
  Those who walk in darkness will face sudden destruction, inescapable judgment, and wrath. Paul's purpose is to remind the
  Thessalonians that because of their standing in Christ, they
  have a different destiny than an unbelieving world. Paul seems
  to be telling them, "You do not need to worry about these
  things; God has different plans for you." To be sure, His different plans culminate in a heavenly home, but given the context,
  Paul apparently is also reassuring them that God would deliver
  them from having to experience any wrath associated with the
  Day of the Lord.

One final observation is necessary before a closer look at the
passage. Admittedly, much debate exists concerning these matters.
Where one lands on his timing of the rapture is not a test of fellowship. For every argument in favor of placing the rapture before the

Day of the Lord, there are arguments against it. One truth is not up for debate, however: Jesus is coming again. The church must live in eager expectation of this event. Trials and tribulations *will be* a part of your journey while you wait expectantly for Him (Rom 8:17; Phil 1:29; 1 Pet 4:12-19). But since you and I live with the hope of salvation, we agree with Paul: "I know the One I have believed in and am persuaded that He is able to guard what has been entrusted to me until that day" (2 Tim 1:12).

As we turn our attention to the text, remember that Paul had just informed the Thessalonians that Christ could come at any moment. This obviously triggered a question similar to that of the disciples who asked Jesus, "Tell us, when will these things happen? And what is the sign of Your coming and of the end of the age?" (Matt 24:3). In addition to their curiosity about signs and seasons, the Thessalonians had a more significant question about the Day of the Lord: Would they have to experience the terrible events associate with that day? To address their questions, Paul has three objectives in mind as he pens 1 Thessalonians 5:1-11: to remind them of the swiftness of God's judgment (5:1-3), to exhort them to live faithfully (5:4-8), and to encourage them to remain confident in God's deliverance (5:9-11).

God's Judgment Is Declared
1 THESSALONIANS 5:1-3

A few years ago while out for an evening on the town, my wife and I set out to find an ATM to get some cash. Determined to save a few bucks in associated ATM charges, I was on a mission to find one associated with my bank. With every new street came the hope and expectation of the great discovery, but ultimately my efforts proved fruitless. Frustrated and prepared to concede defeat, I glanced heavenward only to see some very large, brightly illuminated letters attached to the top of a skyscraper. To my surprise, it was the name of my bank. I not only found my bank; I found the world headquarters of my bank! For one hour I was circling the streets of the city in search of something that was right in front of me the whole time. All I had to do was look up to see it.

In a sense, the same is true when it comes to knowing God. God gives every human being sufficient information to know that He exists. If you would only "look up," you would see Him. As David declared in Ps 19:1-6, creation is a living testimony to the existence of God. Because

God has made Himself known, human beings are accountable for how they respond to Him. Paul states this truth plainly when he writes,

> *For God's wrath is revealed from heaven against all godlessness and unrighteousness of people who by their unrighteousness suppress the truth, since what can be known about God is evident among them, because God has shown it to them. For His invisible attributes, that is, His eternal power and divine nature, have been clearly seen since the creation of the world, being understood through what He has made. As a result, people are without excuse.* (Rom 1:18-20)

God has given sufficient notice that judgment day is coming. Some look up and see it, and others choose to ignore it, but no one outside of Jesus Christ will escape the dreadful consequences of that day.

A Solemn Warning (1 Thess 5:1-2)

The text begins with an implied question: When is Jesus coming again? On the surface it sounds like a fair question. After all, if the Thessalonians could know the "times and the seasons," they could prepare for Christ's coming. Paul reminded them that they already had enough information to be fully prepared: "You do not need anything to be written to you," he replies. "For you yourselves know . . ." (5:1-2). There is a bit of irony here. **They were ignoring the information they already had to ask for information they did not need**. Dates and times were not what they needed. Instead, they needed to remember that the Lord's coming was imminent. John MacArthur makes this point:

> Being spiritually prepared for the return of Christ does not involve date setting, clock watching, or sign seeking. God has chosen not to reveal the specific time of end-time events so that all believers will live in constant anticipation of them. (Macarthur, *1 and 2 Thessalonians*, 143)

The Thessalonians had the information; what they needed was preparation.

Before we come down too hard on the Thessalonians for their unhealthy curiosity about dates and times, we would do well to recall how often we are guilty of having the same inquisitiveness. For example, I wonder how many Christians spend their lives studying the *what* of Christianity but never get down to living out the *why* of Christianity. Other Christians zealously search for God's will but carelessly leave their

Bibles unopened. If we ignore the little responsibilities that God gives us now, what makes us think that He will give us bigger opportunities later (Luke 16:10)? Paul challenges the Thessalonians to live in the light of the information that God provided. His statement "you yourselves know" is quite similar to what we saw in chapter 4 where He told them that they needed no further instruction about how to love each other (4:9). There comes a point when you have all the information that you need. The real issue then becomes what you do with that information.

Paul was convinced that his prior teaching on the Lord's coming was sufficient. Dates and times were not part of God's revelation (Matt 24:36; Acts 1:7). There are at least two practical reasons for this. First, knowing that His coming was hundreds or thousands of years in the future would only stifle their urgency and passion. As we have seen, a spirit of indifference had already settled over some in the church (4:11-12). The last thing this church needed was more deadbeat Christians. Second, if they had advance knowledge that His coming was soon, it could lead them to make rash decisions or even cause widespread panic. God never intended for you to know *when* Christ is coming—He always intended for you to know *that* Christ is coming. The Bible does not give dates and times; it gives a promise: Christ is coming. An *indifferent* church lacks motivation and a *panicked* church lacks peace. However, an *expectant* church is filled with passion. That is exactly the means by which God designed the church to pursue its mission—with passion and expectancy.

While the Thessalonians did not need to have a knowledge of the times and seasons, they did need to have an understanding of the Day of the Lord. Doubtless Paul had taught them that the Day of the Lord represented a future time of God's judgment. Listen to how Amos describes this day:

> *Woe to you who long for the Day of the LORD! What will the Day of the LORD be for you? It will be darkness and not light.*
> *It will be like a man who flees from a lion only to have a bear confront him. He goes home and rests his hand against the wall only to have a snake bite him.*
> *Won't the Day of the LORD be darkness rather than light, even gloom without any brightness in it?* (Amos 5:18-20)

Paul had provided the Thessalonians with enough knowledge to know that the Day of the Lord would bring God's severest judgment on the ungodly. For a church that was already suffering intense persecution, the thought of experiencing anything worse than their current trials obviously brought great concern. Therefore, one of Paul's primary objectives is to reassure them that God would deliver them from any coming judgment.

Paul describes the Day of the Lord as a "thief" (5:2). The coming of a thief is never a joyful, announced event. No thief ever informs a victim of his intentions before the crime. The Day of the Lord is going to surprise some people. Yet when Paul speaks of those who will be surprised, he does not have in mind the Thessalonians. Their response will be much different. "But you, brothers, are not in the dark," Paul writes, "for this day to overtake you like a thief" (5:4). God does not keep His people in the dark about future events. This of course does not mean that they will know every detail, but the Christian knows that both Jesus and judgment are coming. Thus Paul seeks to reassure the Thessalonians about what they know and to encourage them to faithfulness in light of Christ's coming. As Gordon Fee suggests, Paul's admonition about the Day of the Lord is not intended to threaten the Thessalonians, but to encourage them to live obediently "in the face of their present hardships . . . [and] to reassure them about their own future" (Fee, *First and Second Letters*, 190).

An Indifferent Response (1 Thess 5:3a)

The shift from "you" to "they" in verses 2 and 3 is noteworthy. An unbelieving world responds to God with a frank indifference. God's solemn warnings of judgment are often met by the world's yawn. This response is vividly portrayed by the words "peace and security." Oblivious to God's imminent judgment, and thinking that life is just fine, the world goes about its business. However, Paul says that the Day of the Lord will overtake them "like a thief in the night" (v. 2). Before they have time to figure out what's happening, they will be swept away by "sudden destruction."

Indifference toward God is always deadly. Jesus repeatedly warned of the dangers of indifference. For example, He warned of the dangers of choosing the wrong pathway to follow:

> *Enter through the narrow gate. For the gate is wide and the road is broad that leads to destruction, and there are many who go through it. How narrow is the gate and difficult the road that leads to life, and few find it.* (Matt 7:13-14)

Jesus also warned of the danger of indifference when choosing a foundation on which to build:

> But everyone who hears these words of Mine and doesn't act on them
> will be like a foolish man who built his house on the sand. The rain
> fell, the rivers rose, the winds blew and pounded that house, and it
> collapsed. And its collapse was great! (Matt 7:26-27)

Indifference toward God, however, is no less deadly than willful rejection of God. Either way the consequences are the same (5:3b). Turning your back on a problem does not make it go away. Cries of "peace and security" are powerless to change your circumstances. If a windswept forest fire is raging toward the front of your home, sipping lemonade on the back porch won't make the fire go away. In the same way, living your life with good intentions may be a noble pursuit, but if you are travelling on the wrong pathway or building on the wrong foundation, you are only moments away from devastating consequences.

A Sobering Result (1 Thess 5:3b)

Just as there is a contrast between those who heed God's warnings and those who ignore them, there is also a contrast between what people think the future holds and what will actually take place. Paul moves from an unbeliever's reassuring shouts of "peace and security" to his or her surprising shock when "sudden destruction" comes. Such a turn of events should not be surprising. That is what thieves do. Without warning, they interrupt your peace and take away your security. The thief/pregnancy imagery illustrates the inescapability of divine judgment for those who have rejected Christ. As Stott puts it, "The thief gives you no warning, and labor pains give you no escape" (Stott, *Gospel and the End*, 109). Thus when the Day of the Lord begins, it will move unalterably to its inescapable end.

God's People Respond
1 THESSALONIANS 5:4-8

In chapter 5 Paul uses vivid vocabulary to contrast the destiny of those who honor God with those who choose to ignore Him. Note how he describes the future judgment of those who ignore God: surprise, destruction, darkness, pain, and no escape. Now contrast those concepts with how Paul describes the future destiny of those who honor

God: light, salvation, and alive with Christ. The differences are striking. Paul singles out these differences to make a very important point: the Thessalonians had no need to fear future judgment. Why? Because when they embraced Christ, He transformed them from children of wrath to children of God (Eph 2:3-6). As Paul told the Colossians, the Father "rescued [them] from the domain of darkness and transferred [them] into the kingdom of the Son He loves" (Col 1:13). Hence, their future inheritance would not be the darkness of wrath; their future inheritance would be a kingdom of light.

Remember, they feared being subjected to the judgments of the Day of the Lord. Paul showed them that the judgments of that day are reserved only for those who walk in darkness (5:4). By contrast, the Thessalonians have been transferred into a new kingdom. They are "sons of light and sons of the day." They therefore have nothing to fear. God's sanctifying work was empowering them to live confidently in the present and to look hopefully at the future.

Christians should never be caught off guard by future events because they recognize that God is moving human history toward a final consummation. Knowing that this consummation is soon—albeit not knowing when—provides incentive and motivation to make the most of every day. In other words, Christians live with the end in mind. Paul reveals two ways that they can do this: they walk in the light, and they live with expectancy.

They Walk in the Light (1 Thess 5:4-5)

Paul's discussion about future events can be confusing unless we keep the context in view. As we have discovered, the Thessalonians were confused about their present circumstances and their future fate. They were suffering greatly on account of their new faith (2:14). Yet they believed that Jesus would return to deliver them from any such suffering (1:10). The delay of His return coupled with the intensity of their suffering led them to conclude that they were now in the midst of the Day of the Lord.

To address their confusion, Paul does not choose to unfold all of the specifics that will mark this terrible time in human history (we might wish he had!). Instead, he focuses on helping them to live confidently in light of these coming events. As verse 4 begins, the conjunction *but* marks a significant contrast between those who are ignorant of future events and those who are expecting them. These contrasts were briefly examined in the previous section (5:3-4). To bring them comfort, Paul reminds the Thessalonians that the light of God's promises is shining on their future. They did not need to spend time in fear of being caught suddenly by the Day of the Lord. God had placed their future destiny in plain sight. Paul writes, "But you, brothers, are not in the dark, for this day to overtake you like a thief" (5:4). Again, what is worth repeating is that God never intended for Christians to live with uncertainty about the future.

Pause and let this truth sink in. When we stop worrying about tomorrow, we are truly liberated to live for today. Let me help you to see this truth by way of a practical illustration. Think for a moment about a time when you were unable to watch the big game on TV. Although you may have missed it live, you were still able to record the game so that you could watch it later. Desiring not to know the score until you have watched the game, you attempt to avoid all TVs, radios, computers, and smart phones. With remote in hand (to fast-forward through commercials), you settle into your favorite chair to view the action. However, as you turn on your TV, you somehow forgot that it was tuned to ESPN, and before you could switch it, the final score of the big game scrolls across the bottom of your screen. Your evening is ruined . . . or is it? The good news is that you now know that your team won the game. The bad news is that the anticipation and thrill of watching the game is gone. But if you are a true sports fan, you will most likely still enjoy watching the game, but you will now watch it with a different attitude and perspective. In fact, it might even be a little more enjoyable to watch. When your team suffers a setback, you will recognize that it is only temporary. When your team falls behind, you won't become discouraged because you know the final outcome. In a real sense, when the future is not in doubt the present is much more enjoyable.

The Thessalonians' present discouragement was the result of their future uncertainties. But God did not intend for them to stumble around in the darkness of uncertainty. No matter how difficult their present circumstances might become, they could face them with the promise of a secure future. The Day of the Lord was not going to overtake them like a thief. God had opened their eyes to see how it was going to happen. They could now face their future with hope, their present with purpose, and their past without regret. All of this was possible because they were walking in the light of Christ. Light always has a way of changing our perspective (Ps 119:105; John 1:4-5; 9:5).

They Live with Purpose (1 Thess 5:6-8)

Being a Christian means something. It's one thing to say that you walk in the light, but it's another thing to prove that you walk in the light. Thus Paul reminds the Thessalonians that a Christian's new nature will be reflected by a Christian's new conduct. One of the most transforming days in a believer's life is when he moves past the *why* of salvation and begins to grasp the *what* of salvation. The Thessalonians were in danger of allowing their *end times* confusion to distract them from their *present day* living. And they clearly did not need more distractions. Their city was full of them. As I have mentioned, sexual immorality was right outside the window. Every day a thousand different things were competing for their attention. To borrow the words of singer Rich Mullins, the "stuff of earth" was competing for their allegiance ("If I Stand," 1988). Paul was challenging them to be true to their first love. He was imploring them to let their lifestyle reflect their loyalty to Christ. To challenge them in their loyalty to Christ, Paul makes a transition from their *standing* ("sons of light" and "sons of the day") to their *living* ("stay awake and be serious"). God expects them to live a sober life and to practice a serious faith.

They live their lives soberly. When it comes to following God's instruction, Christians do not "sleep" like the rest of the world (5:6). Sleep carries with it the connotation of a blissful ignorance. Some people live their lives with the mantra, "If the pressures of life become too difficult, a good nap will make them disappear." Of course, you know by experience that your problems never sleep. Paul employs the metaphor of sleep to describe how an unbelieving world views God. While God sounds the sirens of judgment, the world takes a nap. But as we have discovered, sleep is powerless to delay the Day of the Lord or to lessen its severity. While an unbelieving world slumbers, "sudden destruction" will come like a thief in the night (5:2-3). Jesus describes it this way:

> As the days of Noah were, so the coming of the Son of Man will be. For in those days before the flood they were eating and drinking, marrying and giving in marriage, until the day Noah boarded the ark. They didn't know until the flood came and swept them all away. So this is the way the coming of the Son of Man will be. (Matt 24:37-39)

Jonah learned the dangers of sleeping while God was talking. He surmised that if he slept long enough God would take His message to someone else (Jonah 1:5). He found out that God has a way of waking you up when He wants to get your attention. Turning your back on a problem will not make that problem go away. Jesus taught His disciples not to turn their backs to the reality of His return. They were to be living in a constant state of readiness. He said,

> Therefore be alert, since you don't know when the master of the house is coming—whether in the evening or at midnight or at the crowing of the rooster or early in the morning. Otherwise, he might come suddenly and find you sleeping. And what I say to you, I say to everyone: Be alert! (Mark 13:35-37)

Watchfulness, however, involves more than merely waiting for what is coming. Watchfulness means doing something while we wait. Paul instructs the Thessalonians to be "serious" (5:6). The idea here is to live a self-controlled life. It relates directly to their behavior (1 Pet 4:7). Again note with care how the imminence of Christ's coming should affect our behavior. Paul makes this point plain in his exhortation to the Romans:

> Knowing the time, it is already the hour for you to wake up from sleep, for now our salvation is nearer than when we first believed. The night is nearly over, and the daylight is near, so let us discard the deeds of darkness and put on the armor of light. Let us walk with decency, as in the daylight: not in carousing and drunkenness; not in sexual impurity and promiscuity; not in quarreling and jealousy. But put on the Lord Jesus Christ, and make no plans to satisfy the fleshly desires. (Rom 13:11-14)

God has not intended for His people to sleep their lives away. He has called them to be sober. Even if Jesus delays His coming, the motivation to live faithfully still exists.

They take their faith seriously. Those who fail to take their Christianity seriously need to carefully consider Paul's instruction in this passage. The imagery portrayed by his use of darkness and light is telling. Christians are radically different from non-Christians. "Since we belong to the day," Paul argues, "we must be serious and put the armor of faith and love on our chests, and put on a helmet of the hope of salvation" (5:8). To paraphrase: "If we say that we are Christians, then let's get serious about it!" Commenting on this verse, Calvin describes how seriously Christians must view their faith:

Casting off the cares of the world, which burden us because
of their weight, and throwing off base lusts, let us rise up to
heaven with freedom and alacrity. It is spiritual sobriety when
we use this world so sparingly and temperately that we are not
entangled in its allurements. (Calvin, *1 and 2 Thessalonians*, 53)

Just as the soldier avoids the affairs of civilian life, so also the Christian
avoids the allurements of the world (2 Tim 2:4). The way that some
Christians mess around with worldly allurements makes us wonder how
seriously they take their faith.

In verse 8 Paul suggests that the Christian faith is a battle. By
employing the imagery of a soldier's armor, he challenges the Christian
to prepare for this battle. A soldier who recognizes the dangers of the
battlefield would never venture into combat without being prepared.
In the same way, believers who take their faith seriously understand the
importance of spiritual preparation. The picture that Paul paints here is
similar to the one he used to describe the nature of a Christian's warfare
in Ephesians 6:10-18. The fact that he instructs the Thessalonians to
"put on" this armor indicates that such an act requires discipline.

Concerning the purpose of this armor, Paul identifies two areas
of great vulnerability for the Christian: the heart and the head. The
Christian virtues of faith, love, and hope are the three defenses available to the believer. Faith and love form the breastplate that protects the
heart, and hope is the helmet that protects the head (5:8). Faith reflects
confidence. Love declares loyalty. Hope provides security. This triumvi-
rate of Christian virtues forms the essence of Christianity. Believe what
God says by faith; do what God requires out of love; and trust what God
promises because of hope. Paul therefore encourages the Thessalonians
to guard their hearts and their heads by remembering their relationship
with Christ.

Peter gave a struggling group of believers a similar reminder when
he wrote, "Honor the Messiah as Lord in your hearts. Always be ready
to give a defense to anyone who asks you for a reason for the hope that
is in you" (1 Pet 3:15). A settled heart will always produce a steadfast
hope. When we believe God by *faith* and respond to Him out of *love*, the
natural outcome is a life filled with *hope*. For the Christian, hope is not
wishful thinking; it is a steadfast conviction that God will always keep
His word. If we believe God enough to obey what He commands, then
we will also believe Him enough to never lose hope. Considering the
Thessalonians' confusion, Paul was telling them to look past the trials

of the present and see the hope of the future. This, however, would be impossible if they did not "put on" the armor of faith, love, and hope. Usually the first things to go when we get discouraged are the very things that you need to keep you from getting discouraged in the first place. If we want to live in hope, then we must take our faith seriously.

God's Deliverance Comes
1 THESSALONIANS 5:9-11

If you have ever had the unfortunate experience of being pulled over by a policeman then you know the full range of emotions that sweep over you when you see the blue lights in your rearview mirror. Surprise, frustration, and guilt might be a few words to describe these emotions. Of course, you probably could add a few more of your own. Now think about the different emotions that you experienced when the policeman told you that he was *not* going to give you a ticket. Can you say, "RELIEF"? Maybe you actually deserved the ticket, and maybe you did not, but the response that you received from the policeman was not what you were expecting.

Paul has been addressing some very difficult issues in this section of Thessalonians. As already noted, end times passages like this often create more questions than they answer. However, amid the complexities of this text are some very plain and sobering truths. One of these truths is that God will pour out His righteous judgment on those who walk in darkness. This judgment will come surprisingly, swiftly, and inescapably (5:2-4). This somber warning troubled the Thessalonians. Their initial concerns about the Day of the Lord were what prompted Paul to write this in the first place. Now after hearing how terrible this day would be, they had to be wondering if they would be able to endure it. The warning lights were flashing and judgment day was coming. Against this backdrop, Paul's words in verse 9 must have brought them great relief: "For God did not appoint us to wrath, but to obtain salvation through our Lord Jesus Christ." With a few strokes of his pen he gave them reassuring words of comfort, hope, and peace.

They Are Delivered from Wrath (1 Thess 5:9a)

The "wrath" Paul describes in verse 9 could be a wrath of tribulation associated with the Day of the Lord, or it could be a wrath of condemnation associated with hell and final judgment. Either way, we must conclude that this is indeed good news. Having said that, the context seems to favor that Paul has in mind the wrath associated with the Day of the Lord (5:1-3). The Thessalonians clearly knew that Christ had pardoned their sin, purchased their redemption, and delivered them from death (1:4-5). Their present struggles do not appear to be related to questions about their eternal destiny. As the letter reveals, their present struggles were related to questions about future events, namely, the destiny of their dead friends and the coming Day of the Lord. Paul's purpose was to give them enough knowledge of future events to bring them comfort and encouragement (4:18; 5:11). Clearly those who walk in darkness will experience the sudden and inescapable wrath of God (5:3; Rom 1:18). Conversely, those who walk in light will "obtain salvation." He reassures them that they have a different destiny than that of an unbelieving world. They were "appointed" for salvation through Christ.

Before moving on, consider the implications of verse 9 as they relate to Paul's discussion about Christ's return in 4:13-18. Although there is far from universal agreement concerning how to interpret these texts, for us to consider how the two passages fit together is important. Generally speaking, there are two ways to view this: (1) 1 Thessalonians 4:13-18 refers to the rapture of the church *prior to* the Day of the Lord; (2) 1 Thessalonians 4:13-18 speaks of the rapture of the church *following* the Day of the Lord. Although some of these issues have already been introduced, let's briefly reconsider each as they relate to Paul's statement about God's wrath.

(1) Deliverance from wrath points to the rapture of the church. Those who maintain this view conclude that since the church will be raptured prior to the unfurling of God's wrath (4:13-18), Christians will miss the Day of the Lord. For them, Paul's statement that "God did not appoint us to wrath" is directed toward the Thessalonians' concerns about the Day of the Lord. His message to them is that their fears are unfounded because Christ will come for them *before* this day occurs. This view seems to fit Paul's theme of encouragement (4:18; 5:11). It also appears to be very similar to Jesus' promise to keep His church "from the hour of testing that is going to come over the whole world" (Rev 3:10). This does not mean that *no* Christians will experience the Day of the Lord. Clearly, there will be those who will begin to follow the Lord during this time (Rev 6:11; 7:2-4; 13:7-8; 14:13). However, the purpose of Paul's statement in verse 9 is to show the Thessalonians that God's special plans for His people do not include the Day of the Lord.

(2) The church will experience the Day of the Lord. Those who believe that the church will go through the Day of the Lord view 4:13-18 differently. For them, Christ will come for His church following the Day of the Lord. They argue that deliverance from wrath in verse 9 does not speak of the rapture but of the work of Christ in salvation. Since Paul clearly mentions both salvation and wrath together, the logical reading of the text would point to God's deliverance from His ultimate wrath—hell. Additionally, the biblical record clearly shows how God supernaturally protects His people in the midst of trials (e.g., the plagues in Egypt). So God is more than capable of caring for His people during the outpouring of His wrath during the Day of the Lord.

To be sure, not everyone agrees on these issues. Oh, that Paul were more specific in his instruction! However, the main tenets of his teaching are unambiguous. On these tenets there is consistency: Jesus is coming again; the Day of the Lord will bring God's judgment and vindicate God's people; and Jesus delivers His children from wrath. The church should be encouraged by these promises.

They Are Delivered from Sin (1 Thess 5:9b-10)

Verses 9b-10 would be encouraging if they were read alone, but when you consider these verses in the context of the entire passage, they take on a more profound sense of meaning. Leon Morris provides an important insight that will help you to see this passage in its proper light:

> One of the things that gave salvation so full a meaning to
> New Testament Christians was that they were sure of the
> wrath of God, and knew that Christ had rescued them from
> a terrible fate. In modern days men are often prone to take
> Christianity lightly because they have emptied the wrath of its
> content. To remove the wrath of God from the scene is to rob
> life of a good deal of its serious purpose. (Morris, *Epistles of
> Paul*, 95–96)

You will never fully appreciate what Christ has done for you until you first grasp why He had to die. Paul says that Jesus "died *for* us" (5:10; emphasis added). He became your substitute and died in your place. He did this so that you could obtain salvation (5:9b). Apart from His death "for us," we stand guilty before God as "children under wrath" (Eph 2:3). Jesus' death delivers us from what we rightly deserve—judgment. Morris' statement is so true. Until you recognize how hopelessly doomed you are apart from Christ, you will never fully appreciate how miraculous the cross of Christ really is.

Bringing this back to the Thessalonians, we can now see how profoundly encouraging Paul's words would be. He gives them the hope they were looking for. "Whether we are awake or sleep," he writes, "we will live together with Him" (5:10). This single statement answers their troubling questions. He is saying to them in the clearest way possible, "If you die [sleep], you will be with Jesus. And if you are alive [awake] when He comes, you will be with Jesus." Everyone who belongs to Him will one day be with Him. Jesus Himself gave His followers this promise:

> My sheep hear My voice, I know them, and they follow Me. I give them eternal life, and they will never perish—ever! No one will snatch them out of My hand. My Father, who has given them to Me, is greater than all. No one is able to snatch them out of the Father's hand. (John 10:27-29)

They Are Delivered from Discouragement (1 Thess 5:11)

Paul adds his exclamation point to the end of this passage with the statement, "Therefore encourage one another and build each other up as you are already doing" (5:11). If these words sound familiar, they are. Paul used the same words at the end of chapter 4. In both texts Paul begins by addressing the Thessalonians' confusion about future events and ends with a strong note of exhortation (4:18; 5:11). Again, Paul gives them truth in order to bring them from confusion to confidence. A strong dose of God's Word is always the appropriate remedy for a confused and troubled heart.

How unfortunate it is that passages like this often create more confusion than they provide encouragement. It's easy to get caught up in debates about signs and seasons. However, the true test of whether we get it is not that we gathered all the facts but ultimately whether or not we get the point. **And the point of this passage from beginning to end is that our only hope is Jesus**.

Conclusion

Let's conclude by considering three practical ways that a passage like this can translate from the page of Scripture to the heart of a Christian.

God has called the church to comfort and not to conflict. Like the Thessalonians, we need to wake up, to sober up, and to look up. We have work to do and a Savior to please. It's time to lay aside petty disputes and silly disagreements. You and I cannot possibly be building one another up if we are constantly tearing one another down.

We have a limited opportunity to make a maximum impact. If we truly believe that Jesus' coming is imminent, then we will desire to make every moment count. The time to do something significant for God is now. Allow Him to show you what your task is, and don't delay when He reveals it to you. We were created for far more than most people realize. May God plant in you an insatiable desire to find out what your calling is, and may you not rest until you find it.

God provides the security, but you must take the risks. If you have any question about your future as a Christian then you need to listen again to Paul's statement: "For God did not appoint us to wrath, but to obtain salvation through our Lord Jesus Christ, who died for us, so that whether we are awake or asleep, we will live together with Him" (5:9-10). How is that for maximum security? Life is too short to play it safe. Mark Batterson gets it right when he asserts,

> Faith is the willingness to look foolish. Noah looked foolish building a boat in the middle of a desert. The Israelite army looked foolish marching around Jericho blowing trumpets. A shepherd boy named David looked foolish charging a giant with a slingshot. The Magi looked foolish tracking a star to Timbuktu. Peter looked foolish getting out of a boat in the middle of the Sea of Galilee. And Jesus looked foolish wearing a crown of thorns. But the results speak for themselves. Noah was saved from the flood; the walls came tumbling down; David defeated Goliath; the Magi discovered the Messiah; Peter walked on water; and Jesus was crowned King of kings. (Batterson, *Circle Maker*, 64–65)

With God, risk taking is not a foolish leap into the unknown, it is a bold step into a life of total dependence on Him.

Reflect and Discuss

1. How are the questions and concerns that prompted Paul to write this passage for the Thessalonians similar to questions Christians have today?
2. What are the promise and threat implied by the "Day of the Lord"?

3. Why doesn't Paul go into details about the "times and the seasons"? How do you think knowing the exact hour of Jesus' return would affect people?

4. How does Paul contrast the fates of believers and unbelievers in this passage?

5. Explain how a firm hope in the future will enable you to live confidently today.

6. How does the hope of Christ's coming encourage Christians to live soberly and seriously?

7. How would you explain to a child that faith, love, and hope are like armor that protects her head and heart?

8. What does Paul mean by the statement, "God did not appoint us to wrath"? What are some ways in which Christians have viewed this statement?

9. What is the connection between 4:13-18 and 5:1-11?

10. What is the ultimate point of this passage? How does this message speak to the church today?

A Healthy Church

1 THESSALONIANS 5:12-22

Main Idea: A healthy church is identified by how its people relate to one another and to God.

I. **The Value of Healthy Relationships (5:12-15)**
   A. Leaders who take their calling seriously (5:12)
      1. A pastor works.
      2. A pastor leads.
      3. A pastor admonishes.
   B. People who love one another devotedly (5:13-15)
      1. People to pastors (5:13)
         a. Recognize his calling.
         b. Respect his work.
         c. Rest in his leadership.
      2. People to people (5:14-15)
         a. Warn the irresponsible.
         b. Comfort the discouraged.
         c. Help the weak.
         d. Be patient with everyone.
         e. Refuse to retaliate.

II. **The Importance of Personal Devotion (5:16-22)**
   A. Joyful in outlook (5:16)
   B. Persistent in prayer (5:17)
   C. Grateful in attitude (5:18)
   D. Sensitive to the Spirit (5:19)
   E. Obedient to Scripture (5:20)
   F. Committed to discernment (5:21-22)

Facebook is an amazing thing! As of January 2014, the company boasted more than 1 billion active monthly users, which means that nearly one out of every 6 people on the globe is connected to Facebook. Many people check their Facebook page as their first task in the morning and their last task at night. Facebook has so woven its way into the fabric of this world that, for many people, to imagine their lives without it would be difficult if not downright impossible. Arguably, the success of Facebook is directly attributable to the innate human craving for relationships. Of course, you might wonder just how meaningful relationships can be via the medium of social media. Yet, for millions of people, Facebook is the place to which they go to connect with others.

For those who serve as pastors, Facebook has afforded an opportunity to see their church members on their turf. What you see can sometimes be quite enlightening. For instance, what you see via a Facebook post on Saturday may be very different from what you see at church on Sunday mornings. Through photos, posts, and personal musings, you now have the opportunity to see others just as they are. Sometimes I wonder if people actually realize that what they post online is available for the world to see! Still, Facebook allows people just to be themselves—so what you see is what you get.

Let's turn this thought to the church. If someone could look into the inner workings of your church, what would they see? I'm not talking about what you want them to see; I'm talking about what they would really see. In other words, if your church posted "real pictures" on its Facebook page, what story would those pictures tell? **Churches are just like people. There is the "real you," and then there is the "you" that you want others to think you are. In the same way, there is your real church, and then there is the church that you want others to think you are**.

The purpose of Paul's instruction in 5:12-22 is straightforward: he desires for the Thessalonians to be a "real church." After taking them on a journey from present to future and from earth to heaven (4:13–5:11), you can imagine how easy it would be for them to want to absorb all of this. But without missing a beat, Paul quickly brings them back to earth by reminding them that they have lives to live and a mission to pursue. He dives right in by giving them practical instruction about everyday living in the body of Christ. In this passage Paul probes no deep theological mysteries nor does he unveil any prophetic utterances. In fact, he does not even address worship styles, building architecture, or dress codes; instead he gets right to the heart of the church—its interpersonal relationships and its internal devotion. How much do you love one another, and how much do you love God?

The Value of Healthy Relationships
1 THESSALONIANS 5:12-15

Someone has said that church would be easy if it weren't for people. While in a humorous way that might be true, with all joking aside, if it weren't for people, there wouldn't be church. But the fact remains that when you bring people together with varying personalities, styles, likes, and preferences, problems are sure to ensue. Have you stopped to consider that the church is the only institution on earth where a person has to admit how bad they are before they can actually join? Paul reminds the Corinthians of just what a miracle the church really is:

> *Do not be deceived: No sexually immoral people, idolaters, adulterers, or anyone practicing homosexuality, no thieves, greedy people, drunkards, verbally abusive people, or swindlers will inherit God's kingdom. And* some of you used to be like this. *But you were washed, you were sanctified, you were justified in the name of the Lord Jesus Christ and by the Spirit of our God.* (1 Cor 6:9-11; emphasis added)

Given the checkered past of the church's constituency, that the church is able to accomplish anything is no small feat. Yet despite its many people and the challenges they bring, Jesus still guarantees the church's success (Matt 16:18). However, for the church to accomplish its mission outside of its walls effectively, it must first be healthy inside its walls. And one of the key factors affecting the internal health of the church is how God's people relate to one another. With this in mind, Paul shows the Thessalonians two specific areas within the church where proper interpersonal relationships are essential: how the leaders view their calling, and how the people relate to one another.

Leaders Who Take Their Calling Seriously (1 Thess 5:12)

God has woven into the fabric of life the need to have leaders. From marriages and sports teams to corporations and churches, leadership is essential. Without leadership, marriages suffer, sports teams lose, corporations flounder, and churches fail. Leadership makes life better.

If ever a group of people needed bold leaders, the Thessalonians did. Facing persecution from without and searching for answers within, this infant church needed guidance. Since Paul knew that he would not always be there to answer their questions and to calm their anxieties, he urges the Thessalonians to follow the leadership of "those who labor among you and lead you in the Lord" (5:12). This statement implies that pastors had already been appointed and were presently leading the Thessalonian church (cf. Titus 1:5). Paul reminds them that a healthy relationship between pastor and people is essential for the church to do its work and accomplish its mission. However, for these relationships to work, each group had to understand its specific role within the church. He begins by highlighting the responsibilities of the pastor: he works, he leads, and he teaches.

A pastor works. Concerning those who lead, Paul writes, "Now we ask you, brothers, to give recognition to those who labor among you and lead you in the Lord and admonish you" (5:12). The Greek word translated "labor" means "to exert energy to the point of weariness or fatigue." It implies that a pastor is not afraid of sweat and hard work. He is not in it for paychecks, perks, or a nine-to-five job. In fact, his ministry is not a job—it's a calling. And his calling is his life and passion. Speaking to a group of potential pastors, Charles Spurgeon described such a calling:

> If any student in this room could be content to be a newspaper editor, or a grocer, or a farmer, or a doctor, or a lawyer, or a senator, or a king, in the name of heaven and earth, let him go his way; he is not the man in whom dwells the Spirit of God in its fullness, for a man so filled with God would utterly weary of any pursuit but that for which his inmost soul pants. If on the other hand, you can say that for all the wealth of both the Indies you could not and dare not espouse any other calling so as to be put aside from preaching the gospel of Jesus Christ, then depend upon it, if other things be equally satisfactory, you have the signs of this apostleship. We must feel that woe is unto us if we preach not the gospel; the word of God must be unto us as fire in our bones, otherwise, if we undertake the ministry, we shall be unhappy in it, shall be unable to bear the self-denials incident to it, and shall be of little service to those among whom we minister. (Spurgeon, *Lectures*, 26–27)

Paul's life was a living testimony to the kind of passion required of those in ministry. He practiced what he preached in the presence of the Thessalonian Christians. Take note how he described his personal work ethic: "For you remember our labor and hardship, brothers. Working night and day so that we would not burden any of you, we preached God's gospel to you" (2:9). Look at the vocabulary Paul employs to describe his ministry: labor, hardship, and work. Although he had a right to live off the gospel, he chose instead to provide his own financial support by working as a tentmaker so as not to burden the churches (Acts 18:3). And as Phillips suggests, Paul most likely worked on tents during the day and then turned around and preached the gospel all night (Phillips, *Exploring 1 and 2 Thessalonians*, 139). No pastor would ever make such a commitment if he were not sure of and passionate about his calling.

A pastor leads. Paul's reference to those who "lead you" (5:12) suggests that pastors assumed a significant place of responsibility within the Thessalonian church. The word translated "lead" has several potential meanings. It could mean "to preside, lead, and direct" or "to protect and provide." It is difficult to know exactly which meaning Paul had in mind. However, the word is used four times in Paul's instruction to Timothy concerning elders within the church (1 Tim 3:4,5,12; 5:17). Three of those usages refer to an elder "managing" (leading) his family. The fourth usage is in 1 Timothy 5:17 where Paul speaks of an elder as a "leader" of the church. While it is possible that Paul has in mind to protect and care for the church, the more likely meaning is that just as elders must lead and direct their families, so also they have the unique calling to preside over or direct the affairs of God's church. Regardless of how this leadership is exercised, we know that is not to be done in a dictatorial manner. Peter makes this clear:

> *I exhort the elders among you: Shepherd God's flock among you, not overseeing out of compulsion but freely, according to God's will; not for the money but eagerly; not lording it over those entrusted to you, but being examples to the flock.* (1 Pet 5:1-3)

Paul underscores this sober responsibility by emphasizing that all pastoral leadership must be done "in the Lord" (5:12). Beale describes the significance of this prepositional phrase:

> This position of authority is not to be performed in a dictatorial or sinful way, but the elders are over the rest of the believers in the Lord. Their authority can be exercised only in so far as the Lord has given them authority to act. . . . Church leaders are not autonomous sovereigns but represent Jesus'

authority. They are commissioned by Christ to carry out their oversight of the flock according to his will and not their own. (Beale, *1–2 Thessalonians*, 160)

A pastor admonishes. The third pastoral responsibility that Paul identifies is admonishment. The Greek word translated "admonish" means "to put in the mind" or "to warn." Paul uses the same word again in 5:14 to refer to the Christian's response to those who are unruly in the church. The word carries with it the idea of confronting a sinful habit or warning against a bad behavior. Interestingly, admonishment is always closely tied to the work of preaching, teaching, and applying scriptural truth (Col 1:28; 3:16).

Correcting inappropriate behavior and confronting sinful attitudes is indeed one of the tougher aspects of ministry. Still, pastors have the solemn responsibility to address these things when they are present. Paul's charge to "preach the word" (2 Tim 4:2 ESV) involves more than just encouraging and instructing; it also involves correcting. The word translated "preach" or "proclaim" is used more than 60 times in the New Testament. The word connotes the image of a herald who has been given the task of announcing a king's message. Because the message comes directly from the king himself, the herald is expected to proclaim the message as given. Such an image says much about the weighty responsibility of the pastor. When God's laws are broken, His Name is misrepresented, or the purity of His church is threatened, the pastor's responsibility is to speak the truth. God-called men have a God-given mandate to proclaim His message. They must have the courage to confront sin and correct behavior.

With the pastor's responsibilities to the people established, Paul will now turn his attention to the people's responsibilities to the pastor. The leadership of even the most gifted shepherd proves impotent if the sheep are unwilling to follow. But as F. F. Bruce rightly notes, this is not a one-way street. Pastors and people have a mutual responsibility to honor and respect each other. Bruce writes,

It will make for the effective life and witness of the church and for peaceful relations among its members if its leaders are recognized and honored and their directions followed. The corollary of this is that the leaders should be the kind of people who deserve to be recognized and honored by their fellow Christians. (F. F. Bruce, *1 and 2 Thessalonians*, 120)

People Who Love One Another Devotedly (1 Thess 5:13-15)

For God's people to expand the breadth of their influence on the world, they must first grow in the depth of their love for one another. Jesus said it this way: "By this all people will know that you are My disciples, if you have love for one another" (John 13:35). For the Thessalonian church to continue its vibrant ministry outside the walls, the church needed to remember not to neglect loving those inside the walls. Paul turns his attention to this matter by addressing two very important relationships in the church: people to pastors, and people to people.

People to pastors (5:13). In one sentence the writer of Hebrews offers an important insight into the nature of Paul's exhortation to the Thessalonians:

> *Obey your leaders and submit to them, for they keep watch over*
> *your souls as those who will give an account, so that they can do this*
> *with joy and not with grief, for that would be unprofitable for you.*
> (Heb 13:17)

In this statement we see a vivid picture of both the pastor's responsibility to His people and the people's responsibility to the pastor. Under the watchful eye of God, a pastor leads, keeps watch over, and joyfully cares for his church. Likewise, out of obedience to God, the people follow, respect, and honor the leadership of their pastor. Anyone who has experienced the friction created by poor pastor-people relationships will recognize the damage that such conflict can cause to the testimony of Christ and His church. At the same time, anyone who has experienced a healthy pastor-people relationship will testify to the joy and unity that it has brought to the church. Paul's focus is on the latter. He thus encourages the people to respond positively to their shepherd by recognizing his calling, respecting his work, and resting in his leadership.

Recognize his calling. As we have noted above, those who have been called to lead God's church shoulder a significant weight of responsibility. Because of the nature of their calling, the church must recognize these leaders for the strategic work that they do on its behalf. To this end, Paul instructs the church to give them proper "recognition" (5:12). The word carries a more profound meaning than simply to acknowledge what the pastor does; it means that the church should know and value *who* the pastor is. Albert Barnes illustrates how the church should view their leader:

They should not regard him as a distant man, or as a stranger among them. . . . They are to "know" and regard him as their spiritual teacher and ruler; not to be strangers to the place where he preaches the word of life, and not to listen to his admonitions and reproofs as those of a stranger, but as those of a pastor and friend. (Barnes, *Notes*, 56)

Barnes makes a very important point. The pastor-people relationship in unhealthy churches often takes on the unfortunate "us against him" mentality. God did not design His church to function in that environment. While there is no certainty that any such problems existed in Thessalonica, the context does seem to indicate that Paul was trying to prevent any such occurrence (see 5:13b). Nothing destroys a church's witness like contentiousness. Regardless of who is to blame for such "us against him" posturing, such an attitude seldom leads to a positive outcome for the future of that church.

Although it is impossible to prevent completely, pastors can still do much to create an environment where contentiousness is minimized. If they desire for people to know and value them, then pastors must take the time to get to know and value their people. In an effort to keep a "holy distance" from their people, pastors might find themselves in the unfortunate position of being isolated from them. This is never a good thing. In fact, it is contrary to the calling of a pastor. Peter reminds pastors that they are to be attentive shepherds who lovingly guide, feed, and care for their sheep (1 Pet 5:2). You cannot care for your sheep if you do not spend time with your sheep. And if you do not desire to spend time with sheep, then you better not be a shepherd. You cannot shepherd God's people if you don't share your life with them (2:8).

Respect his work. According to Paul, pastors must be regarded "very highly in love because of their work" (5:13). I. Howard Marshall notes that such honor is granted "not because of any qualities which they may possess due to birth or social status or natural gifts but only on the basis of the spiritual task to which they are called" (Marshall, *1 and 2 Thessalonians*, 148–49). Because of the nature of their calling, pastors are to be held in the highest honor. One might wonder how many congregations actually view their pastors in this way. Furthermore, one might also wonder what would happen if they did. The results might be surprising. A number of years ago *Our Daily Bread* featured an article titled, "Getting Rid of the Pastor." Apparently, some members of a local congregation approached another pastor to seek advice about how to get rid of their pastor. Seeing through their request, this pastor offered them the following wise counsel:

> Look your pastor straight in the eye while he is preaching and say "Amen!" once in a while. He'll preach himself to death. Pat him on the back and tell him his good points. He'll work himself to death. Rededicate your life to Christ and ask your minister for a job to do. He'll die of heart failure. Get the church to pray for him. Soon he'll become so effective that a larger church will take him off your hands. (Richard DeHaan, *Our Daily Bread*, July 2003)

Admittedly, respect must be earned. Nevertheless, churches have the responsibility to esteem their leaders not because of title or status, but "because of their work." However, even if a pastor does not receive the respect that his calling deserves, he must still treat his people with the dignity and respect that they deserve. John Phillips shares this powerful insight from the life of William Carey:

> When William Carey was aboard ship on his way to India, he was surrounded by peers of the realm and diplomats, the high British officials who ruled the Indian subcontinent. He was looked upon as a nobody. One snobbish individual sneered at the missionary, "Just a shoemaker, aren't you, Carey?" he said disdainfully. "No sir," replied William Carey. "I am not a shoemaker. I am only a cobbler." Nobody knows the name of that civil servant, but the whole church honors William Carey. (Phillips, *Exploring 1 and 2 Thessalonians*, 139–40)

Pastors would do well to remember that the final evaluation of their ministry has nothing to do with how people treated them and everything to do with how faithfully they fulfilled their calling by loving their people.

Rest in his leadership. The logical outgrowth of a church that loves and respects its pastor is "peace" (5:13b). Again, we cannot be certain that Paul saw potential conflict on the horizon. Even if no immediate issues were pressing him to pen these words, it did not preclude the possibility of such issues arising in the future. Either way, Paul desired nothing more than for the Thessalonians to be at peace with one another. Their young church was the target of enough opposition from the outside—why would they manufacture their own conflict on the inside? Internal conflict only breeds unrest and turmoil (1 Cor 1:10-13; Titus 3:9-11). When we work toward healthy relationships and mutual respect, the result is peace and rest (Ps 133:1-3; John 17:21; Rom 12:10-18; Col 3:12-15).

People to people (5:14-15). For pastors and people to get along is one thing, but it is an entirely different thing for people within the church to get along. Far from the homogeneous exclusivity of a country club or civic organization, the church is a melting pot of ethnic diversity, various socio-economic statuses, and very opinionated people. A recent *Forbes .com* post listed the "job" of a pastor as the fifth toughest leadership role in America (Asghar, "Ranking"). A senior pastor who was interviewed in the post made the following insightful statement about his role:

> You're scrutinized and criticized from top to bottom, stem to stern. You work for an invisible, perfect Boss, and you're supposed to lead a ragtag gaggle of volunteers towards God's coming future. It's like herding cats, but harder. (Forbes.com, Feb. 25, 2014)

Anyone who has ever served in ministry can appreciate both the candor and the humor of his statement. Added to the diversity of people within the church are the challenges associated with keeping all of those people on the same page. Without a doubt, it is a formidable challenge to lead a "ragtag gaggle" of volunteers to accomplish a common objective.

Paul knew the high stakes that were involved in establishing a vibrant church in Thessalonica. He also knew that for the church to share the love of Jesus with a lost city, the people first needed to reflect His love in their relationships with one another. Doing this would require that they learn how to navigate the waters filled with problem people within the church. It's easy to love the people with whom you agree, but special grace and wisdom are needed to deal with those who bring challenges to the unity of the fellowship.

Warn the irresponsible. Paul begins this next series of exhortations with a note of urgency. He writes: "We exhort you brothers: warn those who are irresponsible" (5:14). His use of the word *exhort* indicates that this is more than a simple request. You'll recall that previously he "asks" (not exhorts) them to give proper recognition to their leaders (5:12). The word *ask* is not a word of urgency but a word of request. Although the difference between these two words is subtle, it is significant. On one hand, Paul "asks" the church to pursue healthy relationships with its leaders, but on the other hand, he "exhorts" them to deal swiftly with certain people within the fellowship. It seems that although the issue of showing proper respect for leaders is *important*, the matter of dealing with problem people in the church is *urgent*. Clearly he implies that, if left unchecked, these people had the potential of negatively impacting the testimony of the church. Pretending that problem people are not in the church does not make them go away. Unfortunately, the path of least resistance is often the path that will eventually bring the most resistance. Still, many churches learn this lesson the hard way by not taking the time to confront the carnal or to comfort the hurting. The biggest threats to the health and well-being of a church often come from within and not from without.

The word translated "warn" is not unfamiliar to us. Paul used the same word to describe one of the functions of pastors/elders (5:12). The Greek word can mean "to reprove, admonish" or "to caution." However, it is usually used in reference to confronting sin or correcting behavior. Paul instructs the Thessalonians to warn the "irresponsible." The only other time this word is used in the New Testament is in 2 Thessalonians where Paul writes,

> *Now we command you, brothers, in the name of our Lord Jesus Christ, to keep away from every brother who walks irresponsibly and not according to the tradition received from us. . . . In fact, when we were with you, this is what we commanded you: "If anyone isn't willing to work, he should not eat." For we hear that there are some among you who walk irresponsibly, not working at all, but interfering with the work of others.* (2 Thess 3:6,10-11)

Although we cannot be certain as to the precise identity of these individuals, likely Paul has in mind the lazy busybodies who were meddling in everyone's business. The word *irresponsible* pictures a soldier who steps out of line and behaves in a disorderly manner. Based on the meaning of the word, perhaps Paul simply had in mind any church member whose ungodly behavior was threatening the unity and integrity of the church.

Today, the "irresponsible" take on many forms—from the gifted pew-sitter who never gets involved, to the opinionated busybody who criticizes everyone. These are the ones who threaten to withhold their tithe when they get upset, seek to undermine the authority of their leaders by stirring up dissension, refuse to use their spiritual gifts while critiquing those who do, and show up for business meetings but not for worship. Since the irresponsible have the potential to undermine God's work and to divide the fellowship, they must be warned. Considering the danger that these individuals posed to an infant Thessalonian church, we can see why Paul urgently exhorted the church to deal with these people.

Comfort the discouraged. Serving alongside the irresponsible were the "discouraged" (5:14b). This word most likely refers to one who is worried, fainthearted, or fearful. In this sense, the discouraged would be the antithesis of the irresponsible. The *irresponsible* would be those overly self-confident individuals who clamor for attention; whereas the *discouraged* would be those who lack self-confidence and choose to remain on the fringes. Perhaps these people were once busily serving the Lord but have since allowed life's pressures to steal their joy and stifle their passion. The Thessalonians were facing the pressures of persecution from the outside (3:2-4) and the pain of grief on the inside (4:13-14). Given these challenges, likely there were more than a few discouraged Christians in the fellowship.

Discouraged people need to be comforted (5:14). The Greek word translated "comfort" means "encourage." According to Paul, helping discouraged people is not that difficult. Often all they need is a simple word of encouragement. Concerning this, Swindoll offers a helpful suggestion about the *gift of encouragement.* He writes,

> This gift may be wrapped in an affirming word, a gentle
> touch, a smile, or a shoulder to lean on. It may simply be our
> presence. Too often we isolate ourselves; like strangers in an
> elevator, we feel uncomfortable even making eye contact or
> speaking politely to one another. In the family of God, though,
> these things must be different. Let's free ourselves to touch
> one another, particularly the [discouraged], who need to
> know someone cares. (Swindoll, *Contagious Christianity*, 81)

Regardless of how we choose to help those who are hurting and discouraged, we have the responsibility both to rejoice with those who rejoice and to weep with those who weep (Rom 12:15).

Let's consider for a moment how this might play itself out in your church. Suppose your church is pursuing a new church plant in a neighboring town or city. The majority of the congregation is on board and ready to go. However, there are a few members who express their doubts about the plan. You might hear them say something like, "We really don't have the money or resources to fund this project." Or, "We have tried this before and it failed." Most would respond by summarily dismissing both them and their comments and would choose to move forward with their own plans. We might even be tempted to rebuke them for being stubborn or divisive. While moving forward despite their opposition may be necessary, it would not be right for the church to ignore these people in the process. Perhaps these individuals are not being *divisive* at all. Instead they may be among the *discouraged*. Maybe they have been burned in the past by a similar decision in a previous church and fear that it could happen again. Or maybe there is some other issue holding them back. Whatever their reason, it could be that their opposition has less to do with the plan itself and more to do with their own personal hurts, struggles, and faithlessness.

Church work is sometimes messy because you must deal with people, and people bring baggage to church. All people are products of past hurts, present struggles, and future fears. Sometimes they are able to overcome these, but sometimes they get the best of them and they become discouraged. If the church is to be a place where everyone can be real, then you must remember that sometimes people need encouragement. Not every person who asks questions or expresses doubts is being divisive. We would do well to remember that sometimes people ask questions with a stated reason even though a different but genuine reason lies in the background. These stated public reasons are not always the same as the internal private ones. Sometimes the real reason behind a question is a person's internal struggle with doubts, hurts, or fears. Rather than running such a person over in an attempt to get the work done, we must be willing to roll up your sleeves, get our hands dirty, and spend some time "comforting the discouraged." Hence, as Hiebert notes, Paul challenged the Thessalonians to deal with their discouraged members accordingly:

> These timid, discouraged individuals needed to be encouraged, cheered up, stimulated, helped along. They did not need to be warned and rebuked like the idle, but rather needed to be encouraged through the use of helpful words to continue the battle for the Lord. (Hiebert, *1 and 2 Thessalonians*, 252)

Help the weak. In comparison to those who are discouraged, the "weak" are those who lack strength. Although Paul may be referring to physical weakness (Phil 2:26), more likely he has in mind spiritual weakness (Rom 14:1-6). Paul instructs the church to "help" them ("lay hold of" or "hold firmly to"). The city of Thessalonica was no place for the spiritually faint of heart. So the spiritually strong were encouraged to stand alongside those who are spiritually weak. As Michael Martin so aptly puts it, "The church should support these 'weak' brothers as beloved fellow strugglers, not desert them as ignorant or unimportant stragglers" (Martin, *1, 2 Thessalonians*, 178).

Be patient with everyone. If Christians are going to take seriously their responsibility to warn the irresponsible, comfort the discouraged, and help the weak, then they are going to need to be "patient" (5:14c). The word *patient* means to "have a long fuse." The patient person is someone who does not "blow up" easily when dealing with challenging circumstances or difficult people. Patience is one of those virtues that, though knowing its importance, you struggle to put into practice. We often demand patience in how others respond to our shortcomings and then lack patience in how we deal with theirs. As damaging as unruly, discouraged, and weak believers can be to a church, a spirit of impatience will only make matters worse. Patience is one of God's attributes. The prophet Joel describes this divine attribute: "[God] is gracious and compassionate, slow to anger, rich in faithful love, and He relents from sending disaster" (Joel 2:13). These words do not mean that God will allow sin to go unpunished; nor do they suggest that God will fail to hold sinners accountable. They do mean, however, that God has a "long fuse" and is controlled or restrained in His response to sinners (Exod 34:6; Num 14:18; Ps 86:15; Jonah 4:2; Nah 1:3; Rom 2:4). Since we have been redeemed by Jesus Christ and adopted into God's family, we ought to reflect our heavenly Father in everything, including our patience in dealing with one another.

Refuse to retaliate. Of all the admonitions in this section of Paul's letter, the one that we may find the toughest to obey is found in verse 15: "See to it that no one repays evil for evil to anyone, but always pursue what is good for one another and for all." Interestingly, Paul directs this admonition to the entire congregation. Considering the context in which Paul makes this statement, it is not difficult to see why he had the entire church in mind. One of the most difficult aspects of church life is learning how to get along with one another. While we may rightly expect that all Christians will love one another, this is sadly not always the case. Unfortunately, people within the church are capable of inflicting great hurt on other Christians. Everyone faces the very real possibility of being hurt by a fellow church member. The irresponsible may enjoy their irresponsibility, the discouraged may find comfort in their discouragement, and the weak may have no desire to grow strong. Despite our best intentions to help, some simply do not want our help and may even resent us for getting into their business. Sometimes this resentment is expressed through anger, slander, gossip, or even false accusations.

How then are we to respond when we become the object of another person's resentment or anger? Here is where Paul's command enters the picture. We must pursue only what is good for everyone. Period. He says nothing about this pursuit being contingent on whether or not we think someone deserves your kindness. We must resist the urge to fight fire with fire by repaying evil with evil. We cannot control how others treat us, but we can control how we respond to them. We must do our part and then trust God to do His part. As Paul told the Romans,

> *Bless those who persecute you; bless and do not curse. . . . Do not repay anyone evil for evil. Try to do what is honorable in everyone's eyes. If possible, on your part, live at peace with everyone. Friends, do not avenge yourselves; instead, leave room for His wrath. For it is written: Vengeance belongs to Me; I will repay, says the Lord.* (Rom 12:14,17-19)

The Importance of Personal Devotion
1 THESSALONIANS 5:16-22

Paul moves the discussion from the Thessalonians' interpersonal relationships with one another to their spiritual relationship with God. He gives a series of eight imperatives directed at each member's personal devotion to God. All these imperatives are stated in the present tense, calling for continuous action. Because they are in the imperative, they are clearly meant to be commands and not suggestions. Therefore, these are not habits that the Christian is to practice occasionally; these are identifying characteristics that mark a Christian's life. Paul underscores this fact when he asserts, "For this is God's will for you in Christ Jesus" (5:18b).

Joyful in Outlook (1 Thess 5:16)

For many Christians the command to "rejoice always" is perplexing. Christians like to talk about such biblical truths but often struggle to put them into practice. Given life's hurts, pains, and sorrows, one may legitimately question how a person could possibly always rejoice. The answer is not as difficult as it may appear. **Joy is not something that we *work on*; Joy is something that we *live in*.** We are able to experience constant joy because of the presence of God's Spirit in you (Gal 5:22). Our joy is never generated from the outside in but always from the inside out.

Persistent in Prayer (1 Thess 5:17)

The command to "pray constantly" has also been the source of misunderstanding and confusion. Does Paul mean that you should always be praying—like 24/7? Or is he suggesting that you memorize written prayers and recite them incessantly, as is the practice of some religious groups? What is at the heart of this imperative? We know that Paul does not have in mind that Christians should be praying at every single moment of the day. This, of course, would be impossible. We can also be sure that Paul is not advocating the "vain repetitions" of memorized prayers. The Bible condemns such a practice (Matt 6:7 KJV). When Paul commands that we pray, we are to keep on praying—earnestly, passionately, and expectantly. Jesus commands you to pray in this way:

> *So I say to you, keep asking, and it will be given to you. Keep searching, and you will find. Keep knocking, and the door will be opened to you. For everyone who asks receives, and the one who searches finds, and to the one who knocks, the door will be opened.* (Luke 11:9-10; see also Luke 18:1-8)

Mark Batterson explains why God wants you to pray in this way:

> God has determined that certain expressions of His power will only be exercised in response to prayer. Simply put, God won't do it unless you pray for it. We have not because we ask not. . . . The greatest tragedy in life is the prayers that go unanswered because they go unasked. (Batterson, *Circle Maker*, 17)

If we truly expect that God will answer our prayers, then we had better learn to pray with such tenacity and persistence that we allow nothing to hinder us from bringing even our boldest requests to God.

The fact that Paul commands us to pray in this manner reveals two significant truths about God. First, God wants to hear from you. Let that thought soak in for a moment. The God of this universe wants to hear *from you*. On the basis of your relationship with Jesus Christ, you have been granted an all-access ticket into His presence (Heb 10:19-22). Second, if God expects that you will ask Him for things, then it follows that He has the ability to give you what you ask. In fact, He has the ability to give you more than you ask (Eph 3:20). Think about your most pressing needs, your most formidable opponents, or even your most out-of-reach dreams. If God desires that you bring those matters before Him, then you can be sure that He has more than enough ability to do something about them. As Jeremiah so aptly puts it, *nothing* is too difficult for our God (Jer 32:17).

Grateful in Attitude (1 Thess 5:18)

At first blush this appears to be a very unusual command. Given how tough life is, we might wonder how it could even be possible for a person to give thanks for *everything*. While we may concede the need to give thanks for *some* things, we would certainly question the legitimacy of giving thanks for *all* things. When we read the verse carefully, however, we might be surprised to learn that Paul says we are to "give thanks *in* everything" and not *for* everything. This imperative speaks more about our perspective toward life than it does about our attitude toward our circumstances. To obey this command we must keep the big picture in view, and to keep the big picture in view we must understand how God's providence works.

J. I. Packer defines *providence* as

> The unceasing activity of the Creator whereby, in overflowing bounty and goodwill, He upholds His creatures in ordered existence, guides and governs all events, circumstances and free acts of angels and men, and directs everything to its appointed goal, for His own glory. (Packer, "Providence," 990)

Calvin states it a little more succinctly when he writes,

> For what is fitter or more suitable for pacifying us, than when we learn that God embraces us in Christ so tenderly, that he turns to our advantage and welfare everything that befalls us? (Calvin, *1 and 2 Thessalonians*, 297)

Only God could take the thousands of details of a person's life (some good and some bad) and weave them into the beautiful tapestry of His perfect plan. From the human perspective, many of life's occurrences—especially the painful ones—appear to have little intrinsic value. However, if we had God's perspective, we would be able to view each of these details in a different way. **Providence affirms that no detail is irrelevant or insignificant. God is using everything for our ultimate good and His everlasting glory** (Rom 8:28). Hence, to "give thanks *in* everything" is to affirm our resolute belief that God is overseeing every detail of our lives. Paul, by no accident, concludes this verse by reminding us that such an attitude is "God's will for you in Christ Jesus" (5:18b). What more could please the heavenly Father than for Him to know that we trust Him so much that we are willing to live each moment in a constant state of thankfulness?

Sensitive to the Spirit (1 Thess 5:19)

With this imperative concerning how we respond to the Holy Spirit, Paul turns from commanding the Thessalonians what they should be doing in verses 16-18 to what they should avoid (or stop) doing (vv. 19-20). In the first three imperatives he places an emphasis on the manner in which the action is to be performed: *always* rejoicing, *constantly* praying, and *in everything* giving thanks. In these next two imperatives he places an emphasis on the subject being discussed: as for the *Spirit*, do not stifle Him; and as for *prophecies*, do not despise them.

Paul's command, "Do not stifle the Spirit," could be translated, "Do not put out the Spirit's fire." The Greek word translated "stifle" is used in several places in the New Testament to speak of putting out a fire (Mark 9:48; Heb 11:34). In a very simple but straightforward manner, Paul is commanding the church to avoid any activity that will thwart the Spirit's work. By using the present tense, Paul directs this injunction squarely at a specific issue in the Thessalonian church. What exactly Paul has in mind is the subject of much discussion. Some see Paul's command directed specifically toward members of the Thessalonian church who were frowning on their fellow church members for exercising certain gifts of the Spirit (cf. 1 Cor 12–14). In this sense, Paul would be admonishing them not to stifle the Spirit's activity as He manifested His work through those gifts. Those who adopt this view also see a close connection between this verse and Paul's discussion about prophecy in the verse that follows. While such an argument is intriguing, no information in hand indicates that this was an issue in Thessalonica. We might surmise that if Paul had in mind the need to address a major issue relating to the gifts of the Spirit, he would have addressed it in such a way as to leave no question, just as he did with other issues that troubled the church (4:13-18). It makes sense then to see this imperative as a general admonition to live a Spirit-filled life. Perhaps this command relates directly to the first three imperatives in verses 16-18, as Marshall suggests:

> It is . . . possible that the specific commands . . . were needed because the church was not sufficiently open to the inspiration of the Spirit. . . . Paul wanted them to experience more joy in the Lord. They needed the power of the Spirit to build them up. (Marshall, *1 and 2 Thessalonians*, 158)

Marshall is indeed correct. Incessant joy, persistent prayer, and genuine gratitude are all evidences of the Spirit's work.

Obedient to Scripture (1 Thess 5:20)

Walter Kaiser notes that prophecy can mean either "*foretelling*" or "*forthtelling.*" The former speaks to the specific function of the prophet who predicted the future activities of God. The latter speaks to ongoing activity of the prophet who spoke as "a preacher of righteousness to his generation and his culture" (Kaiser, *The Christian and the Old Testament*, 128). More than two thirds of all prophetic activity in the Bible is forthtelling rather than foretelling.

Paul's reference in this imperative is most likely a rejection of the preached word. To what extent they were "despising prophecies" cannot be determined with certainty. Paul may even be attempting to prevent this from happening rather than to correct something that was already happening. Perhaps some thought that those with the gift of preaching were receiving too much attention. Or maybe the presence of false teachers led them either to abandon preaching altogether or to minimize its importance. Whatever the issue, Paul did command them to place a high value on the proclaimed word. But for whatever reason, they were not valuing the preached word as they had been taught. This fact is evident by Paul's use of the word *despise* (5:20). This word has the sense of "treat with contempt" or "look down on." Paul never taught the church to treat prophesies with contempt, but he did challenge the church to "test" them (5:21). He knew that the health of the church would ultimately be determined both by its commitment to preach and by its desire to honor God's Word. Although written more than 30 years ago, Walter Kaiser's sobering words are as relevant today as when they were first written:

> It is no secret that Christ's Church is not at all in good health in many places of the world. She has been languishing because she has been fed, as the current line has it, "junk food"; all kinds of artificial preservatives and all sorts of unnatural substitutes have been served up to her. As a result, theological and Biblical malnutrition has afflicted the very generation that has taken such giant steps to make sure its physical health is not damaged by using foods or products that are carcinogenic or otherwise harmful to their physical bodies. Simultaneously a worldwide spiritual famine resulting from the absence of any genuine publication of the Word of God (Amos 8:11) continues to run wild and almost unabated in most quarters of the Church. (Kaiser, *Toward an Exegetical Theology*, 7–8)

The church will only be as strong as its commitment to preach, teach, and obey Scripture.

Committed to Discernment (1 Thess 5:21-22)

Paul brings this section to a fitting conclusion by highlighting the need for proper discernment. He commands the church to put everything to the test. The word translated "test" means "examine closely for the purpose of determining authenticity." Some of its many uses in the New Testament include testing to see what pleases the Lord (Eph 5:10), testing to evaluate the genuineness of faith (2 Cor 13:5; 1 Pet 1:7), and testing to determine the nature of God's will (Rom 12:2). Paul may very well be referring to testing the various "prophecies" that were circulating among the Thessalonians (2 Thess 2:1-2; see also 1 Cor 12:10). If this is the case, then he is commanding them not to dismiss such messages summarily but to evaluate their truthfulness carefully. Calvin agrees with this view when he writes,

> Paul . . . prohibits them from condemning anything without first examining it . . . [and] he admonishes them to exercise judgment, before receiving what may be brought forward as undoubted truth. (Calvin, *1 and 2 Thessalonians*, 300)

While there is much credence to this view, seeing Paul's statement as a command to put *everything* to the test seems best. For the believer, all of life must be viewed through the lens of Scripture. Before making any decision, accepting any teaching, choosing any course of action, or setting off in any direction, the first question that every Christian must ask is, What does the Bible say? Those things that prove to be "good" must be embraced. Those things that prove to be "evil" must be rejected (5:21-22). The word translated "stay away" has the sense of "abstain or hold oneself away from." Paul used the word when he instructed the Thessalonians to "abstain" from sexual immorality.

Conclusion

For the local church, the principles set forth in this passage are more than just practical—they are indispensable. Imagine what the church would look like if its people obeyed these commands to confront, comfort, encourage, and help one another. God has called His people to develop deep and meaningful relationships with one another. He desires for the church to be more than a superficial gathering of people; He desires for the church to be a family—a family devoted to one another and to Him. For a family to function properly each member must do his or her part. Paul taught that God's family includes both horizontal responsibilities (people to people) and vertical responsibilities (people to God). When those within the church embrace their responsibilities at least three things will happen:

- Its leaders will take their calling seriously (5:12-13).
- Its members will love one another genuinely (5:14-15).
- The entire church will love God devotedly (5:16-22).

Reflect and Discuss

1. Why does Paul command the church to give recognition to those who serve as pastors? How should people respond to their pastor?
2. According to this passage, what are the responsibilities of the pastor?
3. Why do you think that people within the church are reluctant to develop meaningful relationships with one another?
4. What does Paul mean by "warn those who are irresponsible"? What do "irresponsible" people look like in today's church? What would be the consequences of ignoring their existence?

5. Describe the difference between the "discouraged" and the "weak." Why are many people reluctant to come alongside and help those in these categories?

6. Why did Paul conclude the section on interpersonal relationships by admonishing the church not to "repay evil for evil"?

7. Why do you think that so many Christians struggle with finding joy in life? What can they do to experience joy and to express gratitude?

8. Explain how the Christian can practice the command to "pray constantly."

9. What are some ways that the church is guilty of neglecting the importance of preaching the Word of God?

10. What are some practical ways Christians can obey the command to "test all things"?

Living in the Light of Christ's Coming

1 THESSALONIANS 5:23-28

Main Idea: Only God Himself can empower you to live a holy life as you anticipate the coming of Jesus Christ.

I. **The Promise of God to His People (5:23a,24)**
   A. The source of sanctification—God Himself (5:23a)
   B. The scope of sanctification—His work (5:24)

II. **The Work of God in His People (5:23b)**
   A. Sanctification secures our standing.
   B. Sanctification ensures our progress.
   C. Sanctification guarantees our future.

III. **The Presence of God through His People (5:25-28)**
   A. Praying for one another (5:25)
   B. Encouraging one another (5:26)
   C. Growing with one another (5:27-28)

Some time ago, a generous church member offered to fly me in his personal airplane to a speaking engagement. After taking off, he set the autopilot to the appropriate heading, altitude, and airspeed, and then we sat back and enjoyed the journey. Apart from takeoff and landing, the airplane virtually flew itself. Technology is an amazing thing! Unfortunately, what is true of airplanes is not true of Christianity. There is no autopilot in the Christian life. Following Christ is not as simple as saying your prayers and reading a few Scriptures only to sit back and watch your faith fly itself. You don't soar past your problems, cruise through your relationships, and then glide effortlessly into spiritual maturity. Christianity requires hard work. In fact, Jesus made no secret of the level of commitment required to take this journey:

> *If anyone comes to Me and does not hate his own father and mother, wife and children, brothers and sisters—yes, and even his own life—he cannot be My disciple. Whoever does not bear his own cross and come after Me cannot be My disciple.*
> *For which of you, wanting to build a tower, doesn't first sit down and calculate the cost to see if he has enough to complete it? Otherwise,*

after he has laid the foundation and cannot finish it, all the onlookers will begin to make fun of him, saying, "This man started to build and wasn't able to finish."

Or what king, going to war against another king, will not first sit down and decide if he is able with 10,000 to oppose the one who comes against him with 20,000? If not, while the other is still far off, he sends a delegation and asks for terms of peace. In the same way, therefore, every one of you who does not say good-bye to all his possessions cannot be My disciple. (Luke 14:26-33)

Jesus demands nothing less than for His followers to be "all in" in their relationship with Him.

As we have seen, the second half of Paul's letter is directed at the Thessalonians' commitment to Christ. Paul seems to be saying, "If you are all in for Jesus, then your life will reflect your commitment." Paul has been revealing to them how their faith is to be fleshed out in the course of their lives. He has covered a lot of territory and addressed some major themes in the space of only two chapters. These themes include moral purity (4:3-8), brotherly love (4:9-10), grief and death (4:13-14), interpersonal relationships (5:12-15), and basic Christian virtues (5:16-22).

Paul had to anticipate that the Thessalonians would be somewhat overwhelmed at the thought of measuring up to the things that he had been teaching. This thought was doubtlessly on his mind as he penned the closing words of his letter. With words that are measured and focused, he seeks to reassure them that God is interested in their spiritual success. In fact, God is so interested in their success that He promises to be personally involved. He will fulfill His purposes in them and through them by His work of sanctification.

The Promise of God to His People
1 THESSALONIANS 5:23A,24

One of the most transforming truths that you will ever hear is that God is interested in you (Rom 8:31-32). When the implications of this truth grip your heart, they will change the way you think and influence the way you live. Contrary to the lyrics from Bette Midler's hit song, God is not "watching us from a distance" (Julie Gold, "From a Distance," 1985). He is actively involved in every detail of your life, including your personal sanctification. In his closing prayer Paul reminds the Thessalonians of this life-changing truth: "Now may the God of peace *Himself* sanctify you completely. . . . He who calls you is faithful, who also will do it" (5:23a,24; emphasis added). This is not the first time that the Thessalonians heard Paul pray in this way. There is a close connection between this prayer and his previous prayer for their sanctification in 3:11-13. In both passages Paul purposely places an emphasis on God as the source of the believer's sanctification.

The Source of Sanctification—God Himself (1 Thess 5:23a)

Paul begins his prayer by addressing God as the "God of peace." Charles Wannamaker insightfully observes that by using the word *peace,* Paul is referring to God not merely as One who brings order into our confusion, but as "the source of all well-being for the people of God" (Wannamaker, *Epistles,* 205). He thus bestows His peace on those who are reconciled to Him through saving faith in Jesus Christ. The believers in Thessalonica had come to know God not as an angry and distant deity, but as a loving and compassionate Father. Chuck Swindoll paints a beautiful picture of what it means when we view God in this way:

> Our God has compassion filling His eyes because His wrath
> has been appeased at the cross. We don't have to drag our
> good deeds before Him like sacrificial offerings, hoping He's
> in a good mood that day. He demands nothing more of us for
> salvation than that we receive His love and forgiveness as a gift.
> Christ's blood has done the work of atonement, and God is
> satisfied. (Swindoll, *Contagious Christianity,* 97)

When the Thessalonians embraced the gospel, God set them apart for holiness. And as we will see later, He began His work of sanctification in them. Now that He is their Father, they could find comfort in knowing that their "God of peace *Himself*" was going to equip and empower them to live holy lives. To emphasize this truth, Paul places the pronoun *Himself* at the beginning of the sentence in Greek to identify God as the primary source of their sanctification.

That God Himself was going to sanctify them was not to imply that the Thessalonians had no role in the process. Paul had just outlined for them a series of commands to obey (4:3-10; 5:12-22). While sanctification is the work of God, believers must still assume an active role in this process by obeying God's Word, following God's will, and surrendering to God's Spirit. Concerning the individual's active role in sanctification, Paul writes,

> *So then, my dear friends, just as you have always obeyed, not only in my presence, but now even more in my absence, work out your own salvation with fear and trembling. For it is God who is working in you, enabling you both to desire and to work out His good purpose.* (Phil 2:12-13)

So on the one hand, God's Spirit is committed to bring about our complete sanctification. On the other hand, we are also called to pursue passionately a life that honors God, knowing that "He who started a good work in you will carry it on to completion until the day of Christ Jesus" (Phil 1:6).

The Scope of Sanctification—His Work (1 Thess 5:24)

Paul reminded the Thessalonians that God always finishes what He starts: "He who calls you is faithful, who also will do it" (5:24). What a remarkable commitment God makes to us! He's not going to rest or quit until He brings to final completion the work that He began when He saved you. Your ultimate security is not found in your not letting go of God, but in God not letting go of you. And He promises never to let go of you. Calvin drives this truth home: "For he does not promise to be a Father to us merely for one day, but adopts us with this understanding, that he is to cherish us ever afterwards" (Calvin, *1 and 2 Thessalonians*, 305). When God calls you, He keeps you; and when He saves you, He sanctifies you. The assurance you have is that God never begins anything that He does not intend to finish.

> *He will also strengthen you to the end, so that you will be blameless in the day of our Lord Jesus Christ. God is faithful; you were called by Him into fellowship with His Son, Jesus Christ our Lord.* (1 Cor 1:8-9)

The Work of God in His People
1 THESSALONIANS 5:23B

Having identified "the God of peace Himself" as the source of our sanctification, you must now consider what actually transpires in the work of sanctification. Paul had previously informed the Thessalonians that

God's will is for them to be sanctified (4:3). Here, however, Paul prays for God to work through them to accomplish His will: "Now may the God of peace Himself sanctify you completely" (5:23). God sanctifies completely by transforming both who we are (our standing) and what we do (our living). As Hiebert notes, Paul uses the word *completely* to demonstrate that God desires to transform "every part of their being, leaving no area untouched by the pervasive power of divine holiness" (Hiebert, *1 and 2 Thessalonians*, 268).

To take this thought of complete sanctification a little deeper, Paul includes these words in his prayer: "May your spirit, soul, and body be kept sound and blameless for the coming of our Lord Jesus Christ" (5:23). Unfortunately, the debate over the precise meaning of "spirit, soul, and body" has often clouded Paul's strongly worded and passionate request for God to completely transform His people from the inside out.[15] The point is, while we can work hard at reforming our behavior and altering our appearance, there is nothing we can do to transform our spirit, soul, and body. Fixing up our outside may make us feel better for the moment, but it can do little to give us lasting peace. However, what we are incapable of doing, God is able to do "completely." Only God has the power both to transform us and to keep us "sound and blameless" until the coming of Christ. As Morris states,

> Paul is not thinking of a sanctification that may last a little
> time here on earth. . . . [He] looks for them to be preserved
> blameless not only through the changes and trials of this
> earthly life, but also on that dread day when they stand before
> the eternal judge. (Morris, *First and Second*, 183)

To understand better the significance of Paul's prayer we must take a closer look at how sanctification works in a person's life. Sanctification

---

[15] For centuries theologians have debated whether human beings consist of two parts (body and soul) or three parts (body, soul, and spirit). The dichotomist position claims that human beings are made of only two parts—body and soul/spirit (Isa 26:9; Matt 10:28; Luke 1:46-47). The trichotomist position claims that human beings are made up of three parts—body, soul, and spirit (1 Thess 5:23; Heb 4:12). While unanimity on the matter remains elusive, you must affirm that Scripture is unambiguous in its affirmation that human beings consist of both a material aspect (body) and an immaterial aspect (soul and/or spirit). For a summary of the various perspectives of dichotomy versus trichotomy, see Erickson, *Christian Theology*, 538–57.

has three dimensions—past, present, and future. Each of these dimensions carries with it a specific dimension of God's work in us.

Sanctification Secures Our Standing

The moment that you put your faith in the Lord Jesus Christ and are born again, you are instantly set apart for God (1 Cor 1:2; 6:11). God forgives your sin, changes your nature, adopts you as His children, and clothes you with His righteousness. This is called *positional* sanctification. When the Thessalonians heard the gospel, received the message, and turned from idols to God, they were saved (1:2-10; 2:12-13). At the moment they believed the gospel, God saved, sealed, and sanctified (Heb 10:10). They were now "dead to sin but alive to God in Christ Jesus" (Rom 6:11). Positionally, they had a new standing with God. When their standing changed, so did the trajectory of their lives. The exciting thing about the gospel is how quickly your life can change. God can change the standing of even those with the hardest of hearts if they will turn to Christ in repentance and faith. The Corinthian church experienced firsthand how Jesus could "wash" and "sanctify" the sinful hearts of robbers, drunks, adulterers, and foul-mouthed thieves (1 Cor 6:9-11).

Sanctification Ensures Our Progress

God does not save you to sit and soak in your salvation; He saves you to go and live out your salvation. That is why sanctification is not only *positional*—in the past when God saved you—it is also *progressive*—in the present as God changes you. This is clearly Paul's focus as he asks God to make the Thessalonians more like Jesus Christ through the sanctification of their "spirit, soul, and body." God loves us far too much to allow us to remain as we are. God will untiringly chip away at our sin and imperfections until we look more and more like Jesus (John 17:19). Without God's ongoing work of sanctification, the Thessalonians would never be able to measure up to God's standards. God, however, would leave no stone unturned as He continued His work in their "spirit, soul, and body" until they would ultimately stand in His presence.

Sanctification Guarantees Our Future

The ultimate goal of sanctification is our future *glorification*. What God did in the past at salvation and what He is doing in your present transformation is preparing you for your future with Him. As John puts it, "We know that when He appears, we will be like Him because we will see Him as He is" (1 John 3:2). Paul offers a similar word to the Philippian church:

> *Our citizenship is in heaven, from which we also eagerly wait for a Savior, the Lord Jesus Christ. He will transform the body of our humble condition into the likeness of His glorious body.* (Phil 3:20-21)

While the Thessalonians were anticipating the day when they would see Jesus, they needed reassurance that God is able to empower, protect, and preserve them until that day. Paul reminds them that God is able to "keep" them "sound and blameless" (5:23). The word *keep* means "watch over" or "guard," as with something that is very precious. *Blameless* carries the idea of being "without fault or accusation." He is thus reassuring the Thessalonians that God Himself will protect them until the coming of Jesus Christ and prepare them for that great day. Jude had this in mind when he wrote,

> *Now to Him who is able to protect you from stumbling and to make you stand in the presence of His glory, blameless and with great joy, to the only God our Savior, through Jesus Christ our Lord, be glory, majesty, power, and authority before all time, now and forever. Amen.* (Jude 24-25)

The Thessalonians could therefore rejoice that at Christ's coming, God was going to bring their sanctification to its ultimate completion. John Polhill offers a fitting summary of this section when he writes,

> God had set the Thessalonians apart in Christ; He chose them (1:4). And He would remain true to his calling them; he would keep them as his own, blameless until the coming of Christ. (Polhill, *Paul*, 195)

The Presence of God through His People
1 THESSALONIANS 5:25-28

No matter how high you can jump theologically, what matters the most is how straight you walk when you hit the ground. Throughout this epistle, Paul has expounded some deep theological truths—some with present implications for how we live today, and others with future implications for how we will face tomorrow. He takes us on a journey from the moral purity of the human heart to the heights of heaven at the return of Christ. He teaches us how to view death, and he challenges us to make the most of life. He demonstrates the differences between those who love the darkness and those who walk in the light. And he contrasts the judgment of the Day of the Lord with the joy and expectation of seeing Jesus. His teaching has been both profoundly deep and immensely practical. Yet as Paul ends his letter, he comes right back to the local church. He endeavors to keep the Thessalonians firmly planted in their calling. Thus, in his parting words, he draws their attention to three tasks that the Thessalonians must not forsake: praying, encouraging, and growing.

Praying for One Another (1 Thess 5:25)

Paul ends his letter in much the same way that he began his letter—by praying. The slight difference is that in the opening chapter he offers prayer on their behalf (1:2; see also 3:12-13; 5:23), while here he also asks for prayer on his behalf. He begins verse 25 with the term *brothers*, which he has used more than a dozen times throughout the letter. "Brothers" is placed at the beginning of the sentence most likely to emphasize his earnest request for their prayers. It's as if he is saying, "Brothers, we are not just asking for your prayers—we *need* your prayers." Paul's request reveals two things about him. First, he was never too important to identify with God's people. Imagine how the news of Paul's request must have reverberated through the Thessalonian church. From personal experience, I know what an honor and encouragement it is to be asked to pray for others, especially those whom I admire and respect. Second, Paul's request for prayer reveals that He saw his work as part of God's greater work. Paul never lost sight of the strategic mission and importance of the local church.

Although Paul did not name a specific request for which they should pray, the Thessalonians must have been aware of the challenges of his ongoing ministry (cf. Rom 15:30-32; Eph 6:19-20; Col 4:3-4; 2 Thess 3:1-2). Paul's greatest allies in his ongoing work were the untold number of Christians who were privately and corporately praying for him. Not

everyone can go on missionary journeys like Paul, but through intercessory prayer everyone can partner with those who do.

Encouraging One Another (1 Thess 5:26)

As you know, the church is a living, growing spiritual body (Eph 2:19-22;
4:11-16; 5:23-33; 1 Cor 12:12-27). Like our physical bodies, it comprises
many parts, each with its own specific function. As has been made clear
in this letter, each member of the body of Christ comes with his own
set of hurts, habits, and hang-ups, including being fearful, discouraged,
and irresponsible (5:14). Considering the varying backgrounds, personalities, and preferences of those within the body of Christ, it is a miracle
that the church is able to accomplish anything. Yet through the power
of His Spirit, God not only equips His people to do His work, He also
enables them to love one another while they do it.

God expects His people to build close relationships that are marked
by mutual love and accountability. **God did not establish His church to
be a place; He established His church to be a people—a people who love
Him and love one another**. To those outside the church, Paul's request
to "greet all the brothers with a holy kiss" might seem a bit unusual
(5:26), but those who are a part of the body of Christ understand the
profound love that Christians have for one another. The cold formality
and palpable superficiality that you may experience in some churches
do little to encourage the simple shake of a hand, let alone the giving of
a holy kiss! As the apostle John affirms, one of the most visible signs of a
redeemed heart is a genuine love for others:

> *This is how we have come to know love: He laid down His life for us.
> We should also lay down our lives for our brothers. If anyone has this
> world's goods and sees his brother in need but closes his eyes to his
> need—how can God's love reside in him?* (1 John 3:16-17)

By giving them this affectionate request, Paul reminds the
Thessalonians to express their love for one another visibly. As Marshall
points out, while we may not practice the same custom today, we still
must be careful so as not to miss the point:

> What is important is that the members of the church should
> have some way of expressing visibly and concretely the love
> which they have for one another as fellow-members of the
> body of Christ. (Marshall, *1 and 2 Thessalonians*, 165)

Growing with One Another (1 Thess 5:27-28)

Paul's final command is written in such a way so as not to be misunderstood: "I charge you by the Lord that this letter be read to all the brothers" (5:27). That this command is written in the first person singular most likely indicates that Paul has personally penned these words. Up until this point, Paul likely employed an amanuensis, or secretary, to record his words (cf. 2 Thess 3:17; 1 Cor 16:21; Gal 6:11-18). With very strong language, he commands them to have the letter read to the church.

To understand why Paul was so bold in his command is not difficult. Although Paul was the human author of the letter, its message was divinely inspired (2 Tim 3:16; 2 Pet 1:20-21). This message came from God to the church, and since God had spoken through Paul, the letter represented divine truth. Since the letter addressed many specific concerns and issues within the fellowship, the leaders were obligated to make certain that everyone was exposed to its teaching. While God's Word touches every area of our lives, it cannot do its work if it is not heard. And to be heard it must be proclaimed (Rom 10:14). Paul knew that there was enough misinformation circulating throughout the church. Therefore what the church needed was not another opinion, but a word from God Himself.

Put yourself in the Thessalonians' shoes on the day that Paul's letter is read to the church. Suppose that you are one of the members who had lost a loved one. Imagine the weight that is lifted from your shoulders when you hear that your loved one will not miss out on the glorious return of Christ. Perhaps you are one of the busybodies who have been meddling in everyone's affairs, but after hearing Paul's letter, you are convicted to stop bothering others and to start helping them. Maybe you have been contemplating sexual sin, but because you now recognize that God's will for you is to remain morally pure, you flee from sexual immorality. Of course, you could name dozens of other ways that Paul's letter would speak to a person, but that is exactly what God's Word does. That is why the writer of Hebrews states,

> *For the word of God is living and effective and sharper than any double-edged sword, penetrating as far as the separation of soul and spirit, joints and marrow. It is able to judge the ideas and thoughts of the heart.* (Heb 4:12)

In typical Pauline fashion, Paul ends his letter on a note of God's grace. Without God's grace, Paul is just another man and 1 Thessalonians is just another letter; but because of God's grace, Paul is the apostle sent from God and 1 Thessalonians is God's Word to us. Paul began the letter with grace (1:1), and now he ends his letter with God's grace (5:28). For Paul, grace was not merely an invocation and a benediction—it was his life.

Conclusion

Let's conclude by highlighting four takeaways from this passage.

God has taken a special interest in you. His construction project on you begins from the moment He saves you. And it's more than a renovation project that will last for only a few months—it's a transformation project that will last for a lifetime. He doesn't break for lunch, and He never takes a vacation. He won't break His contract, and He won't let you down. God uses only the finest materials, and He never takes shortcuts. He promises to bring to completion the work that He began in you.

The time to get serious about your personal holiness is now. Your sanctification is not in doubt, for God guarantees it. If God guarantees your sanctification, then why would you resist? To resist God's hand makes no sense. You will only find yourself fighting a battle that you cannot win. His sanctifying work can either be a blessing or a battle. If God is committed to complete the good work that He began in you, then perhaps it's time to partner with Him in the process.

Recognize that God is sanctifying others also. God is not only at work in our lives, He is also working in the lives of others. When we are tempted to lose our cool because of their lack of progress, we would do well to remember that we also are works in progress.

Nothing is accidental. God oversees the affairs of our lives even to the smallest of details. If He is at work in us, then we can be confident that He is also at work around us. Only God can take the thousands of seemingly insignificant details of our lives and weave them together to bring about our ultimate good. Even when we cannot see the good, we can still take comfort that God is good. Although we cannot give thanks *for* everything, we can still give thanks *in* everything. The apostle Paul sums it up perfectly:

> *Who can separate us from the love of Christ? Can affliction or*
> *anguish or persecution or famine or nakedness or danger or sword? As*

it is written: Because of You we are being put to death all day long; we are counted as sheep to be slaughtered. No, in all these things we are more than victorious through Him who loved us. For I am persuaded that not even death or life, angels or rulers, things present or things to come, hostile powers, height or depth, or any other created thing will have the power to separate us from the love of God that is in Christ Jesus our Lord! (Rom 8:35-39)

Reflect and Discuss

1. How would you define Christian sanctification to a non-Christian? How is it different from self-righteousness?
2. When does the work of sanctification begin? When does it end?
3. Explain how God is involved in the work of sanctification. What role do you play?
4. What is the difference between positional sanctification and progressive sanctification?
5. What guarantee does God make to His people about sanctification? Does such a promise allow Christians to take their sanctification for granted?
6. Has someone you respect as a spiritual leader ever asked you to pray for him or her? How did that affect your opinion of that person?
7. What can the contemporary church learn from Paul's admonition to greet one another with a "holy kiss"?
8. Why did Paul command the church to read the letter? Do you think Paul was aware that he had written inspired Scripture?
9. With the context of the book in view, describe some ways that the people might have responded after hearing the letter read.
10. How does Paul's reference to grace in the final verse reflect both Paul's life and his ministry?

2 Thessalonians

Good News about God's Church

2 THESSALONIANS 1:1-5

Main Idea: When a church is grounded in its faith it will be fruitful in its work.

I.   **A Faith That Is Real (1:1-3a)**
  A.   Real faith is grounded (1:1-2).
  B.   Real faith is growing (1:3a).
II. **A Love That Grows Strong (1:3b)**
III. **A Hope That Goes Deep (1:4)**
IV. **A Future That Is Secure (1:5)**

A few years ago, a businessman from my church handed me a little booklet titled, *Why Go to Work?* The booklet was written to encourage persons in the marketplace to rethink both why God expects for them to work and how God wants them to view their work. As I thumbed my way through the booklet, the following words caught my eye:

> God in His love and grace gives His own the privilege of
> participating with Him in what He is doing. They are deceived,
> however, if they believe that they can contribute anything to
> what He is doing. (Vision Foundation, *Why Go to Work?* 25)

What a sobering statement! That you would view your work as contributing to God's work is to suggest that God somehow needs you to ensure His success. The sobering truth is that God really does not need you to accomplish His work; He can get along perfectly fine without you.

God, however, is not content to go it alone. He graciously extends to you an invitation to participate with Him in what He is doing in the world. You get the amazing privilege of joining with Him in a venture that is guaranteed to succeed. That assurance is what makes your participation in the work of His church so fulfilling. Despite the many challenges and setbacks, you can be confident that His work will succeed. In other words, because you know that you are on the winning team, you are not afraid to give your all on the field.

As we turn our attention to Paul's second letter to the Thessalonian church, we see a church that continues to live out its faith. This infant church had welcomed God's invitation to participate with Him in proclaiming the gospel to their city (1 Thess 1:5), and although they were not without their challenges, their love for one another was growing, and their passion for the Lord was increasing. But where good things are happening for Christ, opposition is sure to follow, and the Thessalonians were no strangers to opposition, both from without and from within. Many of the issues addressed by Paul in his first letter persisted. In many ways their struggles only increased in the short time since Paul wrote his first letter. Persecution continued to challenge their faith (2 Thess 1:5-10), false teachers continued to stir up confusion about the Day of the Lord (2:1-3a), and lazy Christians continued to be a drain on the fellowship (3:6-12). Despite these significant challenges, Paul begins his letter by stating, "We ourselves boast about you among God's churches" (1:4). Only a few months had passed since they received his first letter, and apparently word came back about how the church had responded to his instructions. Although there were a number of matters that required his clarification, Paul could take much comfort in the news that the church was alive and well. In the first five verses he identifies four reasons why he was so thankful for them: they had a faith that was real, a love that was growing, a hope that was deep, and a future that was secure.

A Faith That Is Real
2 THESSALONIANS 1:1-3A

The city of Thessalonica had a strategic importance for the advancement of the gospel. Because of its bustling port on the Aegean Sea and its prime location on the Egnatian Road, tens of thousands of sailors, travelers, and immigrants were constantly making their way in and out of the city. Additionally, its stable government, bustling economy, and multicultural diversity made it an attractive place for Greeks, Romans, and Jews to live. With such a diverse population base, a thriving, outwardly focused, gospel-centered church had the potential to make a significant impact not only on the city, but also on the cities and regions beyond.

Of course, this is what brought Paul, Silas, and Timothy to Thessalonica in the first place. They knew that a vibrant, gospel-centered church in Thessalonica was strategic for the advancement of the gospel throughout the Roman Empire. After only a few weeks in Thessalonica, their goal of establishing a church was realized. But, as every Christian knows, whenever God begins to encroach on enemy territory, the enemy fights back, and he does so relentlessly. Satan was working tirelessly to extinguish the work of Christ in Thessalonica. He stirred up an angry mob of Jews who forced Paul and his companions to hastily leave the city. But he was not content merely to see Paul depart the city; he desired to destroy the church that Paul, Silas, and Timothy left behind.

Satan wants to do the same to your church and to you. It is no accident that your most intense moments of satanic attack often come after your most exhilarating experiences of spiritual victory. You would do well to remember that your enemy is not seeking ways to give you a bad day; he is on an all-out mission to give you a bad life (1 Pet 5:8).

Although he was not caught off guard by Satan's strategy, Paul was still the object of his tireless efforts to snuff out the gospel in Thessalonica (1 Thess 2:18). Paul knew that if Satan were attacking him, he would also be doing everything possible to destroy the faith of the new converts.

Satan's primary strategy in Thessalonica was to turn up the heat of persecution. The persecution began the moment they heard the gospel, and it never let up (1 Thess 1:6-7; 2:14; 3:3-4; 2 Thess 2:3-4). The reality of this persecution is what makes Paul's opening words in 2 Thessalonians all the more meaningful. Even under the incessant pressure and intense pain of persecution, the Thessalonians' faith held strong. Persecution, pressure, and trials will always reveal the genuineness of your faith. As Peter puts it, present trials purify you even more, so that "the genuineness of your faith—more valuable than gold, which perishes though refined by fire—may result in praise, glory, and honor at the revelation of Jesus Christ" (1 Pet 1:6-7). While the heat of persecution will purify a genuine faith, it will always wither a false faith. Just as the heat of the sun will ultimately wither a plant that lacks deep roots, so also will persecution reveal the shallowness of a superficial commitment to Christ (Matt 13:3-9).

What was it about the Thessalonians' faith that made Paul so proud? He makes two observations in the first three verses: their faith was grounded because of their standing with God, and their faith was growing because of their passion for Jesus.

Real Faith Is Grounded (2 Thess 1:1-2)

Paul begins 2 Thessalonians in nearly identical fashion to the way he began 1 Thessalonians: "Grace to you and peace from God our Father and the Lord Jesus Christ" (v. 2; cf. 1 Thess 1:1). "Grace" is God's gift, which grants you the privilege to have a relationship with Him, and "peace" is the result as you acknowledge His grace by trusting in the work of Christ on your behalf. Those who acknowledge God's grace and rest in Christ's peace enjoy the blessings of being "in God our Father and the Lord Jesus Christ" (v. 1). This means that we are granted access into His family, the church. As a family, we have a Father who not only loves and leads us, but He also brings us together to accomplish a common purpose.

If we read hastily past these opening words, we may miss the weight of what Paul is saying. He is not wasting his words. Paul wants the Thessalonians to be gripped by the reality of their relationship with God through Jesus Christ. Everything that will follow in this letter will be built on that foundation. Michael Martin states this well:

> Although these words do not anticipate the specific content
> of the letter, they do remind the readers of the foundation
> on which the letter stands. It reminds them that their faith in
> Jesus is well placed, for he is God's Anointed One. Their place
> in the kingdom of God is secure, for the gospel is the message
> of what God himself has done through his Christ. And his
> gospel does not suffer from the vagaries and inconsistencies of
> human works and so-called wisdom. Therefore the believers'
> task is clear: they must continue to obey the Christ whom
> they have owned as Lord. Neither persecution (1:5-10) nor
> false teaching (2:1-11) nor human weakness (3:6-15) can be
> allowed to discouraging the church from persevering in their
> commitment to the one who called them into his kingdom.
> (Martin, *1, 2 Thessalonians*, 197)

A church must never tire of speaking about and resting in the grace and peace of God the Father and the Lord Jesus Christ. No challenge is too great for any church that remains anchored to these wonderful truths.

Real Faith Is Growing (2 Thess 1:3a)

We would be hard pressed to find a pastor who would not wish for his church the commendation Paul bestowed on the Thessalonian church: "We must always thank God for you, brothers. This is right, since your faith is flourishing." Two things jump out of this verse. First, their faith was "flourishing." The verb emphasizes healthy and prolific growth. They are not growing a little bit—they are growing a lot. Second, Paul notes that it is "right" to give thanks to God for them. The verse could read that he is "under obligation" to give thanks for them. He is not rendering thanksgiving unto God on their behalf out of mere duty; he gives thanksgiving to God because they deserve it.

This raises the question as to why Paul felt so obligated to commend them to God for their faith. Paul seems to want to encourage them to keep growing in the face of the many difficulties that they are facing. The more I reflect on the many challenges that this young church faced, the more I am in awe at their level of zeal, tenacity, and commitment to Christ. Satan was throwing the kitchen sink at this church. They were being chased on the outside by their persecutors and being challenged on the inside by false teachers. The temptations of a secular city were lurking around every corner, and doubts about the future were lingering in their minds. Considering these pressures, the Thessalonians possibly began to doubt their ability to remain faithful. William Barclay suggests that the Thessalonians had most likely sent a message to Paul conveying these doubts. He contends that Paul's opening words were written specifically to build them up and to encourage them to keep pressing on:

> Paul's answer was not to push them into the slough of despond by agreeing with them; it was to pick out their virtues and their achievements in such a way, that these despondent, frightened Christians would square their shoulders and fling back their heads and say, "Well if Paul thinks that of us we'll make a fight of it." (Barclay, *Letters*, 243)

Based on the enthusiastic way in which Paul applauds their growth in the first four verses, one can imagine that His words of encouragement must have brought much relief to this weary church.

A Love That Grows Strong
2 THESSALONIANS 1:3B

In one of the first letters written to the New Testament church, the apostle James wrote these penetrating words:

> *What good is it, my brothers, if someone says he has faith but does not have works? Can his faith save him? If a brother or sister is without*

> *clothes and lacks daily food and one of you says to them, "Go in peace,*
> *keep warm, and eat well," but you don't give them what the body*
> *needs, what good is it? In the same way faith, if it doesn't have works,*
> *is dead by itself. But someone will say, "You have faith, and I have*
> *works." Show me your faith without works, and I will show you faith*
> *from my works.* (Jas 2:14-18)

James's words provide the criterion by which genuine faith is measured: genuine faith will always produce genuine works. This truth is vividly portrayed in the lives of the Thessalonians. Their "flourishing" faith was producing a visible, "increasing" love (1:3b). These are two of the most distinguishing characteristics of genuine conversion. They are placed alongside one another repeatedly throughout Scripture. For example, to the Ephesian church Paul writes, "This is why, since I heard about your faith in the Lord Jesus and your love for all the saints, I never stop giving thanks for you as I remember you in my prayers" (Eph 1:15-16). He echoes similar words in his letter to the Galatians: "For in Christ Jesus neither circumcision nor uncircumcision accomplishes anything; what matters is faith working through love" (Gal 5:6). And to the Corinthians he says, "Now as you excel in everything—faith, speech, knowledge, and in all diligence, and in your love for us—excel also in this grace" (2 Cor 8:7).

Paul was following the pattern set by Jesus, who declared to His disciples,

> *I give you a new command: Love one another. Just as I have*
> *loved you, you must also love one another. By this all people will*
> *know that you are My disciples, if you have love for one another.*
> (John 13:34-35)

In this statement, Jesus reveals how faith and love work together. Faith is our response to Jesus' invitation to be His disciples (Luke 14:26-33), and love is the proof that our faith is real. Faith requires that we look up and see Him for who He is, and love requires that we look around and see others for who they are. This, of course, was what brought Paul such joy as he reflected on the Thessalonian church: their love for one another was telling the real story of their faith. This result was exactly what Paul had prayed for when he asked God to "increase" their love for one another (1 Thess 3:12); and it was the same response for which he had hoped when he called them to love one another "even more" (1 Thess 4:10). The Thessalonians had fulfilled his hopes and God had answered his prayers. No wonder Paul would say, "We must always thank God for you brothers. This is right" (1:3).

A Hope That Goes Deep
2 THESSALONIANS 1:4

By now you have most likely noted a recurring theme in the Thessalonian letters: Paul's emphasis on faith, love, and hope. This theme was first introduced in 1 Thessalonians 1:3-4:

> *We recall, in the presence of our God and Father, your work of faith, labor of love, and endurance of hope in our Lord Jesus Christ, knowing your election, brothers loved by God.*

At the conclusion of 1 Thessalonians, Paul repeats this theme again: "But since we belong to the day, we must be serious and put the armor of faith and love on our chests, and put on a helmet of the hope of salvation" (1 Thess 5:8). For Paul, faith, love, and hope are often linked together (1 Cor 13:13; Col 1:4-5).

Not surprising, then, is the discovery that Paul also commends the Thessalonians for their "endurance and faith in all [their] persecutions and afflictions" (1:4). A genuine faith will produce more than an external love for others; it will also produce an internal hope and trust in God. The Greek word translated "endurance" does not carry the idea of a passive acquiescence to adverse circumstances, nor does it suggest a gritting of the teeth until the trial passes. As Barclay explains, the word

> describes the spirit which does not only patiently endure
> the circumstances in which it finds itself; but which masters
> them and uses them to strengthen its own nerve and sinew. It
> accepts the blows of life, but in accepting them it transforms
> them into stepping stones to new achievement. (Barclay,
> *Letters*, 244)

The person who has a genuine faith in God will view affliction and suffering through the lens of an enduring hope—not the kind of endurance that waits to thank God when the trial passes, but the kind of endurance that thanks God even if the trial does not pass. The very sobering reality of the Christian faith is that the possibility exists that God will not allow your trials to pass. There are tens of thousands of Christians all over the world who live under the incessant daily pressure of trials and persecution. This was true of the Thessalonian Christians. They received the gospel through persecution, they were following Christ in persecution, and they were trusting God to deliver them from persecution. For them, trials were more than a bad day at work, and persecution was more than a passing insult from a friend—consequential persecution and trials were a way of life. God may have the same kind of life in store for us. The question is, Do we have the kind of hope that will endure?

We will view everything that happens to us as either an opportunity or an obstacle. Obstacles are things that block our pathway, frustrate our plans, and make our lives difficult. God sometimes places obstacles in our path to accomplish His purposes in us, or even to discipline us (Heb 12:7-21). But if we trust in His sovereignty, we will view the things that happen to us not as obstacles that keep us from getting what we want, but as opportunities to depend more desperately on God to meet our needs. Hardship, trials, and persecution will reveal the genuineness of your conversion and the true depth of your faith. Trying times and adverse circumstances will draw the truly converted to God instead of driving them away from God. Paul knew this to be true from personal experience:

> I will most gladly boast all the more about my weaknesses, so that
> Christ's power may reside in me. So I take pleasure in weaknesses,
> insults, catastrophes, persecutions, and in pressures, because of Christ.
> For when I am weak, then I am strong. (2 Cor 12:9-10)

James said that you should "consider it a great joy" when you face hardships and trials because they bring forth the fruit of endurance, maturity, and ultimate happiness (Jas 1:2-10,12). We can live with an expectant hope because our trials are working for us and not against us. Paul gives us the perspective that we need for facing our trials:

> Therefore we do not give up. Even though our outer person is
> being destroyed, our inner person is being renewed day by day. For
> our momentary light affliction is producing for us an absolutely
> incomparable eternal weight of glory. So we do not focus on what is
> seen, but on what is unseen. For what is seen is temporary, but what is
> unseen is eternal. (2 Cor 4:16-18)

Given the opportunity, most people would gladly opt for a life free from burdens and pain. Some people even believe that if they have enough faith, then such a life is guaranteed. Their reasoning goes something like this: "If I fulfill my end of the deal by living faithfully, then God will meet His end of the deal by blessing me abundantly." Whether they admit this or not, many who serve the Lord in full-time ministry believe that this is true. They mistakenly assume that smooth sailing is ahead if they only walk with God, proclaim His Word, and love His people. To be honest, I believed this when I accepted my call to ministry. But 20 minutes into my first pastorate, I learned otherwise. And now, more than 20 years later, I am convinced more than ever that neither ministry nor Christianity is for the fainthearted.

Perhaps now we can begin to get a better picture as to why Paul was willing to "boast" about the Thessalonians "among God's churches" (1:4). Their growing faith and increasing love did not occur in a sterile environment. On the contrary, they were growing in the midst of some very trying conditions. A storm of persecution had settled in and showed little sign of letting up, but rather than being blown away by the storm, they remained firmly anchored to the unshakable foundation of their hope and genuine faith. Any seasoned mariner will tell you that the best way to ride out a storm is to anchor deep. The writer of Hebrews reminds us that we have an anchor and a hope that is "safe and secure," and His name is Jesus (Heb 6:19-20).

A Future That Is Secure
2 THESSALONIANS 1:5

We will have difficulty understanding why God uses hardship, suffering, and pain to accomplish His great purposes from our limited earthly perspective. While we may concede their immediate value in producing humility before Him and fostering dependence on Him, most of us never stop to consider that God uses our pain to produce something much bigger than what we presently see. Listen to how John Stott explains this:

> It takes spiritual discernment to see in a situation of injustice
> (like the persecution of the innocent) evidence of the
> just judgment of God. Our habit is to see only the surface
> appearance, and so to make only superficial comments. We
> see the malice, cruelty, power and arrogance of evil men who
> persecute. We see also the sufferings of the people of God,

who are opposed, ridiculed, boycotted, harassed, imprisoned, tortured and killed. . . . We are tempted to inveigh against God and the miscarriage of justice. "Why doesn't God do something?" we complain indignantly. And the answer is that he *is* doing something and will go on doing it. He is allowing His people to suffer, in order to qualify them for a heavenly kingdom. He is allowing the wicked to triumph temporarily, but his just judgment will fall upon them in the end. Thus Paul sees *evidence that God's judgment is right* in the very situation in which we might see nothing but injustice. (Stott, *Gospel and the End*, 147; emphasis in original)

Those are powerful words. In the remainder of chapter 1 we will see how Paul describes the judgment of the wicked. But before jumping ahead to examine this in much greater detail, let's first explore the matter of how suffering counts us "worthy of God's kingdom" (1:5).

A careful reading of verse 5 reveals that our suffering, God's judgment, and our worthiness to enter His kingdom are inseparably linked together. Paul writes, "It is a clear evidence of *God's righteous judgment* that *you will be counted worthy of God's kingdom*, for which you also are *suffering*" (1:5; emphasis added). What may appear at first to be a confusing statement is actually one of the most comforting statements that you will find in the Bible. Only God can take the concepts of "suffering" and "judgment" and turn them into words of comfort and expectation. That is exactly the point that Paul is conveying to the Thessalonians. Their suffering was not what secured their salvation; their suffering was the evidence of a salvation already secured when they identified themselves as followers of Jesus Christ (Rom 8:17; 1 Pet 1:6-9; 2:21). Stated another way, they were not *made* worthy of the kingdom because they suffered; they were *counted* worthy of the kingdom because they suffered.

As strange as this may sound to our ears, their suffering was evidence that God loved them, not a sign that He had abandoned them. Paul is reassuring them that their suffering has an eternal purpose. This paints an entirely different picture of suffering than many of us have of it. We can imagine how such a picture would dramatically influence the way in which we live. With this picture of suffering in mind, listen to how Paul challenges the Philippians:

> Live your life in a manner worthy of the gospel of Christ . . . not being frightened in any way by your opponents. This is a sign of destruction

for them, but of your deliverance—and this is from God. For it has
been given to you on Christ's behalf not only to believe in Him, but
also to suffer for Him. (Phil 1:27-29)

Paul could thus rejoice with and brag about the Thessalonians because their enduring faith in the face of suffering was yet another sign of their genuine conversion.

Now that we have a clearer picture of the connection between our earthly suffering and our eternal glory, we are in a better position to understand what Paul means by "God's righteous judgment." While possibly Paul has in mind God's future judgment of the unrighteous (1:6-10), more likely he is speaking about the righteous judgment of believers by means of God's loving discipline. In this sense, the present trials of the Thessalonians would fall under the chastening hand of God. As Leon Morris puts it, such chastening would not necessarily be punitive but would instead be part of God's refining process in the lives of His people as He "uses tribulations to bring His own people to perfection" (Morris, *Epistles of Paul,* 116). Adding to this thought, James Grant offers the following helpful insight:

> God has designed suffering to work for us and not against us.
> He has designed it to change us, to consume our dross and
> refine our gold. He will supply his all-sufficient grace through
> the fiery trials of life, and those trials are actually evidence
> that God is for us and not against us. (Grant,
> *1 and 2 Thessalonians,* 159)

The writer of Hebrews helps you see why God disciplines His people:

> *Endure suffering as discipline: God is dealing with you as sons.*
> *For what son is there that a father does not discipline? But if you*
> *are without discipline—which all receive—then you are illegitimate*
> *children and not sons. Furthermore, we had natural fathers discipline*
> *us, and we respected them. Shouldn't we submit even more to the*
> *Father of spirits and live? For they disciplined us for a short time*
> *based on what seemed good to them, but He does it for our benefit, so*
> *that we can share His holiness. No discipline seems enjoyable at the*
> *time, but painful. Later on, however, it yields the fruit of peace and*
> *righteousness to those who have been trained by it.* (Heb 12:7-11)

Did you catch the statement "so that we can share His holiness"? God uses discipline to bring about your sanctification by producing the "fruit of peace and righteousness." Therefore, the presence of pain, suffering, and trials are actually proof that God keeps His promise to keep you "sound and blameless for the coming of our Lord Jesus Christ" (1 Thess 5:23). Through His loving, albeit sometimes heavy, hand of discipline, God is preparing His people for their future home in heaven.

C. S. Lewis wrote, "God whispers to us in our pleasures, speaks in our conscience, but shouts in our pains: it is His megaphone to rouse a deaf world" (Lewis, *Problem of Pain*, 91). Clearly God was using His megaphone to get the attention of the Thessalonian Christians. Their pain was proving their legitimacy as God's own people. By their faithful endurance they were demonstrating their worthiness to be citizens of God's kingdom. God could have stopped the persecution but chose to use it as a tool in their preparation for the glory that was to come (1 Thess 5:23-24).

God has an eternal purpose for your affliction and pain, but what about an earthly purpose? Is there any present value to your "momentary light affliction" (2 Cor 4:17)? Let's briefly consider two of God's earthly purposes for your pain:

God uses pain to draw us into a more intimate union with Him. Our natural inclination will always be to allow the lesser (though not always unimportant) things of life to crowd out the more important things in life. At the top of this list is our daily walk with God. Nothing in life should be more important than this. Yahweh is a jealous God (Exod 34:14) and is not content to play second string on your team or to play second fiddle in your band. Isaiah reminds us, "This is what the LORD, the King of Israel and its Redeemer, the LORD of Hosts, says: I am the first and I am the last. There is no God but Me" (Isa 44:6).

God yearns jealously for your friendship (Jas 4:4-5) and thus refuses to allow lesser gods to take His place. He also loves you too passionately to allow you to walk away from Him. Therefore, because He yearns for you jealously and loves you passionately, He will use whatever means necessary to bring you back to Him. And the tool that He often uses is pain and suffering. Timothy Keller makes the point well:

> Some suffering is given in order to chastise and correct a
> person for wrongful patterns of life (as in the case of Jonah
> imperiled by the storm), some suffering is given not to correct
> past wrongs but to prevent future ones (as in the case of
> Joseph sold into slavery), and some suffering has no purpose
> other than to lead a person to love God more ardently for

himself alone and so discover the ultimate peace and freedom. (Keller, *Walking with God*, 47)

The process of preparing you for heaven begins at the moment of conversion and lasts until you finally see Jesus. God is not going to allow your personal sinfulness to derail His purifying work in you. He may choose to use pain, persecution, or both, but God always finishes what He starts.

God uses pain to make us more like Jesus. The fall corrupted and distorted the image of God in us. Jesus came to do for us what we could not do for ourselves: to restore fully that broken image. Paul describes what happens when we put our faith in Christ:

> *You took off your former way of life, the old self that is corrupted by deceitful desires; you are being renewed in the spirit of your minds; you put on the new self, the one created according to God's likeness in righteousness and purity of the truth.* (Eph 4:22-24)

From the moment of your conversion, God begins the work of shaping and pruning you to be more and more like Jesus (Rom 8:29). Because God is passionate about you reflecting the image of His Christ, you can be confident that He will take the necessary measures to remove anything that distorts His image. When His hands meet your resistance, you can anticipate that discipline will follow. And there is no question that God's discipline will always achieve its intended purposes both in this life and in the life to come (Rom 8:30-39).

Conclusion

How do we evaluate the effectiveness of a church? If we ask ten people that question, we are likely to get ten answers. However, if we are looking for an objective means for determining the overall health of a church, then I suggest we look to the Thessalonians. After all, any church that the apostle Paul was willing to boast about "among God's churches" deserves our careful consideration. Above everything else, the Thessalonian church was a gospel-centered church: their faith in God was rooted in the gospel, their love for one another flowed from the gospel, and their hope for the future was because of the gospel. From this gospel-centered focus we see three essential characteristics for every healthy church: gospel preaching, gospel people, and a gospel passion.

Gospel preaching. Preaching and teaching must be centered on the life, death, and resurrection of Jesus Christ. The gospel is not an addendum to be hastily added to the end of a sermon; the gospel is the scarlet thread of redemption that must run through every sermon preached. While not every biblical text is evangelistic, every biblical text will be gospel-centered. This raises the question, How evident is the gospel in your church? Would a gospel-centered focus be evident from the moment that a person walks in the door, listens to a sermon, and meets your people? Go back and reread the Thessalonian letters, and you will discover that this church was built on the gospel.

Gospel people. The most effective means by which to measure the depth of gospel preaching in a church is to take a long, hard look at the people in the church. Genuine conversion will always be marked by life transformation. God did not call the church to be a building, but He did call the church to be a body. The church is not a *place* where a crowd gathers to worship; the church is a *people* who take their worship with them wherever they go. Gospel preaching always bears the fruit of gospel people who are deep in their love for God and wide in their love for others. The Thessalonians personified the gospel by loving God with all their heart and loving others as they loved themselves (Luke 10:27).

Gospel passion. God never commanded the people on the outside of the church to come inside, but He did command the people on the inside of the church to go out. God calls those who put their trust in Jesus Christ not to sit and play it safe, but to get up and take some risks. However, you will never take the kinds of risks that the gospel demands until you first rest in the hope that the gospel provides. You will never be passionate about something in which you don't fully believe. You may be able to fake your passion for Christ for a season, but it will be sure to wither when the heat of affliction comes. How far you are willing to go and how much discomfort you are willing to experience for the sake of the gospel will say much about what you truly believe.

Reflect and Discuss

1. What is the difference between contributing to God's work and participating in God's work?
2. Why was Thessalonica the prime location to plant a church? What are the advantages that your own church could avail itself of?
3. What are some possible reactions that a church may have to adversity and persecution?

4. What is the significance of Paul's mention of grace and peace in his salutation? How does this apply to you as you live out your faith?
5. What are the distinguishing characteristics of genuine conversion?
6. Based on his first letter to the church, why is Paul so delighted to learn that their love for one another was increasing?
7. Describe the various ways that your hope enables you to face both your challenges and your opportunities.
8. What are some of the reasons Paul was so willing to boast about the Thessalonian church? How might someone boast about your church?
9. What did Paul say to the Thessalonians to encourage them to be faithful in the midst of their persecutions?
10. How does this passage challenge the way you view the presence of pain in your life? What can affliction and pain teach you about how God deals with those He loves?

When God Balances the Books

2 THESSALONIANS 1:6-12

Main Idea: When Jesus is revealed from heaven, He will bring relief to those who love Him and retribution to those who reject Him.

I. **The Hopeful Future of Those Who Are Faithful (1:6-7,10-12)**
   A. Relief from our enemies (1:6-7a)
   B. Rest from our sorrows (1:7b)
   C. Rewards for our faith (1:10-12)
      1. We will be with Him when He comes.
      2. We will serve Him until He comes.
II. **The Fateful Future of Those Who Do Evil (1:6,8-9)**
   A. God's judgment is just (1:6).
   B. God's judgment is fearful (1:6,8-9).
   C. God's judgment is final (1:9).

How much longer?" Have you stopped to consider how those three simple words hold such a prominent place in your life? For children on a long road trip in the family car, they represent the great gulf fixed between them and the fun awaiting them at the end of the journey. For the sports team that is attempting to run out the clock, they represent the only obstacle between their team and the final trophy presentation. For the parents paying for their child's education, they represent the months remaining until graduation.

At some point in your life, the question, How much longer? has either passed through your lips or weighed heavily on your mind. The question relates to your inability to know if and when things will get better. This is especially true for God's people as they view the pain, affliction, and suffering that is often associated with following Christ. God's people have always desired to know "how long" until God would bring an end to such injustice, to right all wrongs, and to judge those who harm His followers. Listen to how the prophet Habakkuk asked this question:

How long, LORD, must I call for help and You do not listen
or cry out to You about violence and You do not save?

Why do You force me to look at injustice?
Why do You tolerate wrongdoing? (Hab 1:2-3)

King David had a similar question for God:

LORD, how long will You forget me?
Forever?
How long will You hide Your face from me?
How long will I store up anxious concerns within me,
agony in my mind every day?
How long will my enemy dominate me?

Consider me and answer, LORD my God.
Restore brightness to my eyes;
otherwise, I will sleep in death.
My enemy will say, "I have triumphed over him,"
and my foes will rejoice because I am shaken. (Ps 13:1-4)

The good news is that God is not offended by such questions. In fact, you may be surprised to learn that He told us to ask them. To illustrate this truth, Jesus shared the following parable:

"There was a judge in a certain town who didn't fear God or respect man. And a widow in that town kept coming to him, saying, 'Give me justice against my adversary.'

"For a while he was unwilling, but later he said to himself, 'Even though I don't fear God or respect man, yet because this widow keeps pestering me, I will give her justice, so she doesn't wear me out by her persistent coming.'"

Then the Lord said, "Listen to what the unjust judge says. Will not God grant justice to His elect who cry out to Him day and night? Will He delay to help them? I tell you that He will swiftly grant them justice." (Luke 18:2-8)

The point of the parable is inescapable: If an "unjust judge" will respond to persistent requests of a widow, how much more will the loving Father respond to the requests of His own children? God is not only expecting you to bring your questions to Him, He is also waiting to answer you when you do.

Although we have no indication that the Thessalonians asked Paul the question, How long? we can assume that they must have been thinking about it. Whatever the source of their suffering, we know that it was intense. They had to be longing for God to bring judgment on their adversaries and to grant their church relief from its afflictions. Paul's words must have been encouraging: "It is righteous for God to repay with affliction those who afflict you and to reward with rest you who are afflicted" (1:6-7). Remember that Paul just told them how God was using their present suffering to demonstrate their worthiness for their future glory. While it was comforting to know that their suffering was worth it, knowing that God was going to bring retribution to their adversaries and relief to their pain had to give the Thessalonians hope for the future.

As we examine this text more closely, we must keep Paul's main thought in view. We find this in verse 7 where he says, "This will take place at the revelation of the Lord Jesus from heaven." This verse points to the final and climactic event in human history, when Jesus Christ returns to earth, renders complete justice, and ultimately establishes His eternal reign.[16] When this event occurs, Paul mentions two specific things that will happen: God will grant final relief to those who love Him, and He will bring retribution to those who do not. This passage thus portrays two very different eternal destinies: that of unending joy for the people of God and that of unmitigated judgment for the enemies of God.

The Hopeful Future of Those Who Are Faithful
2 THESSALONIANS 1:6-7A,10-12

There is the story of an encounter between two farmers, one a believer and the other an atheist. At harvest time the atheist's fields were rich with crops while the Christian's fields produced a paltry little. The atheist taunted the Christian by telling him that apparently it did not pay to serve God. The Christian replied, "It does pay to serve Him, but

---

[16] The event portrayed here appears to be different from the one described in 1 Thess 4:13-18, where Paul refers to the *parousia* ("presence" or "coming"). In the present text Paul uses the word *apokalupsis* ("unveiling") to indicate that Jesus will be revealed in a way much different than that of His incarnation (e.g., 1:8). A number of other notable differences exist between this passage and 1 Thess 4:13-18: In the 1 Thessalonians passage Christ returns in the air and for His church with no mention of judgment. However, in the 2 Thessalonians passage, Christ returns to the earth and with His church for the purpose of bringing judgment. For a helpful article exploring the relationship between the rapture and the Day of the Lord, see Robert L. Thomas, "Imminence in the NT," 191–214.

you must remember that God does not always settle His accounts in October."

One of the most difficult things to do when walking through painful times is to keep the proper perspective. A loss of perspective is almost always followed by a loss of purpose. When our mind becomes fixed on what we don't like about our circumstances, we will invariably fail to consider what God may be doing in our circumstances. Paul wants the Thessalonians to view their present circumstances through the lens of God's future promises. The amazing thing about Scripture is that God unveils pre-written history. When you open your Bible, you are able to see into the future. God has the perfect perspective about everything:

> For I am God, and there is no other;
> I am God, and no one is like Me.
> I declare the end from the beginning,
> and from long ago what is not yet done,
> saying: My plan will take place,
> and I will do all My will. (Isa 46:9-10)

With God the future is far from uncertain. And through His Word, He has graciously provided a preview of what is coming. Armed with knowledge of His plans, the Christian can view the future with expectancy and not uncertainty.

Concerning God's plans for His people, Paul informed the Thessalonians that at Jesus' return, He is going to bring His followers complete relief from their enemies, ultimate rest from their sorrows, and the just rewards for their faithfulness. Let's examine each of these promises more closely.

Relief from Our Enemies (2 Thess 1:6-7a)

Most of us are familiar with the expression, "Things are not always as they seem." Through personal experience we learn very early in life that looks can be deceiving. As we grow in our understanding of how God works, we quickly begin to realize that God is often at work in ways that we cannot see. So even though our eyes may tell us one thing when viewing the world, we know that there is so much more to the picture. Of course, this is the reason Paul exhorted the Corinthians not to fix their eyes on the temporary things (2 Cor 4:18).

Still, looking beyond temporary things is one of the most difficult things for us to do. For example, consider how many of the typical

Christian prayer requests are directed toward the temporal aspects of life. While there is nothing sinful about praying about these things, such as our desire for good health and our yearning for more stuff, Jesus taught that we are to take our prayers to a much different level. He knows that we need things like food, clothing, health, and shelter, and He expects that we will seek Him for these needs and trust Him to meet them. But Jesus expects that our prayers will be focused on much more significant matters like glorifying His Name, expanding His kingdom, and accomplishing His will (Matt 6:9-13,32-33). We must learn to view the temporary things through the lenses of God's eternal plans.

With a proper perspective on eternity, we will recognize that what we see tells only part of the story. While apparently those who oppose the gospel and trouble God's people have the upper hand, behind the scenes God is orchestrating human history to accomplish His purposes. At Jesus' coming, God will bring final relief to all believers who have suffered at the hands of the ungodly. He is going to answer the prayers of His people who have cried out to Him, "How long until You judge and avenge our blood from those who live on the earth?" (Rev 6:10). As Charles Ryrie rightly notes, though the Thessalonians' "present adversaries seem so powerful, there is One who is mightier than all, who will mete out punishment on their tormentors when He appears in great power and glory" (Ryrie, *First and Second Thessalonians*, 99).

Rest from Our Sorrows (2 Thess 1:7a)

The concept of rest may mean different things to different people. For example, for the weary student who has just pulled an all-nighter preparing for her final exam, the word *rest* may conjure up images of a bed and a pillow. Or for new parents listening to the incessant cries of a newborn infant down the hall, the word *rest* may be an illusive dream. For the marathon runner whose legs are burning and feet are aching, rest is waiting just across the finish line. While rest may mean different things to different people, I think all would agree that rest is typically a good thing.

Imagine the Thessalonians' reaction when they heard that God was going to give His people "rest" when the Lord Jesus was revealed from heaven. What do you think crossed their minds? For people in the throes of affliction and pain, the thought of rest doubtlessly brought them relief. In fact, the word that Paul uses for *rest* often describes the releasing of a bowstring and thus can mean "loose" or "relax." In other words, if you are longing for a stress-free life, just wait until Jesus returns!

Paul says that God will bring ultimate relief to every believer "at the revelation of the Lord Jesus from heaven with His powerful angels." On that day God will provide eternal rest for His people. The apostle John peels back the curtains and gives us a glimpse of that day:

> Look! God's dwelling is with humanity, and He will live with them. They will be His people, and God Himself will be with them and be their God. He will wipe away every tear from their eyes. Death will no longer exist; grief, crying, and pain will exist no longer, because the previous things have passed away. (Rev 21:3-4)

The fact that Paul points to a future rest is not to suggest, however, that there will be no rest in this life. Paul taught the Thessalonians that their present sorrows were preparing them for their future glory (1:5). In even our most troubling times, God still has a purpose. So though we may not rest *from* our sorrows, we can certainly take comfort that we can rest *in* our sorrows. Paul knew how to remain hopeful in sorrow. His words to the Corinthian church have provided comfort to countless believers: "I take pleasure in weaknesses, insults, catastrophes, persecutions, and in pressures, because of Christ. For when I am weak, then I am strong" (2 Cor 12:10). Similarly he admonished the Romans to look past their suffering and ahead to their future glory: "For I consider that the sufferings of this present time are not worth comparing with the glory that is going to be revealed to us" (Rom 8:18).

Rewards for Our Faith (2 Thess 1:10-12)

As difficult as it may be for us to grasp, the relief granted from our enemies and the rest provided from our sorrows will pale in comparison to the reward we will receive for our faith. Paul's description of this reward surpasses our comprehension: ". . . in that day when He comes *to be glorified by His saints and to be admired by all those who have believed,* because our testimony among you was believed" (v. 10; emphasis added). The present sufferings of following Christ mean nothing without this promise. But when we view the present through the lens of promises like this, we gain a better understanding of how it is possible to see the good in our pain. God is going to turn the tables completely. For those who now face affliction, persecution, and pain, God will one day grant the privilege of sharing with Jesus in the manifestation of His glory (2 Cor 4:17).

We will be with Him when He comes. A number of suggestions have been offered to explain what Paul means by his statement that Jesus will be "glorified *by* His saints." Some see this as referring to the saints' worship and adoration of Christ. So when Christ returns, His saints will be praising, worshiping, and glorifying Him. Just as they proclaimed the wonder of His glory in this life, so also will they continue to do so through eternity, including the day when Jesus is revealed from heaven.

Others, however, see Paul as suggesting that Jesus is glorified by the work that He has done *through* and/or *in* His saints. When viewed in this way, His saints are seen as those who by their transformed character reflect or radiate His glory. Stott offers the analogy of a light bulb by suggesting that Jesus' glory shines through His people like an electrical current travels through its filament:

> For when the current is switched on, it becomes incandescent.
> So when Jesus is revealed in his glory, he will be glorified in
> His people. We will not only see, but share his glory. We will be
> more than a filament which glows temporarily. . . . We will be
> radically and permanently changed, being transformed into
> his likeness. . . . We will glow forever with the glory of Christ,
> as indeed he glowed with the glory of the Father. (Stott, *Gospel
> and the End*, 149–50)

However you choose to interpret this verse, the point that cannot be missed is that Jesus alone is the source of glory; and at His coming, His glorified people will display it in its fullest sense. Calvin affirms this:

> Christ will not have this glory for himself alone but it will
> possess all the saints. . . . When the Son of God is manifested
> in the glory of His kingdom, he will gather them into the same
> fellowship with himself. (Calvin, *1 and 2 Thessalonians*, 79)

The apostle John pointed to the day of Christ's appearing:

> *Dear friends, we are God's children now, and what we will be has not
> yet been revealed. We know that when He appears, we will be like Him
> because we will see Him as He is.* (1 John 3:2)

We will serve Him until He comes. Throughout his epistles, Paul has a unique way of transitioning from heavenly discussions about future promises to the daily responsibilities of present life. For example, after teaching the Corinthians about the promise of a future resurrection and their subsequent glorified bodies, Paul immediately brings them back to earth by reminding them of the importance of taking up a weekly collection at church (see 1 Cor 15:58–16:1). Future promises must always be met by practical obedience. While we long for heaven, we must also remember that we have work to do until we get there. If we are not careful, like Peter at Jesus' transfiguration, we may find ourselves wanting to build three tabernacles in heaven so that we don't have to go back to earth (Matt 17:4). Of course, Peter could not persuade Jesus to stay in heaven, as He had not yet completed the work that He came to do on earth.

In verses 6-9 Paul took the Thessalonian believers on a journey to their heavenly home, but before they could get too comfortable there he immediately brings them back to Thessalonica. To make the transition from the future promise of being glorified with Christ to the present reality of their current circumstances, Paul uses the phrase, "and in view of this" (1:11). These five words provide the link between the future and the present. In other words, Paul says, "Now that you know that your future is secure, let's not forget that God is still at work in you and He still has work to do through you." Although Christ's coming was imminent and God's promises were guaranteed, the Thessalonians still had a walk to pursue and a mission to fulfill. In view of this, Paul offers a prayer on their behalf.

His prayer includes two specific requests: First, he prayed that God would consider them "worthy of His calling" (1:11a). This is not the first time that we heard Paul pray in this way (1:5; 1 Thess 2:12). As we have discovered, God uses every circumstance, even our sufferings and afflictions, to prepare us for future glory. Our faithfulness in affliction and steadfast hope in trials reveals the genuineness of our faith. So we demonstrate our worthiness of His calling by passionately pursuing God regardless of our circumstances. We do not prove ourselves worthy of His calling *in order to* be saved, but are proved worthy *because* we are saved. Stated another way, through the progressive sanctification of God's Spirit, He transforms those who belong to Him into the likeness of Christ and thus reveals their worthiness to bear God's name and enjoy God's kingdom (see comments at 1 Thess 5:23b).

Paul's second request is that by His "power" God would "fulfill every desire for goodness and the work of faith" (1:11b). The word *fulfill* means "accomplish or bring to its proper end." Paul is asking God to complete the work that He began in them at their conversion (see Phil 1:6). This prayer is for their ongoing sanctification.

This is no perfunctory prayer. The depth of his requests for the Thessalonian Christians should challenge us to pray in like manner for others. His prayer went well beyond the superficial "Bless my church" requests that are all too common among God's people. He knew that the stakes were high for these young Christians. So instead of asking God to remove them from their danger, He asked God to keep them faithful in their suffering, grounded in their faith, and steadfast in their work. Through his prayer, Paul not only provides us with a pattern for how to pray for the churches, but he also reveals the kind of prayer that is consistent with God's will. When we make God's passion our passion, we can be confident that He will hear us when we pray. King David knew this when he wrote, "Take delight in the LORD, and He will give you your heart's desires. Commit your way to the LORD; trust in Him, and He will act" (Ps 37:4-5). Jesus stated it this way: "If you remain in Me and My words remain in you, ask whatever you want and it will be done for you" (John 15:7).

What then is God's ultimate goal for His church until Jesus returns? Paul says it is "so that the name of our Lord Jesus will be glorified by you, and you by Him, according to the grace of our God and the Lord Jesus Christ" (1:12). What a marvelous thought! Jesus Christ is glorified by the faithful work that His people do for Him; and the church is glorified by the faithful work that Jesus Christ does by His grace in them. Gordon Fee perfectly sums up the main point of Paul's prayer:

> In the midst of the Thessalonian believers' pain and suffering, Paul's prayer for them focuses ultimately on God and his glory. Yet God's glory will be manifest as he fulfills in his people the desire of this prayer. And one should never lose sight of the fact that God's glory is intimately tied to Christ's being glorified in and among his people. (Fee, *First and Second Letters*, 268)

The Fateful Future of Those Who Do Evil
2 THESSALONAINS 1:6,8-9

The story is told of a time when the Viceroy of Naples was visiting Spain. While visiting a harbor, he noticed a group of convicts aboard a large galley ship. As punishment for their crimes, these men were required to pull the oars of the ship. Curious as to what crimes these convicts committed, the Viceroy went aboard and asked each of them to tell him his story. One man begrudgingly said that a corrupt judge was bribed to convict him. Another said that his enemies framed him by paying people to bear false witness against him. Still another said that he was falsely accused by a case of mistaken identity. One after another, the convicts explained why they were innocent and deserved to be set free. Arriving at the last man on board and expecting to hear the same story, the Viceroy was shocked to hear the man exclaim, "I'm here because I deserve to be. I am a thief and a criminal. I committed a crime and I deserve my just punishment." Upon hearing this, the Viceroy shouted to the captain, "How have you allowed this one wicked criminal to be in the presence of all of these innocent men? Release him immediately, lest he corrupt the others!"

Human beings have such a difficult time admitting guilt. From our earliest years as a child to our later years in adulthood, we have an innate tendency to claim our innocence even when we know that we are guilty. No matter how guilty we may be, we will always be able to find an appropriate excuse to legitimize why we did what we did. Over and against this reluctance to be honest about our sin is the reality of a coming day of judgment when God will call the world to ultimate accountability. While the redeemed people of God will receive relief and rest on that judgment day, the fate of the ungodly will be much different. Paul details the fate of the ungodly by pointing to three aspects of God's judgment with language that is direct and vivid: it is just, it is fearful, and it is final.

God's Judgment Is Just (2 Thess 1:6)

Both the hope of life with Christ in heaven and the horror of separation from Him in hell are wrapped up in the justice of God. Paul writes, "It is *righteous for God* to repay with affliction those who afflict you and to reward with rest you who are afflicted" (1:6; emphasis added). God's justice demands that He will always do what is fitting and right. Thus God is completely consistent when He promises to reward the righteous with rest and the unrighteous with judgment. A. W. Tozer explains,

> Justice, when used of God, is a name we give to the way God is, nothing more; and when God acts justly He is not doing so to conform to an independent criterion, but simply acting like Himself in a given situation. As gold is an element in itself and can never change nor compromise but is gold wherever it is

found, so God is God, always, only, fully God, and can never be other than He is. Everything in the universe is good to the degree it conforms to the nature of God and evil as it fails to do so. God is His own self-existent principle of moral equity, and when He sentences evil men or rewards the righteous, He simply acts like Himself from within, uninfluenced by anything that is not Himself. (Tozer, *Knowledge*, 87–88)

So then, given the fact that all human beings are sinful, how can a just God reward one person and judge another? Understanding His purpose in sending Jesus Christ is the key to answering this question.

God does not set His justice aside when He redeems sinners. If God sacrificed His justice to pardon a sinner, then He would no longer be God. But through the substitutionary death of Christ on the cross, God provided a way to show mercy without doing away with His justice. Though all human beings stand guilty before God's perfect holiness, by His mercy He graciously offers them forgiveness and redemption through the death of Jesus Christ. Concerning this, Paul writes,

> For all have sinned and fall short of the glory of God. They are justified freely by His grace through the redemption that is in Christ Jesus. God presented Him as a propitiation through faith in His blood, to demonstrate His righteousness, because in His restraint God passed over the sins previously committed. God presented Him to demonstrate His righteousness at the present time, so that He would be righteous and declare righteous the one who has faith in Jesus. (Rom 3:23-26)

The most significant issue then for all human beings revolves around the question, What will you do with Jesus? A. W. Tozer explains further,

> Because of our sin we are all under sentence of death, a judgment which resulted when justice confronted our moral situation. When infinite equity encountered our chronic and willful in-equity, there was violent war between the two, a war which God won and must always win. But when the penitent sinner casts himself upon Christ for salvation, the moral situation is reversed. Justice confronts the changed situation and pronounces the believing man just. (Tozer, *Knowledge*, 89)

Hence, those who accept God's offer of salvation through Christ receive the reward of God's justice—salvation and the promise of eternal rest

(1:7a); those who reject God's offer also receive the reward of God's justice—judgment and the promise of eternal punishment (1:8).

God's Judgment Is Fearful (2 Thess 1:6,8-9)

The language that Paul uses to describe God's judgment is vivid: "affliction," "vengeance," and "destruction." None of these words carry even the slightest nuance of hope concerning the eternal destiny of those outside of Jesus Christ. The words also appear to indicate an increasing intensity in judgment:

- *Affliction* carries the idea of tribulation or pressure.
- *Vengeance* indicates full and complete punishment.
- *Destruction* points to ruination and "implies the loss of all things that give worth to existence" (Rienecker and Rogers, *Linguistic Key*, 606–7).

God is going to settle His accounts. While it appears that injustice and unrighteousness prevail, God is going to have the last word when He "repays" those who do not know Him and those "who don't obey the gospel of our Lord Jesus" (1:6,8). His judgment will be rendered justly and not vindictively. We desire revenge for injustices done to us, but God desires justice for injustices done to Him. Hence, God's vengeance does not flow from His desire to exact revenge; His vengeance flows from His desire for justice. In fact, as Morris notes, the Greek word translated "vengeance" contains a root word that means "right," and that root, translated "righteous," is found in verses 5 and 6 (Morris, *First and Second*, 203). This means that even in His vengeance, God is doing what is right. Ezekiel notes that God takes "no pleasure in the death of the wicked" (Ezek 33:11). He is so unlike you and me. God is not on some egotistical "power trip" to put all of His enemies in their place. He takes no delight in that. God does delight when His Name is glorified, His Word is vindicated, and His Son is exalted (Matt 6:9; John 14:21; Phil 2:9-11). While He may not delight in the death of the wicked, He will hold those accountable who do not honor Him, His Word, or His Son.

God's Judgment Is Final (2 Thess 1:9)

Before we conclude with this final thought, let me help you to get a picture in your mind that will enable you to grasp the seriousness of what Paul is saying in verse 9. Think back to a time when you were watching your favorite football team attempt to mount a last-minute drive to win the game. You cheer them on as your star quarterback manages the clock perfectly while methodically moving your team down the field for a last second come-from-behind victory. Needing a touchdown to win, your quarterback throws a screen pass to your lightning-quick running back. You cheer excitedly as he zigzags among the defenders and heads for the end zone, but just before he can cross the goal line he gets tackled. You glance over at the clock and notice that time has expired. Your first thought is to quickly scan the field in search of a yellow penalty flag in hopes that your team may get one more play. But hope suddenly gives way to reality when you realize that the game is over and your team just lost. If you have watched enough football games, then you know exactly what I am talking about. It is a sick feeling to know that your team was that close to victory but will not be afforded the luxury of running another play. The game is over.

Now I want you to think about something much more serious. In verse 9 Paul vividly reveals the ultimate fate of every person who does not know God and does not respond in obedience to the gospel of Jesus. Listen to the finality of these words: "These will pay the penalty of eternal destruction from the Lord's presence and from His glorious strength" (1:9). When Jesus comes again, He will pronounce final and ultimate judgment on those who do not know God. Unlike football, there will never be another game or another season with a chance to make up for the shortfall. It's game over—forever! This is "eternal destruction" away from God's presence forever (Rev 20:11-13). John Phillips describes the horror of this final judgment:

> The wicked then, at the Lord's return, will be handed over to eternal ruin. Who can imagine the horrors that will accompany the dissolution of their personality, the gnawings of conscience, the torments of memory, the anguish of guilt, and the terrible knowledge that their doom is deserved, hopeless, and unending. (Phillips, *Exploring 1 and 2 Thessalonians*, 184)

Jesus repeatedly taught about a place of eternal ruin and destruction called hell. He described it as a place of "eternal fire" (Matt 25:41), "eternal punishment" (Matt 25:46), eternal "darkness" (Matt 22:13), eternal pain (Matt 8:12), and eternal separation (Luke 16:19-31). However, of all the biblical descriptions portraying the horrors of hell, perhaps none is more striking than the one Paul gives at the end of verse 9 where he speaks of eternal separation "from the Lord's presence," and "from His glorious strength."

Though the darkness, fire, anguish, and pain will make hell unbearable, the total absence of God's presence is what makes hell what it really is—hell. Paul's emphasis in this text has nothing to do with what you might find in hell and everything to do with what is absent in hell—the presence and glory of God. To have a conscious, definite awareness of God's presence and yet to be completely cut off from Him will be to suffer the worst kind of hell imaginable.

Of course, to know that such a place exists is bad enough, but to realize that untold millions will spend eternity there ought to cause you to shudder. In fact, according to the latest available statistics, nearly 150,000 people die worldwide every day. That equates to more than 4.5 million people a month. Where will these people spend eternity? The uncertainty of how we might answer that question should call us to immediate action. If heaven and hell are real and a personal relationship with Jesus is the only way that anyone can enjoy the eternal rest and reward of heaven and miss the eternal pain and isolation of hell, then nothing that we do could be more important than to tell others about Him. According to Luke, God "has set a day when He is going to judge the world in righteousness by the Man He has appointed" (Acts 17:31). As long as we have breath there is still time on the clock to make each day count, but we know that His coming is imminent. So, until we die and stand before Him, or He comes to gather His church, we must continue to "proclaim Him, warning and teaching everyone" that Jesus Christ is the only way (Col 1:28).

Conclusion

This text has serious implications for how we live today and how we view eternity. Let's briefly consider three implications for each.

How We Live Today

What you see is not always what you get. The fact that injustice appears to have an upper hand in the world does not tell the whole story. We have the tendency to view our world through the lens of our personal experiences instead of through the lens of God's redemptive plan. From the perspective of the Thessalonian Christians, their future did not look very hopeful. Their life was a never-ending story of persecution, affliction, and pain (1:4-5). However, when they began to view things from God's perspective, their picture changed dramatically. God can be seen moving "His" history and subsequently their history forward at His pace and according to His plan (1:6-10). While knowing God's ultimate plan for the future may not make our problems go away, it does provide us with a firm foundation on which to stand in uncertain times. Perhaps we will even be able to proclaim with David,

> *I waited patiently for the LORD,*
> *and He turned to me and heard my cry for help.*
> *He brought me up from a desolate pit,*
> *out of the muddy clay,*
> *and set my feet on a rock,*
> *making my steps secure.* (Ps 40:1-2)

God is more than capable to right our wrongs. The more time that we spend in the presence of people, the more chances there are that someone will hurt us. These hurts may come as persecution from an antagonistic world, or they may be the result of an inconsiderate friend. The question for us is not, What will we do *if* we get hurt? But, How will we respond *when* we get hurt? The good news is that we do not have to play God. He is more than capable to defend us. If we are looking for a blueprint for how to handle our hurts, then look no further than Jesus. Peter tells us how He approached His hurts:

> *For you were called to this, because Christ also suffered for you, leaving you an example, so that you should follow in His steps. He did not commit sin, and no deceit was found in His mouth; when He was reviled, He did not revile in return; when He was suffering, He did not threaten but* entrusted Himself to the One who judges justly. (1 Pet 2:21-23; emphasis added)

Ask this question: If Jesus will be glorified in His saints at His coming, then why not start glorifying Him now? Of course, this was exactly the point of Paul's prayer in 1:11-12. Considering the glorious future that God has planned for His people, we should be looking for every conceivable opportunity to make His name great among the nations. Perhaps a good place to begin is by reevaluating the what, the why, and the how of church. Admittedly, this will not an easy task, but if believers exist for the purpose of glorifying Jesus by fulfilling "every desire for goodness and the work of faith," then they must reach beyond just *doing* church—they must be busy *being* the church.

How We View Eternity

Let's also consider three implications of this passage for how we view eternity.

Heaven will bring us rest from our labor but not from our activity. Heaven not only promises to be a place of rest but it also promises to be a place of activity. Far from floating around on white clouds and strumming harps, God's people are going to enjoy ceaseless activity in His glorious presence. King David was looking forward to this when he prayed,

> *Therefore my heart is glad*
> *and my spirit rejoices;*
> *my body also rests securely.*
>
> *For You will not abandon me to Sheol;*
> *You will not allow Your Faithful One to see decay.*
>
> *You reveal the path of life to me;*
> *in Your presence is abundant joy;*
> *in Your right hand are eternal pleasures.* (Ps 16:9-11)

Jesus is Lord. The one admonition that continues to surface throughout the Thessalonian letters is that we should live today like Jesus is coming tomorrow. While the rest of the world may ask, "Where is the promise of His coming?" we live with expectation in the light of that promise. Until that day we know that the Lord is exalted and seated in heaven at the Father's right hand (Eph 1:20-21; Heb 1:3). He's not twiddling His thumbs to pass the time until the Father gives Him the final command; instead, He is now interceding for us (Heb 7:25), guiding His church (Eph 1:22-23), and preparing a place for His people (John 14:2-3).

Eternity is forever. Paul reveals that those who do not love God or obey the gospel of Jesus will face "eternal destruction" (1:9). The word *eternal* suggests an endless duration. In other words, there will be no end to their torment. There will be no time put back on the clock. There will be no second chances. The Bible warns, "It is appointed for people to die once—and after this, judgment" (Heb 9:27). The only opportunity for any person to respond to God's offer of salvation and forgiveness in Jesus Christ is in this present life. Our eternal destiny depends on it.

Reflect and Discuss

1. Explain why Paul's instruction in this passage would have been so encouraging to the Thessalonians.
2. What does Jesus' return mean for the wicked? What about for the saints?
3. Based on the context of this passage, what is meant by the saying, "Things are not always as they seem"?
4. Explain what Paul means when he says that Christ is going to bring "rest" for His people. What impact should that promise have on you today?
5. How does God use your present suffering to prepare you for glory?
6. What prompted Paul's prayer for the Thessalonians? What is the nature of His prayer? How can you use his prayer as a model for the way you pray for your fellow believers?
7. How is God just in the way He deals both with sinners and with His saints?
8. Describe how Paul details the finality of judgment for those who do not love God. What should your response be to this description?
9. How is God's vengeance so different from your vengeance?
10. Name some of the present-day implications of this text for how believers should live.

Facing the Future without Fear

2 THESSALONIANS 2:1-12

Main Idea: God gives us a glimpse into the future so that we can live hopefully and expectantly in the present.

I. **Deception Distorts Reality (2:1-3a,5).**
  A. False teaching robs us of peace (2:1-3a).
  B. False teaching ruins our perspective (2:5).
II. **Rebellion Intensifies in History (2:3b-4,6-10a).**
  A. The coming apostasy (2:3b,9-10)
  B. The rise of the antichrist (2:3b-4,6-10a)
  C. The removal of the restrainer (2:6-7)
III. **God Controls Our Destiny (2:8b,10b-12).**
  A. The antichrist is destroyed (2:8b).
  B. The rebellious are judged (2:10b-12).

A number of years ago while doing mission work in China, several people from our mission team returned to the hotel excitedly one evening. When asked about the source of their excitement, they revealed that while making their way back to the hotel they were approached by a street salesman who offered to make them a very good deal on "Rolex" watches. His normal price was $20; but because he liked our group so much, he was willing to sell each person a watch for only $10. One by one, each person from our group proudly showed off their newly purchased luxury timepieces. Later that evening as we headed to dinner, I asked one of the men if he would allow me to have a closer look at his watch. While removing it from his wrist I heard the man gasp as he noticed that the crystal had fallen off of his watch! While neither of us thought that $10 would buy him an actual Rolex watch, we both expected that his cheap imitation would last more than two hours! Most people would admit that there is a big difference between the real thing and a cheap substitute. Even though we know that if it seems too good to be true it probably is, we still find ourselves being fooled time and again. Being deceived by a watch salesman is one thing, but being deceived by Satan is an altogether different matter.

The subject matter of 2 Thessalonians 2:1-12 points forward to future world events, particularly as they relate to God's redemptive history. This portion of Paul's letter introduces some new material, including the events surrounding a coming world leader called the "man of lawlessness" (2:3). This individual will be the personification of evil like this world has never seen. Paul's description of his activity is chilling:

> *He opposes and exalts himself above every so-called God or object of worship, so that he sits in God's sanctuary, publicizing that he himself is God. . . . The coming of the lawless one is based on Satan's working, with all kinds of false miracles, signs, and wonders, and with every unrighteous deception among those who are perishing.* (2:4,9-10)

His purpose is twofold: to usurp the place of God and to deceive those who are perishing. But as quickly as he enters the scene of human history, the return of Jesus Christ will bring an abrupt end to his reign of terror (2:8).

In exploring this section more closely, we must remember that while this material may be unfamiliar to the contemporary reader of 2 Thessalonians, it was apparently not new to the Thessalonians themselves. We know this to be true for two reasons, one explicit and the other implicit. First, Paul clearly reminds the Thessalonians to recall his previous instruction about these future events (2:5). At some point in his initial visit to Thessalonica, he taught them many things about God's future redemptive plan, including the Lord's return, the coming lawless one, and the Day of the Lord. We have access to some of this instruction preserved in his letters (1 Thess 4:13-18; 5:1-11; 2 Thess 1:6-10; 2:1-12). In fact, in 2:1 Paul mentions Christ's coming for the sixth time. So, clearly the theme of Christ's return and the specific details surrounding it were not unfamiliar to the Thessalonian believers.

There is also an implicit reason to believe that Paul had given them sufficient instruction about future events. His discussion about the "man of lawlessness" is surprisingly brief. As a result, those outside of Thessalonica are left scratching their heads with more questions than Paul has answers. The implication is that because his previous instruction was more than sufficient, he saw no need to further elaborate.

Concerning his teaching and instruction, we must not miss the significance of what Paul did in Thessalonica. Following their conversion, Paul had a very brief time with these new believers. Though how long he was with them is not certain, it was most likely somewhere between three weeks and a few months. But even in that limited time, Paul apparently taught them extensively about the doctrine of last things. From the prophecy of Daniel to the words of Jesus, Paul no doubt painted a picture of the future, including the rise of antichrist and the abomination of desolation (Dan 7:8,24-25; 9:27; 11:31; 12:11; Matt 24:15-28). So in the midst of their questions about the future, Paul responds to the Thessalonians, "Don't you remember that when I was still with you I told you about this?" (2 Thess 2:5).

The message here to pastors is noteworthy. As challenging as it may be to address the difficult eschatological texts of Scripture, we have a solemn responsibility to teach our people the "whole plan of God" (Acts 20:27). For the Thessalonians to face their future without fear, they needed to be anchored to the unshakable foundation of God's truth. And as we will see, by means of false teaching, someone in the Thessalonian church had attempted to compromise this foundation. The end result was an "upset" and "troubled" church.

With this as a backdrop, remember that Paul is less interested in satisfying our eschatological whims and more concerned with bringing the Thessalonians pastoral encouragement. Since Paul's aim was not to provide every conceivable detail of God's future game plan, we may walk away from the passage with more questions than answers. Still, the text is invaluable as you seek to understand God's ultimate plan for redemptive history.

Deception Distorts Reality
2 THESSALONIANS 2:1-3A,5

From the outset of human history, Satan's goal has been to deceive God's people and to thwart God's purposes (Gen 3:1; John 8:44). Because his purposes are diametrically opposed to the purposes of God, he has dedicated himself to fighting God in every conceivable way. He declared war on Adam and Eve in the garden and on Jesus in His earthly ministry. He continues that war today (Matt 4:1-11; 2 Cor 11:14; 1 Pet 5:8). Satan's battle plan includes two main strategies: exploit our weaknesses, and blind us to God's truth. Although these two strategies almost always work in tandem, the latter typically gives rise to the former. Satan knows that if he can undermine our belief in what God says, then he can exploit our weaknesses as we struggle to live out our lives in obedience to God.

Satan was working assiduously to undermine the Thessalonians' peace about their future. Paul makes this clear as the passage begins:

> *Now concerning the coming of our Lord Jesus Christ and our being gathered to Him: We ask you, brothers, not to be* easily upset *in mind or* troubled, *either by a spirit or by a message or by a letter as if from us, alleging that the Day of the Lord has come. Don't let anyone* deceive *you in any way.* (2 Thess 2:1-3; emphasis added)

We can sense Paul's concern for the Thessalonians: Don't be upset. Don't be troubled. Don't be deceived. He knew that their fretfulness about the future was directly related to their forgetfulness about what he had taught them. Therefore, his goal is to help them refocus on their future by providing them with the lens of God's truth.

However, before we can fully understand what Paul reveals to them in this passage, we first need to recall some background. In 1 Thessalonians 4:13-18 Paul taught the Thessalonians about an imminent event on God's prophetic calendar, that is, the *rapture* or "snatching away" of the church. Paul pointed them to a future day when Jesus would appear in the clouds to call His church to be with Him. He gave the Thessalonians no specific date for this event, but he did give them a suggestion about its timing. Piecing together his flow of thought between 1 Thessalonians 4:13-18 and 5:1-11, likely Paul taught them that Jesus was going to come and gather His church *prior to* the Day of the Lord. As imposing as the Day of the Lord judgments might be, the Thessalonian Christians could view the future with hope knowing that God had no intention for them to be around for these events. Paul twice challenges the church to "encourage one another" with this hope (1 Thess 4:18; 5:11).

To be sure, not everyone agrees that this passage supports a pre-tribulational view of the rapture. Some suggest that it actually makes a stronger case for a post-tribulational rapture.[17] Adherents to that position contend that if Paul believed that Christ would rapture His church prior to the Day of the Lord, his subsequent discussion about the coming "apostasy" and the revelation of the "man of lawlessness" would be superfluous since the Thessalonians would actually miss these events.

---

[17] For a more detailed look at the post-tribulational view, see Gundry, *The Church and the Tribulation.*

They further argue that Paul's provision of the details and timing of both of these events is proof that he was arming the Thessalonians with the insight needed to recognize them when they happened. The post-tribulationist would conclude that Paul's purpose here is not to remind the Thessalonians that they would miss the Day of the Lord, but to prepare them for it. In this regard, Paul thus seeks to reassure them of God's sovereign control over their lives both in the present and in the future when Christ returns to establish His eternal reign.

While such a conclusion is not without merit, it does fail to capture adequately the pervasive theme of pastoral encouragement in Paul's eschatological teaching throughout the Thessalonian correspondence (1 Thess 4:18; 5:11). One might question how the news that things will get worse would bring much comfort to an "upset" or "troubled" Christian. Further, that the Thessalonians were so quickly troubled by the spurious news that the Day of the Lord had arrived does suggest that they had anticipated missing it.

We are now in a better position to understand the significance of Paul's instruction in 2 Thessalonians 2:1-12 with this as the backdrop. Someone in the Thessalonian church, either by a false letter or by false teaching, was claiming that the Day of the Lord had already come. To make matters worse, this letter or teaching had been ascribed to Paul himself. Given their respect for Paul and their ongoing suffering and affliction (2:5-7), the Thessalonians had become convinced that they must have missed the rapture and were now experiencing the Day of the Lord. This fear was taking its toll on the church. We can imagine how the anticipation of facing continued and even worsening persecution was destroying their peace and ruining their perspective, especially considering that they had pinned their hopes on being with Christ.

False Teaching Robs Us of Peace (2 Thess 2:1-3a)

To understand the serious threat that this false teaching posed to the church, recall that Paul described the Thessalonians as "upset," "troubled," and in danger of being deceived. Needless to say, upset, troubled, and deceived people are not part of God's formula for a healthy, vibrant, and growing church. These believers were shaken and confused by this new revelation. As Marshall observes, they were "so perturbed as to lose [their] normal composure and good sense" (Marshall, *1 and 2 Thessalonians*, 186). Perhaps another way to view their state of mind would be to say that they were an emotional wreck.

Their physical and emotional stress was uncalled for, since it resulted from a lie. We can learn from the Thessalonians' mistake. Think about how many times we allow falsehood to steal our joy or rob us of peace. Consider the following hypothetical situation that will help drive this truth home: Suppose your boss comes to you on Friday afternoon at 4:30 and requests a meeting with you at 8:00 on Monday morning. Since your boss never gave you a reason for the meeting, you begin to inquire among your coworkers if any of them has heard anything. One of your coworkers informs you that she has heard a rumor that five people are being let go for financial reasons. With that new information, you are now convinced that you are among those being fired. You dejectedly head home for the longest weekend of your life. You can't eat or sleep. You are irritable with your spouse and grumpy with your children. No matter how much you try, you are unable to get the 8:00 a.m. meeting out of your mind. Questions and doubts begin to fill your mind: Will I have to sell my home? How will I support my family? Why do I deserve this fate? What will everyone think? When Monday finally arrives, you are resigned to the fact that you will be fired. Upon arriving at your boss's office, your boss greets you with these words: "Congratulations, you have been elected as employee of the year!" What? This was definitely not the news that you were expecting. Your anxious, joyless, and miserable weekend was ruined by something that was not even close to being true.

Although the illustration is frivolous, the point is not: when we build our lives on false premises, we are setting ourselves up for many sorrows. Can you see why Paul was so concerned for the Thessalonians? Their emotional instability and mental anguish had nothing to do with the truth. With a firm but pastoral tone, Paul exhorts them, "Don't let anyone deceive you in any way" (2:3). He reminds them that because their future was far from uncertain, they could keep their cool in the midst of trying times, but they needed to allow the light of truth to shine on the darkness of their confusion. The only way to do this is to expose them to the revealed Word of God.

False Teaching Ruins Our Perspective (2 Thess 2:5)

The promise of Christ's return was meant to be a source of encouragement, peace, and hope for the church. Yet confusion about the timing of the Day of the Lord was having the opposite effect. Instead of living joyfully in the present and looking hopefully at the future, the

Thessalonians had lost their perspective. For Paul, this response was unwarranted because he had previously instructed them about God's plan for future events, including the timing of the Day of the Lord. Concerning this, MacArthur wisely notes,

> There was really no excuse for the Thessalonians to have been so gullible, despite the seemingly convincing forged letter. . . . The Thessalonians' gullibility was an emotional reaction to the stress of their situation. However, truth is not determined by emotions or circumstances, but by Scripture. Believers must allow biblical truth and theology to rise above every situation. (MacArthur, *1 and 2 Thessalonians*, 270)

As noted above, what makes the Thessalonians' confusion so troubling is the fact that Paul had repeatedly taught them about the Day of the Lord. Incredulously, he asks, "Don't you remember that when I was still with you I told you about this?" (2:5). His use of the imperfect tense of the verb *told* indicates that his teaching had been continuous. In other words, he did not merely tell them about the Day of the Lord once; it was a recurring theme in his teaching. As a wise pastor, Paul knew that the church needed to recognize how to interpret their present experiences based on their knowledge of future events.

Those who preach and teach must remember that God has given them the assignment to prepare their people to face life's many issues. This commitment requires proclaiming the biblical text both systematically and expositorily. We cannot pick and choose what portions of the Bible we think our people need to hear. Paul's breadth of teaching in Thessalonica serves as a powerful model for a well-rounded and balanced preaching and teaching ministry. Although both letters to the Thessalonians take only about 15 minutes to read aloud, the amount of truth they convey fills volumes. **Hence, just as Paul sought to prepare the Thessalonian Christians with God's truth, so, too, you must prepare your congregation for the inevitable exigencies of life by exposing them repeatedly to the Scriptures.** Peter gives a strong challenge:

> *I will always remind you about these things, even though you know them and are established in the truth you have. I consider it right, as long as I am in this bodily tent, to wake you up with a reminder. . . . I will also make every effort that you may be able to recall these things at any time after my departure.* (2 Pet 1:12-13,15)

The only corrective to false teaching is repeatedly and consistently to expose people to true teaching—God's revealed Word (Jude 3).

Rebellion Intensifies in History
2 THESSALONIANS 2:3B-4,6-10A

This section of Paul's letter is admittedly one of the most difficult in the New Testament to understand. However, what makes these verses so challenging is not the subject matter, but the succinctness with which Paul addresses the subject matter. As already noted, the whole of the apostle's teaching regarding the return of Christ and the Day of the Lord was much more detailed than what is included in the Thessalonian letters. In fact, arguably Paul had been so thorough in his personal instruction that he saw no need to provide more than a quick reminder in his letters. This approach is frustrating to modern interpreters because, as they see it, access to more information would go a long way toward clearing up any confusion. Concerning the challenges that modern interpreters face with this passage, Leon Morris offers a keen insight:

> Our big difficulty in interpreting what he says is that it is a supplement to his oral preaching. He and his correspondents both knew what he had said when he was in Thessalonica, so there was no point in repeating it. He could take it as known, and simply add what was necessary to clear up the misunderstandings that had arisen. We find it very difficult to fill in the gaps and to catch his allusions, which are so difficult, indeed, that many and various suggestions have been put forward in the attempt to elucidate the apostle's meaning. We must bear in mind the gaps in our knowledge and not be too confident in our interpretations of this notoriously difficult passage. (Morris, *First and Second*, 212–13)

Given the inherent challenges facing the interpreter, perhaps the safest place to begin the investigation of this passage is to ask the question, What is Paul's main point?

Regardless of where commentators choose to land in their varying interpretations, they agree that Paul's point is to demonstrate to the Thessalonians that the Day of the Lord had not yet come. Paul's own words speak for themselves: "For that day will not come unless . . ." (2:3b). With this statement, Paul accomplishes two objectives. First, he fires back at the false teachers. Note that his response is not a personal defense of his authority but a theological exposition of the truth. In other words, he is forcing the false teachers to argue with God's Word. This method is always the most effective means by which to confront false teaching. God's Word is more than sufficient to stand on its own. Remember, Paul's response was prompted by a report that the Thessalonians were upset and troubled by the specious claim that the Day of the Lord had already come. To confront the error and to reestablish their footing, Paul recognized that what the Thessalonians needed was not another opinion—they needed truth. He therefore unfolds for them the specific events that must occur prior to the Day of the Lord. His purpose is to allow the light of truth to expose the error of the false teachers.

Paul's second objective in these verses is to set forth a preview of coming events in God's redemptive history. While the commentators acknowledging the inherent difficulties in this passage are many, the truth remains that this passage provides a helpful glimpse into the future. Yes, we must guard against imposing on the text more than what Paul intended, but we must also recognize that God included passages like this in Scripture for our edification and not for our confusion. In other words, there is a message here that we cannot miss.

The Coming Apostasy (2 Thess 2:3b,9-10a)

To make his point that the Day of the Lord had not yet come, Paul points the Thessalonians to three future events: the apostasy, the revelation of the man of lawlessness, and the removal of the restrainer (2:3b,7-8). Using these events as waypoints by which to navigate the understanding of future events, Paul reminds the Thessalonians that none of these events has yet occurred. Any purported teaching claiming that they are now under the shadow of the Day of the Lord is therefore inaccurate. Questions regarding the timing of these three future events are legion, specifically as they relate to "the apostasy" and the "man of lawlessness." Rather than seeking answers to questions that the text does not provide, the best approach is to explore the nature of each of these events.

The idea of "apostasy" was obviously not unfamiliar to the Thessalonians. Paul's simple mention of it with no further explanation indicates that this topic had been previously discussed with them. *Apostasy* is a military term that suggests "the abandoning of a position." When used within the context of the church it points to abandoning or departing from the faith (1 Tim 4:1-2; Heb 3:12). To be honest, modern-day interpreters are at some disadvantage to know exactly what Paul meant when he used this word. Was he referring to a future time during which professing Christians would turn away from their faith? Or was he speaking about a specific historical event that would be characterized by a massive revolt against God? Or was he speaking of something else?

History is replete with examples of those who once professed to know God but then turned away from Him. In this sense, apostasy is nothing new; it has occurred in every period of church history. Paul's use of the definite article suggests that he has in mind something much greater than simply professing believers who fall away from the faith. He appears to be speaking futuristically about a specific period in human history—a time that will be marked by a massive rebellion against God, perhaps even an event gaining wide attention.

Whatever Paul has in mind concerning this apostasy, you can be sure that it will be closely related with the revelation of the "man of lawlessness." Paul ties the two together in the following description:

> *The coming of the lawless one is based on Satan's working, with*
> *all kinds of false miracles, signs, and wonders, and with every*
> *unrighteous deception among those who are perishing.* (2:9-10a)

Fueled by deception and falsehood, the "lawless one" will be Satan's energizing force behind the apostasy. He will be unwavering in his opposition to God and relentless in his revolt against Him. He will also be successful in turning believers away from their once-professed faith. Jesus gives a glimpse into the future with these words of caution:

> *Then many will take offense, betray one another and hate one*
> *another. Many false prophets will rise up and deceive many.*
> *Because lawlessness will multiply, the love of many will grow cold.*
> (Matt 24:10-12)

With this background, we now have a better idea as to why the Thessalonian believers were so shaken by the false teacher who was claiming that they would experience the Day of the Lord. Perhaps we can also sense their relief when they learned from Paul that such teaching was not from God. It is difficult to see how any news other than their total deliverance (rapture) prior to the coming apostasy would be an encouragement to them (cf. Rev 3:10).

The Rise of the Antichrist (2 Thess 2:3b-4,6-10a)

Clearly such a massive revolt against God will not occur without someone very powerful behind it. Paul identifies this driving force as the "man of lawlessness" or "son of destruction." Both descriptions reflect the heinous nature of this man. He is lawless because he despises everything about God's law, and he is the son of destruction because that is his destiny. He will thus have great disregard for the law of God and the dignity of human beings. He will fight to dethrone God, and he will work tirelessly to destroy human beings.

His true character is revealed in the following description: "He *opposes and exalts himself* above every so-called god or object of worship, so that he sits in God's sanctuary, publicizing that he himself is God" (2:4; emphasis added). For this reason, he has been given the title "antichrist." He will oppose everything that God stands for and counterfeit everything that God does:

- God establishes a law; he is the lawless one.
- God stands for creation; he is the son of destruction.
- God demands worship; he sits in God's sanctuary.
- God declares truth; he peddles unrighteous deception.
- Jesus was revealed from heaven; he will be revealed from earth.
- Jesus will come for His church; he will come in Satan's power.

Although he failed in his first attempt to dethrone God (Isa 14:13-15), he will not be deterred from one final attempt at another coup (cf. Rev 13:1-10).

Who will the antichrist be? The simple answer is that we don't know. Every attempt to identify this historical figure has proven to be futile. We know that he is coming; we just do not know who he will be. An unhealthy fixation on the antichrist will only serve to distract us from our focus on knowing, loving, and serving the real Christ. We would do well to heed the apostle John's warning that a "spirit of the antichrist" will characterize every age. He describes it in the following way: "But every spirit who does not confess Jesus is not from God. This is the spirit of the antichrist; you have heard that he is coming, and he is already in the world now" (1 John 4:3; see also 1 John 2:18,22; 2 John 7). While we know that a future historical figure will one day burst on the scene, we also acknowledge that "the spirit of antichrist" is already here. The lawless one may be coming, but lawlessness is already here. The one who opposes Christ may be coming, but people who oppose Christ are already here. We may miss the reign of *the antichrist*, but you will not miss *the spirit of the antichrist*. In light of these challenging days, Paul gives a solemn charge: "Pay careful attention, then, to how you walk—not as unwise people but as wise—making the most of the time, because the days are evil" (Eph 5:15-16).

The spirit of antichrist that is characteristic of the present age will pale in comparison to the coming man of lawlessness. In an ultimate act of defiance against God, he will sit "in God's sanctuary, publicizing that he himself is God" (2 Thess 2:4). Commentators have offered a number of interpretations as to what Paul means when he speaks of sitting in God's sanctuary. Some have identified the sanctuary as that of the literal temple in Jerusalem. Others suggest that Paul is referring to a figurative heavenly temple or perhaps even to the church as the temple of God.

While no view is without its difficulties, apparently Paul has in mind the temple in Jerusalem. A figure like the antichrist would almost certainly desire a worldwide platform from which to blaspheme God. One could find no more prominent place than that which has historically represented the very presence of God. If the temple in Jerusalem is in view, then it is likely that the apostasy to which Paul refers in 2:3 is a reference to what Jesus called the "abomination that causes desolation" (Matt 24:15; cf. Dan 9:27). Though we cannot be certain what this event will be like, we have some historical referent that may give us an idea. In 167 BC the Greek ruler Antiochus Epiphanes desecrated the Jewish temple by erecting a statue of Zeus in the sanctuary and sacrificing a pig on the altar. Driven by his hatred for the Jewish people and his disdain for God, Antiochus sought to bring an end to their worship and their God. Because this act of desecration would have been well known to His disciples, Jesus alludes to it as He describes the coming Day of the Lord. Although He does not speak of the antichrist, He clearly points to a public and heinous act of desecration that would occur in the final days of human history.

Is this the event that Paul had in mind when he wrote about the apostasy? Although the text is not explicit, apparently Paul was foretelling a future event of similar scope and magnitude. Since the antichrist will be a worldwide figure, we can safely assume that his reign of terror will be on a worldwide scale. Paul may have left much to the imagination, but it is difficult to see how his description of the reign of the antichrist could be anything other than a public and prominent display of Satan's power.

Paul makes clear that the antichrist is no ordinary man. Empowered by Satan himself, the antichrist will be Satan's superman. Listen to Paul's description:

> *The coming of the lawless one is based on Satan's working, with all kinds of false miracles, signs, and wonders, and with every unrighteous deception among those who are perishing.* (2:9-10)

This description vividly portrays the power and the activity of the antichrist. A number of observations must not be missed. First, he will have a "coming." He will attempt to mimic Christ in every way possible, including the way that he enters the world stage. Morris calls this a "parody of the incarnation" (Morris, *First and Second*, 232). Second, he will be empowered by "Satan's working." Just as Christ was *filled by God's Spirit* (Luke 4:1), so the antichrist will be *fueled by Satan's power*. Third, he will perform "false miracles, signs, and wonders." Paul uses the word *false* to identify the real motive behind the antichrist's miracles. His attempt to mimic Christ only goes so far. Jesus performed miracles to demonstrate His power to save; the antichrist will perform miracles to accomplish his purpose to deceive.

His sole reason for existence is to deceive those who are perishing (2:10). The antichrist will merely be a reflection of his father—the father of lies (John 8:44). This is why Paul calls him the "son of destruction" (2 Thess 2:3). Both his earthly objective and his eternal end are destruction and ruin. Interestingly, in the biblical record the only other figure who is referred to as the "son of destruction" is Judas Iscariot (John 17:12). MacArthur provides a helpful contrast between the two:

> Judas desecrated the temple with the money he received for betraying Christ (Matt. 27:5); Antichrist will desecrate the temple by committing the abomination of desolation (Matt. 24:15). Judas, apparently without influencing others, went astray, a tragic solitary disaster (Acts 1:18-19); Antichrist will lead the world into destruction (Rev. 13:5-8). (MacArthur, *1 and 2 Thessalonians*, 273–74)

The Removal of the Restrainer (2 Thess 2:6-7)

To remind the Thessalonians that the Day of the Lord had not yet arrived, Paul gave them the following information:

> *And you know* what currently restrains him, *so that he will be
> revealed in his time. For the mystery of lawlessness is already at work,
> but* the one now restraining *will do so* until he is out of the way,
> *and then the lawless one will be revealed.* (2:6-8a; emphasis added)

Based on previous instruction, Paul is reminding them of the impossibility that they were in the Day of the Lord. He bases this argument on the abiding work and presence of the restrainer.

To be honest, Paul's reference to the restrainer has perplexed even the most able Bible commentators. However, what may be baffling to us was clearly obvious to the Thessalonians. Using his previous instruction about the Day of the Lord as a reference point, Paul was building a foundation on which they could regain their hope and reestablish their footing. His message to them is actually quite simple: the Day of the Lord cannot come until the restrainer is removed. That Paul provided no long explanation indicates that his point was self-evident to the Thessalonians. Perhaps this was the evidence the Thessalonians needed to change their perspective about the Day of the Lord. Maybe they nodded their heads in approval and confidently moved on. We, on the other hand, cannot move on so quickly.

While identifying the restrainer is no easy task, a careful reading of the passage does provide some clues. In verse 6 Paul mentions "what" restrains, but in verse 7 he points to "the one" who is doing the restraining. On one hand, he speaks of the restrainer as a force (neuter), but on the other hand, he speaks of the restrainer as a person (masculine). The implication is that *someone* who has the ability to exercise supernatural force is currently holding back the antichrist.

But this only leads to the question, Who is holding back the antichrist? Attempts to identify this person are many.[18] Some see the restrainer as a government, such as the Roman Empire, not as a person. Others suggest that Paul is referring to the nation of Israel or even the preaching of the gospel, while still others argue that Satan himself is holding back the antichrist. Whoever is responsible for holding back the antichrist is obviously very powerful, and that power will not be released until its proper "time" (Mark 13:32-33).

---

[18] I. Howard Marshall provides a helpful and extensive overview of the various interpretations suggested by commentators (*1 and 2 Thessalonians*, 193–200).

Perhaps the best approach in seeking to identify the restrainer is to acknowledge the obvious: God is ultimately the one responsible for holding back the antichrist. G. K. Beale offers an important insight:

> It is clear that God is the ultimate power behind whatever historically particular agent is in mind. This is explicit from the observation that the restrainer will restrain until the revelation of the antichrist at the proper time. . . . This time is certainly set by God, since the whole segment (2:6-12) is placed within a prophecy-fulfillment framework. God will bring history to a conclusion in his own timing. (G. K. Beale, *1–2 Thessalonians*, 217)

Through the power of His Spirit, God exercises His sovereign control over human history. Only when He chooses to remove His hand of restraint will the antichrist be revealed. This conclusion may appear to be an oversimplification of a difficult text, but it takes into account Paul's reference to the restrainer as both a force and a person. Only the Holy Spirit could fit such a description. Since the Holy Spirit is God, His removal from the scene does not indicate His complete absence. Rather, it points to a deliberate lessening of His suppression of evil.

In summary, through the Person and power of the Holy Spirit, God is presently holding back the evil onslaught of the antichrist. Though "the spirit of antichrist" pervades the age, the stage of human history awaits the arrival of the "man of lawlessness." God will one day remove His restraint through the temporal cessation of the Spirit's restraining work; when this happens, the antichrist will be revealed.

God Controls Our Destiny
2 THESSALONIANS 2:8B,10B-12

The antichrist exits the stage of history just as quickly as he entered when God seals his fate with the coming of Jesus Christ. The same fate awaits every person who will be deceived by the antichrist. Even during the dreadful Day of the Lord, God's purposes will prevail. As Paul illustrates in these closing verses, God is methodically moving human history toward its final and perfect consummation. The "man of lawlessness" is simply a means by which God will bring this consummation to pass.

The Antichrist Is Destroyed (2 Thess 2:8b)

Paul announces that the antichrist will meet his final fate at Jesus' coming. He purposely speaks of the "brightness of His coming" to emphasize two aspects of the Lord's return: His presence will be revealed, and His purposes will be fulfilled. Paul clearly wanted to make the point that Jesus was coming not only to reign but also to judge. By the "breath of His mouth" He will effortlessly destroy the antichrist (cf. Isa 11:4). At that moment every aspect of his reign will be rendered inoperative. His temporary seat in the sanctuary of God will be exchanged for his permanent home in the lake of fire (Rev 19:20). How ironic that the "man" who thought that he could conquer *everything* will be brought to *nothing* at Christ's return (Rev 19:11-21).

The Rebellious are Judged (2 Thess 2:10b-12)

By the deceptiveness of his miracles, signs, and wonders, the antichrist will be successful in leading many to follow him (Rev 13:13-14). The full effect of his work will be embraced by the untold numbers of people who would rather believe what is false than to trust in what is true. As devious and deceptive as the antichrist may prove to be, the ultimate responsibility for failing to embrace the gospel falls squarely on the shoulders of anyone who rejects "the love of the truth" (2:10b). As Stott so aptly puts it, "Behind the great deception there lay the great refusal" (Stott, *Gospel and the End*, 172).

The closing verses of this passage reveal a chilling picture of those who will fall prey to the deceptiveness of the antichrist. Whatever else may be said about those who turn away from God, they ultimately make the deliberate choice to love their own sin more than they love God. As Paul puts it, they will perish not because they have not heard the truth, but because "they did not accept the love of the truth in order to be saved" (2:10b). That is a strong statement with significant implications. Human beings are notoriously reluctant to take responsibility for their own actions. Nearly everyone wants to pass blame on to someone else. Paul's reminder is that all will face the inevitable consequences for their own actions. Those who face judgment and condemnation will have no one to blame but themselves. The downward spiral of deliberate disregard for God is clearly illustrated in this passage: rejecting God's truth; believing what is false; enjoying unrighteousness; facing condemnation.

Condemnation is the inevitable outcome of deliberate and willful disregard for and rejection of the truth of the gospel. Whether a person chooses to accept or reject salvation is a matter of the heart. The same is true for those who buy into the deception of the antichrist. Marshall makes this point well: "Whatever one may say about predestination, the lost carry the responsibility for their own perdition" (Marshall, *1 and 2 Thessalonians*, 203).

For those who persist in the path of disobedience, God will send "a strong delusion so that they will believe what is false" (2:11). This admittedly challenging verse reveals much about the ultimate outcome of those who repeatedly and persistently reject God's truth. Paul's statement that "God sends them a strong delusion" can be viewed in one of two ways. First, God will deliberately delude the reasoning of the disobedient to seal their condemnation. The precedent for such action is found in a number of biblical texts (Exod 10:20; Isa 6:9-10), but most notably in Romans 1 where Paul writes, "And because they did not think it worthwhile to acknowledge God, God delivered them over to a worthless mind to do what is morally wrong" (Rom 1:28). For those who persist in willful disregard for Him by loving their sin more than Him, God simply "fixes" or confirms their pathway to eternal destruction. As Hiebert rightly points out, while God did not cause their sin, He "subjects them to the power of the error they chose. God uses their choice of evil as the instrument to punish their sin" (Hiebert, *1 and 2 Thessalonians*, 344).

A second way to view Paul's statement is that God will permit the antichrist to delude the reasoning of the disobedient. Richard Mayhue describes this view:

> God will send them strong delusion (literally "a working of deceit") by having the restrainer step aside (2:6-7) and by letting Satan's undiluted and unchecked lying have its sway over all the earth. God does this by His permissive will, not His determinative will. In other words, Satan will be, for a time, totally free to give the people exactly what they want to believe, i.e. the lie (cf. John 8:44; Rom 1:25; 1 John 2:21). The populace will not be restrained (cf. 2:7) from believing Satan's ultimate deception—the lie that Antichrist is God and salvation is through him. (Richard Mayhue, *Triumphs and Trials*, 191)

Those who choose to believe the antichrist will suffer the consequences of their delusion—eternal condemnation.

In either case one must not miss the point: those who ultimately suffer delusion and judgment do so not because they failed to have the opportunity to be saved, but because they would not believe and receive the truth. God is sovereign even in judgment. From our limited perspective, seeing how God would allow us to travel down a pathway to eternal destruction is difficult. However, if God is able to "work all things together for good," then we must accept that He can use both good things and evil things for His purposes (Rom 8:28). Morris provides a helpful insight:

> God is using the very evil that people (and even Satan) do for the working out of His purpose. They think that they are acting in defiance of Him, but in the end they find that those very acts in which they expressed their defiance were the vehicle of their punishment. . . . God is sovereign. No forces of evil, not Satan himself, nor his Man of Lawlessness, can resist God's might. He chooses people's sin as the way in which He works out their punishment. (Morris, *First and Second*, 235)

Conclusion

John Stott offers a fitting summary of this passage when he writes, "History is not a random series of meaningless events. It is rather a succession of periods and happenings which are under the sovereign rule of God, who is the God of history" (Stott, *Gospel and the End*, 173). Like the Thessalonian Christians, we are afforded the privilege of joining with God in what He is doing in history. But unless we keep the big picture in mind, we, too, can be easily shaken by circumstances outside of your control. We would do well to remember a number of purposes that God is accomplishing in the world.

He is building and strengthening His church. The Thessalonians' anxiety about their present circumstances resulted from their failure to remember God's promises about future events. In a world awash with everything that is false, God has provided the church with the unlimited resources of His truth. He has given believers His future game plan. Armed with the knowledge and insight of His Word, God's people can fulfill their mission with passion and expectancy.

He is using both good and evil to accomplish His purposes. When the world appears to be caving in around us, calamity is simply another means by which God accomplishes His ends. If God can use the vilest of people to fulfill His purposes, then we can be sure that He can also bring good out of our most troubling circumstances.

He is moving history toward a final consummation. The future of this world is not in doubt. Evil may appear to prevail for a season, but looks can be deceiving. God is methodically doing His work in the world. Whether He uses the decree of an unwitting Roman emperor, the vitriol of self-righteous Pharisees, or the lawlessness of the antichrist, we can rest confidently that we do not live in a runaway world. The next time someone asks, "What is this world coming to?" we can answer resoundingly, "This world is coming to Jesus!"

Reflect and Discuss

1. Why were the Thessalonians so upset and troubled?
2. How does Paul seek to clarify their confusion? How important is it for a pastor to be both firm and pastoral when addressing such issues?
3. How are the "apostasy" and the "man of lawlessness" connected?
4. What do you think Paul means when he says that the man of lawlessness will sit in God's sanctuary? Why?
5. Why is Paul's discussion about these future events so brief in this passage? What do you think that he previously told them?
6. Who do you think "the one now restraining" is? Why?
7. How does Satan seek to counterfeit Jesus through the coming and reign of the "man of lawlessness"?
8. What is the ultimate reason people perish?
9. What does Paul mean by suggesting that God will send "strong delusion" to those who do not love the truth? How would you defend this doctrine to a non-Christian?
10. How does a passage like this equip you to live expectantly in the present?

Gospel-Centered People

2 THESSALONIANS 2:13–3:5

Main Idea: Genuinely converted people will bear the fruit of transformed lives.

I. **They Are Transformed by God's Grace (2:13-14).**
   A. God loves and chooses (2:13).
   B. God sanctifies and calls (2:14).
II. **They Are Guided by God's Word (2:15).**
III. **They Are Secure in God's Salvation (2:16–3:5).**
   A. A grounded faith (2:16-17;3:5)
   B. A guarded faith (3:2-3)
   C. A growing faith (3:1,4)

A few years ago my family and I huddled in our den to await the much-anticipated arrival of Hurricane Ike. As the sun set over the Houston area on that September evening, the entire city braced for a direct hit. By eleven o'clock that evening, hurricane-force winds were buffeting the city, knocking out power and sending debris into the streets. For the next eight hours my family and I sat in the dark praying for daylight to come. I can vividly recall counting down the hours until sunrise while listening to the incessant pounding of rain on our roof, the whistling winds outside of our windows, and the sound of falling trees and snapping branches in my yard. Images of a destroyed roof and treeless landscape filled my mind. When the light of morning finally peeked over the horizon, I was able to get my first glimpse at the damage. Remarkably, our house was intact. No missing shingles, no broken windows, and apart from a few fallen limbs, our house and property looked completely normal. After a very long and sleepless night, we were pleasantly surprised by what the daylight revealed. Light has a way of putting even the darkest and stormiest of nights into perspective. Although we had expected the worst, the daylight revealed that our greatest fears were unfounded.

Although they should have known better, the Thessalonians feared being swept away by the Day of the Lord, the storm of God's judgment

(2:2-3). Despite Paul's words promising their deliverance from such a fate (1 Thess 4:13-18; 5:9-11), they were still unnerved by the prospect of having to experience it. While we know their fears were unfounded, no person with insight into the darkness of this period of human history would desire to experience it. The Bible describes the Day of the Lord as a future time of unprecedented calamity and destruction on the created order (Zeph 1:14-18), as well as unmitigated judgment and condemnation for those who reject God (2 Thess 2:9-12). Throughout both letters, Paul sought to reassure the Thessalonians that genuinely converted people do not need to fear this judgment. He continues to reassure them with these words:

> But we must always thank God for you, brothers loved by the Lord, because from the beginning God has chosen you for salvation through sanctification by the Spirit and through belief in the truth. (2:13)

With this statement, Paul reminds them that their salvation is not dependent on *their* not letting go of God, but on *God's* not letting go of them. Just as the morning revealed my storm fears to be unfounded, so also Paul seeks to dispel the darkness of the Thessalonians' confusion with the daylight of God's truth. In this passage Paul reveals three identifying characteristics of genuinely converted believers: they are transformed by God's grace, they are guided by God's Word, and they are secure in God's salvation.

They Are Transformed by God's Grace
2 THESSALONIANS 2:13-14

Do you remember what it was like when you became a Christian? Unfortunately, the further you get from your conversion experience the less likely you are to reflect on what Jesus' death means to you. Much of the Thessalonians' confusion about their future destiny resulted from their lack of understanding about their spiritual identity. Paul takes them back to the basics of their salvation by reminding them of what it means to be in Christ. He does not want the Thessalonians to forget that their salvation provides the only basis by which they have the assurance of escaping the Day of the Lord. So He wastes little time transitioning his thoughts from the deceptive work of the antichrist to the transforming work of the real Christ. Sharing these particular words with the Thessalonians must have proven to be joyful for Paul because, in contrast to those who will fall to the deception of the antichrist, the faithful Thessalonian believers have chosen to embrace the truth. In verses 13 and 14 we find a powerful synopsis of how the gospel transforms a person's life.

God Loves and Chooses (2 Thess 2:13)

If the Thessalonians were looking for a word of assurance concerning their salvation, they were sure to find it in Paul's statement, "But we must always thank God for you, brothers." As the consummate encourager, he restates his words from 1:3. Paul is once again conveying his confidence in their salvation by suggesting that he is under obligation to express gratitude to God for His work in them. His thanksgiving, however, was not based on what they were doing for God, but on what God did for them. While our work for God bears witness to an internal transformation, it must never become the sole basis for our assurance. The hope of our assurance rests squarely on God's unconditional love and sovereign election. In other words, we do not earn God's love or prove ourselves worthy of God's election by what we do for God; both His love and His election are unmerited gifts of what God has done for us.

Salvation then is not a *subjective experience* of doing things for God; rather, it is an *objective standing* based on what God has done for us in Christ. It is a *gift* we receive and not a *right* that we earn. Paul describes this gift:

> But God, who is rich in mercy, because of His great love that He had for us, made us alive with the Messiah even though we were dead in trespasses. You are saved by grace! . . . For you are saved by grace through faith, and this is not from yourselves; it is God's gift—not from works, so that no one can boast. (Eph 2:4-5,8-9)

This thought is amazing: What sin makes impossible, grace makes possible. What we could never do on our own, God does for us at Christ's expense. Paul describes the source of our salvation when he writes these words to Timothy: "He has saved us and called us with a holy calling, not according to our works, but according to His own purpose and grace, which was given to us in Christ Jesus before time began" (2 Tim 1:9).

The Thessalonian believers needed the security that only God could give. God chose them for salvation "from the beginning." Because their names were etched indelibly in the Lamb's Book of Life (Rev 13:8), they were in no danger of experiencing the wrath of God. If the

Thessalonians' future depended on them, then they had every reason to fear. But Paul sought to reassure them that their future depended on God, and as he tells them repeatedly in both letters, God is more than capable to bring to completion the work that He begins.

Why God chooses to love and save anyone is a great mystery that simply cannot be answered this side of heaven. Concerning the salvation of the Israelites, Moses offered these words of explanation:

> The LORD was devoted to you and chose you, not because you were more numerous than all peoples, for you were the fewest of all peoples. But because the LORD loved you and kept the oath He swore to your fathers, He brought you out with a strong hand and redeemed you from the place of slavery, from the power of Pharaoh king of Egypt. (Deut 7:7-8)

Alongside the mystery of why God chooses to save comes the security of knowing what it means to be saved. It would be unthinkable for God to lose anyone whom He chooses to save. The result of resting in this promise provides you with a confidence to face the future without fear. John Stott makes this point well when he writes,

> Let the devil mount his fiercest attack on the feeblest saint, let the antichrist be revealed and the rebellion break out, yet over against the instability of our circumstances and our characters, we set the eternal stability of the purpose of God. (Stott, *Gospel and the End*, 177)

This type of confidence in the purpose of God was the missing link in the Thessalonians' defense against the attacks of the false teachers.

God Sanctifies and Calls (2 Thess 2:14)

The Thessalonians' election by God did not nullify their responsibility to act on the truth. Paul provides a stark contrast between those who perish because they "did not accept the love of the truth" and those who are saved "through belief in the truth" (2:10,13). In both cases we make a deliberate choice, either to accept or to reject the gospel. In the case of those who accept the gospel, we find the mysterious tension between God's work of election (past) with human beings' responsibility to believe the truth (present). Further, to reveal this tension Paul points to the Spirit's activity in every aspect of salvation—from His initial call to salvation to His ultimate work in glorification (2:13-14; 1 Thess 4:7-8; 5:23).

As is the case throughout the Thessalonian letters, Paul's purpose in writing is more pastoral than it is theological. This explains why his message on salvation is short and to the point. The Thessalonians had responded to the calling of the gospel (1 Thess 1:2-5), but they were failing to live in the security of the gospel. They did not need a *how to* lesson about salvation; they needed a *What now?* lesson about salvation. Paul addresses this directly when he writes, "He called you to this through our gospel, so that you might obtain the glory of our Lord Jesus Christ" (2 Thess 2:14). The calling of the gospel and the obtaining of glory go hand in hand. God did not "appoint [them] to wrath" but to salvation and ultimate glory (1 Thess 5:9). Through the gospel, the Thessalonians had the entire trinity on their side. God elected and called them, the Lord Jesus died to redeem them, and the Holy Spirit was sanctifying them. Armed with an understanding of their future security, the Thessalonian believers had no reason to lose heart over the claims of the false teachers. MacArthur sums it up well:

> Based on this sovereign scheme, there was no need for
> the Thessalonians to be insecure about their salvation,
> anxious about the Lord's return, or fearful that they
> were in the Day of Judgment of the ungodly. (MacArthur,
> *1 and 2 Thessalonians*, 288)

They Are Guided by God's Word
2 THESSALONIANS 2:15

The only effective means by which to confront error is to "stand firm" and "hold to" the truth. To have this kind of tenacity and resolve against the strong winds of false teaching requires believers to know both what they believe and why they believe it. Paul speaks of the Thessalonians holding to the "traditions you were taught, either by our message or by our letter." The word *traditions* refers to a body of truth "handed down" (Mark 7:13; Acts 6:14). This truth would include Paul's teaching and any other apostolic word (1 Cor 11:2).

The Thessalonians had a deep reservoir of truth from which to drink. Though his initial stay in Thessalonica was brief, Paul's teaching during this stay was extensive (1 Thess 3:4; 4:1-2; 5:1-2; 2 Thess 2:5; 3:10). In addition to his oral instruction, the Thessalonian believers also had his first letter from which to gain wisdom, instruction, and direction. Of course, Paul's main concern was to provide the Thessalonians with an objective standard of truth by which they could judge the legitimacy of any doctrine or teaching that made its way into the church. Had they exercised this kind of discipline in the first place they never would have been moved from their foundation by false teaching.

The contemporary church would do well to heed Paul's admonition to cling tightly to what has been "handed down" by the apostles and prophets—the Word of God. The proclivity of many Christians is to be constantly on the lookout for some new thing to breathe life into the church. But according to Paul, the answer will not come by finding something new; it will come when the church renews its focus on something old—the Scriptures. Jude captures this when he exhorts the church "to contend for the faith that was delivered to the saints once for all" (Jude 3). Peter challenged his readers to "pay attention" to the prophetic word (2 Pet 1:19). David promised "great reward" to the one who obeys God's Word (Ps 19:11). Jesus affirmed that the one who loves Him will "do" what He commands (John 15:14).

The implication for those who are preachers or teachers is that they will take seriously the calling to "teach" the traditions (2 Tim 2:2). Unless the church is grounded in truth, it will continue to be vulnerable to false teaching (Eph 4:14). Further, since only God's Word has the power to renew life, why would we seek any other means by which to grow the church (Ps 19:7; cf. John 6:68)?

They Are Secure in God's Salvation
2 THESSALONIANS 2:16–3:5

Paul's depiction of the Christian faith reveals a Christianity that is far from passive. When we embrace Jesus Christ as Lord, we begin a lifelong journey of active faith. Our journey begins when we exercise faith by believing the truth (2:13). It progresses as we aggressively "stand firm" and "hold to" the truth (2:15). We will not rest until we reach our ultimate destination when we "obtain the glory of our Lord Jesus Christ" (2:14). This perfectly describes the Spirit's work of sanctification. He sanctifies us *positionally* when we respond to the gospel and are saved. He sanctifies us *progressively* as we yield to Him and are transformed into Christlikeness. We will be saved *perfectly* when we receive the reward of our faith and stand in the presence of Jesus Christ.

Until we receive the reward of our faith, the journey continues. However, to navigate this journey successfully, we need help. Despite our active faith, even our best efforts will fail apart from God's enablement. Paul therefore turns his attention from the Thessalonians' response to God, to God's work in the life of the Thessalonians.

A Grounded Faith (2 Thess 2:16-17; 3:5)

Any mariner will tell you that the best way to keep from getting seasick is to keep your eyes on the horizon. When everything is shifting around you, you must find something stable on which to fix your eyes. The same principle applies when living out our faith. If there is anything certain about our lives, it is that our lives are uncertain. In the midst of our uncertain world we need something certain on which to fix our eyes. As Paul demonstrates in his prayer for the Thessalonians, our certainty comes from the grace and love of "our Lord Jesus Christ Himself and God our Father" (2:16).

Because Paul recognized the impossibility for the Thessalonians to live out their faith in their own strength, he prays for their ongoing encouragement and increasing stability. He identifies both the Lord Jesus and God the Father as the source of this encouragement and stability. Noticeably absent from his prayer are requests for God to lift their burdens or to judge their detractors. He instead prays specifically for God to "encourage" their hearts and "strengthen" them in "every good work and word." In 3:5 Paul adds to this request by praying specifically for God to "direct [their] hearts to God's love and Christ's endurance."

Paul basically had two specific prayer requests for the Thessalonians. First, he prayed for their ongoing spiritual productivity. In this regard he asked for God's intervention in their lives, not to remove any of their burdens, but to bring them encouragement. Second, he prayed for their ongoing spiritual growth. Such growth would be evident by their increasing love for God and their ability to endure suffering by following in Jesus' footsteps (3:5). Hence, Paul's desire for this young church was for them to be diligent in their service for God and deep in their walk with God. For those in spiritual leadership, we can find no more appropriate example of how to pray for your people.

A Guarded Faith (2 Thess 3:2-3)

In His intercessory prayer for His disciples, Jesus makes at first blush what may appear to be a startling request. Listen to His penetrating words:

> *I have given them Your word. The world hated them because they are not of the world, as I am not of the world. I am not praying that You take them out of the world but that You protect them from the evil one.* (John 17:14-15)

There are two very sobering revelations in His request: that Jesus knows how much the world hates His disciples, and that Jesus would desire for His disciples to remain in an antagonistic world.

One of God's great mysteries is how He uses evil and suffering as tools to accomplish His purposes. We have already seen this principle at work in the Thessalonian church when Paul reminded them that God was using their suffering as a means by which they would be "counted worthy of God's kingdom" (1:5). Although Satan is an ubiquitous foe in the Christian life, God provides His people with sufficient strength to overcome. Recognizing that both he and the Thessalonian believers must have God's help in this spiritual war, Paul once again turns his attention to prayer.

With regard to his personal need, Paul asks the Thessalonians to pray for his deliverance "from wicked and evil men" (3:2). For him to request prayer from the Thessalonians says much about how he felt about them. At the same time, the Thessalonians must have been honored by their spiritual father's request for them to pray for him. As a new believer, I can vividly recall one of my respected mentors asking me to pray for him. Although I stumbled over my words as I voiced my prayer, I will never forget how honored I was to be asked to pray. Perhaps you could do the same for a young believer. Enlist his prayer support for the challenges that you face in your life and ministry. At the same time, ask how you can pray for him. One of the most significant joys in the Christian life is the privilege of praying for and with one another. This brings at least three benefits:

We acknowledge our dependence on God. Even on our best days, we are powerless to win any spiritual battle without God's intervention. In this passage Paul reveals dependence on God. We need God's enablement to keep going (2:17), His direction to keep growing (3:5), His protection to keep us safe (3:2-3), and His provision to keep advancing (3:1,4).

We are reminded that we are in this battle together. Spiritual tunnel vision is a very real danger for suffering and hurting Christians. We would do well to recall God's message to a suffering Elijah when God informed him that he was not the only suffering prophet in the land (1 Kgs 19:18). In a strange way, it is comforting to know that you are not the only one who needs to be comforted. In other words, it's comforting to know that you share with one another in the sufferings of Christ (1 Pet 4:12-14).

We are compelled to stay humble. Whether you are an illustrious apostle or an unknown church member in Thessalonica, everyone needs prayer and everyone can pray. As John Phillips rightly notes, prayer grants anyone direct access into God's presence. He writes,

> Prayer links us with the throne of the universe. It connects us with the mind, heart, and will of God. . . . Prayer is one of the forces of the universe, as real as the forces of gravity, electricity and magnetism. God always takes into account the factor of prayer when He is resolving the total equation of the universe. (Phillips, *Exploring 1 and 2 Thessalonians*, 221)

A Growing Faith (2 Thess 3:1,4)

Paul's life passion was to advance the gospel (Rom 1:15-17; 15:20). To hear him request prayer for the "Lord's message" to "spread rapidly" (v. 1) comes as no surprise, but his request goes beyond the *advancement* of the gospel to the *receptivity* of the gospel. To add even more specificity to his prayer request, Paul adds, "just as it was with you." In other words, he knew that if others received his preaching with the same enthusiasm as the Thessalonians, then the gospel would be sure to spread throughout the Roman Empire and beyond. For the gospel to "spread rapidly" at least three ingredients must be present.

There must be a word to be proclaimed. Paul identifies this word as the Lord's message. This message is synonymous with the gospel (1 Thess 1:8). For Paul, the gospel was not an addendum to be tacked on at the end of the sermon; the gospel was the sermon from beginning to end. This of course does not mean that Paul did not expound the Scriptures. He was thoroughly biblical in his approach (Acts 17:1-4; 28:17-29). His messages were thoughtfully prepared and purposefully preached in such a way that the gospel was central. We would do well to follow in Paul's footsteps by evaluating every sermon before we preach it to ensure that it is Christ-centered and gospel-focused.

God must prepare the way. While this might sound obvious, we must not miss the point. Paul's request for the Thessalonians to pray makes clear that he was totally dependent on God to ensure both receptivity to and advancement of the gospel. His request for prayer is in the present tense, which suggests ongoing action. He was asking the Thessalonians to make their prayers for the advancement of the gospel an ongoing priority. They were also exhorted to pray specifically for the message to spread rapidly. Paul envisioned an unobstructed pathway on which the gospel could advance. At the same time, however, he was well aware of the "wicked and evil men" who were seeking to thwart the message and the messenger (v. 2).

There must be receptive people. The preaching of the gospel does not guarantee the rapid advancement of the gospel. Those who hear the message must honor the message by receiving it. Paul's reference to the Thessalonians' receptivity ("just as it was with you") is a reminder to us once again of how the gospel transformed these people. Though Paul, Silas, and Timothy were forced to leave the city under duress (Acts 17:5-10), the message they left behind was doing its work. Even many months later, as Paul pens his second letter, he can still rejoice in the continuing work of the gospel. For God's work to advance, the gospel must be preached and *received.* Perhaps this is a contributing factor as to why some churches grow and others do not. Despite godly leadership and faithful gospel preaching, some churches never see explosive growth. The gospel will never fully take root and spread rapidly without the receptivity of the people. Paul knew this from personal experience. After his successful campaigns in Philippi and Thessalonica, he was greeted by ridicule in Athens (Acts 17:32) and persecution in Corinth (Acts 18:17). The same preacher with the same message experienced different results. Why? Ultimately, the results must be left to the sovereignty of God, but at the same time we cannot ignore the varying degrees of receptivity in each city. Perhaps we now have a better understanding as to why Paul desired that the Thessalonians pray for receptivity to the gospel message. Without it, the message would never spread rapidly.

Conclusion

There are a number of important principles to be gleaned from this passage.

Genuinely converted people will bear fruit. This is a recurring theme in the Thessalonian letters (1 Thess 1:2-10; 2:13; 3:6; 4:9-10; 2 Thess 1:3-4). While the Thessalonians were not a perfect church, there is no doubt that they were a redeemed church (2:13-14). This passage provides a template for us to evaluate how evident the fruit of the gospel is in the churches. Consider these five characteristics of the Thessalonian church:

- They loved Scripture (2:15).
- They were growing in love and perseverance (2:17).
- They were praying for the advancement of the gospel (3:1).
- They were standing firm against the attacks of Satan (3:3).
- They were obedient to God's commandments (3:4).

We would be hard pressed to find any pastor who desires anything less for his church.

We must expect opposition to the gospel. This theme also recurs in the Thessalonian letters (1 Thess 1:6; 2:14,18; 3:7; 2 Thess 1:4-5; 3:3). The "evil one" was working tirelessly to hinder the advancement of God's message in Thessalonica. Yet, despite his efforts, the gospel was flourishing. The presence of opposition does not signal the absence of God. The opposite is often the case. Satan has no need to inject himself into any church where God is not working. Why would he? Where there is no threat there is no need for his intervention. However, where God's Word is advancing and God's people are growing, you are likely to find opposition. In fact, you will most likely discover that the greater the spiritual victory, the more heightened the level of persecution. So while everyone around him is reveling in the glory of God's activity, the wise pastor is exhorting his people to be on guard against the enemy's attack. Contrary to the experience of many Christians, the church is not a playground—it is a battleground. The eternal destinies of people hang in the balance. Why would we expect anything less than the fullest force of opposition against everything we do? Paul did not live his life in a spiritual vacuum. He knew the inherent dangers of ministry. Knowing the dangers you and I also face, listen soberly to Paul's words to the Corinthians:

> *For we don't want you to be unaware, brothers, of our affliction that took place in Asia: we were completely overwhelmed—beyond our strength—so that we even despaired of life. Indeed, we personally had a death sentence within ourselves, so that we would not trust in*

*ourselves but in God who raises the dead. He has delivered us from
such a terrible death, and He will deliver us. We have put our hope in
Him that He will deliver us again while you join in helping us by your
prayers.* (2 Cor 1:8-11)

God sanctifies those whom He saves. Again, this theme runs throughout
1 and 2 Thessalonians (1 Thess 3:12-13; 4:3; 5:23-24; 2 Thess 1:11-12;
2:13,16-17; 3:5). In this passage Paul expresses gratitude to God for sanctifying them by the Spirit (2:13), guaranteeing their ultimate glorification (2:14), encouraging them to persevere (2:16-17a), strengthening
them in their work (2:17b), guarding them from the evil one (3:3), and
directing their path for them to accomplish His purposes in them (3:5).
Indeed, those of us in positions of spiritual leadership should endeavor
to pray for God to do these things in our people. God never intended
for the Christian faith to be a destination; it is a journey whereby God's
people are transformed into the image of Jesus Christ (2 Cor 3:18).

Reflect and Discuss

1. Describe a time when you experienced the truth of God's Word
   relieving you of fear.
2. How does recognizing your identity in Christ provide you with the
   security necessary for living victoriously for Christ?
3. How can Paul's prayer for the Thessalonians (2:16-17) and Paul's
   request for prayer (3:1-2) inform the ways we pray privately and
   corporately?
4. What were the "traditions" to which Paul referred? Why did he
   exhort them to hold onto them?
5. What ingredients are necessary for the Word of the Lord to "spread
   rapidly"?
6. How does the receptivity of the audience factor into the advancement of the gospel message? What can we do to affect receptivity?
7. Why should you expect opposition when you preach or share the
   gospel? What are some ways that this opposition comes today?
8. How does prayer bring God's people together?
9. Based on this passage, identify how God transforms those whom He
   saves.
10. What must the church do to ensure its gospel-centered focus? What
    are some things that would detract a church from having/maintaining
    this focus?

Accountability

2 THESSALONIANS 3:6-18

Main Idea: Christians have an obligation to hold one another accountable for how they pursue their work and how they relate to one another.

I. **Don't Be Lazy (3:6b-10).**
   A. Be informed by the truth.
   B. Be challenged by the example of others.
II. **Don't Be a Burden (3:11-12).**
III. **Don't Be Weary (3:13).**
IV. **Don't Be Negligent (3:6,14-15).**
   A. Hold fast.
   B. Take note and keep away.
   C. Seek restoration.
V. **Don't Be Forgetful (3:16-18).**

Have you ever had an experience like this? It's late and you decide to call it a day by heading off to bed. Prior to making your way into the bedroom, you make one last pass through the house, locking the doors, closing the blinds, and turning off all lights. Upon completing this nightly ritual, you enjoy a restful sleep in the safety and comfort of your home. Refreshed and energized by your good night's sleep, you head out of the house to start your day. Upon entering the garage you discover that while your sleep may have been restful, your home was not secure—you left the garage door open all night! You may have rested well that night, but you did so with a false sense of security.

Paul desired that the Thessalonians find rest in their relationship with Christ. To this end, he sought to warn them and prepare them for a host of exigencies that posed a serious threat both to their peace and to their witness. Throughout his letters, Paul covered numerous topics ranging from their confusion regarding the end times to the sexual purity of each member. He taught them how to rest in the promise of their future glory and how to tirelessly pursue a life of faithful obedience. He encouraged them to look out for one another, and he challenged them to be on the lookout for their enemy. The

Thessalonians could rest knowing that Paul had fully prepared them to live out their faith.

Yet before he concludes his final letter, Paul does not want the Thessalonians to rest with a false sense of security. So he reminds them of a significant danger to the church. He writes,

> *Now we command you, brothers, in the name of our Lord Jesus Christ, to keep away from every brother who walks irresponsibly and not according to the tradition received from us.* (3:6)

Surprisingly, one of the greatest dangers to the Thessalonian church was not a blatant attack from people on the outside, but the carelessness and laziness of people on the inside. Paul refers to these individuals as those who behave "irresponsibly" (3:6,11). They were the unruly church members who were causing problems for everyone else.

This is not the first encounter with these individuals. In fact, they appeared several times in Paul's first letter (1 Thess 4:11-12; 5:14). Some suggest that these people represent those who have quit their jobs in anticipation of the coming of Christ. Others argue that they were poor members of the church who were taking advantage of the affluent members. Whoever these people were and whatever the reason for their irresponsibility, clearly their conduct and their attitude were adversely affecting the church. Paul clearly sees the need to address this issue. As Gordon Fee observes, although Paul does not mention names, he leaves little to the imagination as to whom he has in mind by using language that is direct and to the point. Fee writes,

> In many ways this opening presentation of the issue comes in the strongest language in the entire passage, indeed the entire letter. It is understandably addressed to the community as a whole, since that is the case with the letter as a whole and there would be very little purpose in addressing the slackers themselves in any case. Nonetheless, if they should happen to be present when this letter is read to the whole community, they are about to get an earful. (Fee, *First and Second Letters*, 326)

Believers have an obligation to hold one another accountable for their actions and to deal accordingly with those who reject biblical instruction. Nothing disrupts unity or undermines credibility like believers who fail to conduct themselves in a manner consistent with biblical truth. As difficult as it may be, the church has a responsibility to ensure its own purity by holding those accountable who fail to obey God's Word. This accountability comes in two ways: by exercising church discipline and by providing biblical instruction. This passage includes both, in the form of five admonitions: don't be lazy, don't be a burden, don't be weary, don't be negligent, and don't be forgetful.

Don't Be Lazy
2 THESSALONIANS 3:6B-10

In his letter to the Colossian church Paul sets forth an all-encompassing pattern for how Christians should conduct their lives:

> *Whatever you do, do it enthusiastically, as something done for the Lord and not for men, knowing that you will receive the reward of an inheritance from the Lord. You serve the Lord Christ.* (Col 3:23-24)

Because Christ's followers aim to please Him, they seek to live their lives and do their work with passion and excellence. Christians will thus be guided by a different set of convictions about why they work and a different standard for how they do their work.

Although Paul previously taught the Thessalonians these things, some in the fellowship had failed to take his instruction to heart. Even a cursory reading of this passage reveals Paul's deep concern for how their poor work ethic was reflecting on the Lord and His church. As this passage vividly illustrates, Paul had little tolerance for lazy Christians. He tackles this matter head on by drawing their attention to two reasons why they should avoid laziness: the traditions they received and the example he set.

Be Informed by the Truth (2 Thess 3:6b,10)

"The tradition" refers specifically to Paul's previous teaching on the subject of work. In his first letter Paul gave them the following instruction:

> *But we encourage you, brothers . . . to seek to lead a quiet life, to mind your own business, and to work with your own hands, as we commanded you, so that you may walk properly in the presence of outsiders and not be dependent on anyone.* (1 Thess 4:10-12)

Considering the profound theological instruction found in the Thessalonian letters, we might wonder why Paul would devote such a significant amount of time on the mundane idea of work. For Paul,

Christianity was worthless unless it found its way into the fabric of life. How the church lived said much about what the church believed. If we take God's Word seriously, then we will take it to work with us. That is, how we do our work will reflect on the One we claim to worship.

So adamant is Paul that Christians should lead by their example that he reminds them of his previous injunction: "If anyone isn't willing to work, he should not eat" (3:10). His use of the imperfect tense of the verb indicates the repetitiveness with which he previously issued this command. In the strongest words possible, Paul wishes to persuade the irresponsible Thessalonians to go to work. Those who refuse this directive must be subject to the discipline of the church.

Be Challenged by the Example of Others (2 Thess 3:7-10)

Added to their reluctance to heed Paul's instruction was their unwillingness to learn from his example. With confidence that his life was patterned after God's standard for how to live and work, Paul challenged the Thessalonians to "imitate" him (3:7,9). Morris notes the significance of such a claim:

> No preaching of the gospel can ever be really effective unless the life of the preacher is such as to commend the message. Those who hear must feel that they are listening to one whose life shows his sincerity and the power of the message he brings. (Morris, *First and Second*, 254)

The Greek philosopher Aristotle described the preacher's trustworthiness, sincerity, and credibility as *ethos* (*Rhetoric and Poetics*, 1356a, 1–21). The audience's receptivity to a message is closely connected to the credibility of the one who shares the message. Paul makes clear to the Thessalonians that his credibility is not in doubt, and he appeals to their personal observation of his life to back this up:

> *For you yourselves know how you must imitate us: We were not irresponsible among you; we did not eat anyone's food free of charge; instead, we labored and struggled, working night and day, so that we would not be a burden to any of you.* (3:7-8)

In other words, Paul recognized the vital importance for the matching of his life with his words.

Avoid the temptation to move past these words too quickly. There exists today an unhealthy sense of entitlement among many who claim to be called to serve as ministers in God's church. All too often, before considering a new pastorate, the first question many pastors ask is, "What's in it for me?" While churches have a responsibility to care for those who serve (1 Tim 5:17; 1 Cor 9:3-14), those who are called to lead the church can learn much from Paul's example. Paul, Silas, and Timothy provided for their own needs and at the same time poured their lives into the Thessalonians. Their willingness to support themselves and thus not to burden the church reveals much about the depth of their love for God's people. One could imagine their diligent work at their jobs during the day and passionate preaching of the gospel at night. It is no wonder that Paul notes how they "labored and struggled" to keep from being a burden to the church (3:8). Such a commitment had to be exhausting. To have more concern for the people to whom they preached and the message they were charged to proclaim than for their own welfare reveals much about the character and integrity of these men.

Don't Be a Burden
2 THESSALONIANS 3:11-12

Standing on the platform of his personal integrity and pastoral example, Paul directly addressed the root of the problem in the church: "For we hear that there are some among you who walk irresponsibly, not working at all, but interfering with the work of others" (3:11). As if being irresponsible were not bad enough, such individuals were becoming a burden to those who were seeking to quietly live out their faith. It's one thing to be out of line, but it is an entirely different matter when you become a distraction to the entire church.

With pastoral concern for the health of the church, Paul appealed to the offenders by exhorting them to consider the outcome of their conduct. By spending their time meddling in other people's business, these irresponsible members were actually keeping the conscientious church members from doing their work. Paul uses an interesting wordplay in the Greek language to indicate that those who were not busy were actually being busybodies (3:11). You can imagine the disunity that such persons could cause in a church. Idleness and laziness in the Christian life are never good things. Those who live such a lifestyle will adversely affect the productivity of others.

The appropriate corrective for such a lifestyle is simple: get to work and be quiet (3:12). Those who are not busy must find something to do.

God does not intend for any believer to be unnecessarily dependent on others. Instead, believers are responsible to care for their own needs and lead a quiet life. Instead of meddling feverishly in the affairs of others, they are to reflect a state of inward peace and contentment.

Don't Be Weary
2 THESSALONIANS 3:13

As is often the case, irresponsible and unruly believers have the potential to discourage even the most faithful Christians. Knowing that a discouraged church is unhealthy and unproductive, Paul turns his attention to encourage the faithful. His directive is quite simple: "Brothers, do not grow weary in doing good" (3:13). For those who may become discouraged by the wayward members and so be tempted to lose heart or patience, Paul challenges them to keep doing the right thing. The right thing in this instance may be for the faithful members to continue pursuing their work diligently and be an example to others. Or the faithful members may be challenged to come alongside the wayward for the purpose of correcting and disciplining them. Whatever the case, Paul recognized that for the church to be healthy, its members must never tire of doing the right thing (Gal 6:9). Hence, he appears to be challenging the faithful members to hold those accountable who have chosen to live in a manner unbecoming for a follower of Christ.

If you have been in ministry for any period of time then you know how easily the entire course of a church can be determined by a few disorderly or irresponsible members. As is often the case, these disorderly and irresponsible members never seem to grow weary in wearying others. The unfortunate outcome is that the faithful members become easily discouraged and tacitly concede victory to a few recalcitrant individuals. The very ones who have the responsibility to ensure the purity and integrity of the church are the first ones to give up or give in. Sensing perhaps that such an eventuality was possible in Thessalonica, Paul exhorted the church to do the right thing by addressing the problem before it got worse.

Indeed, sin within the fellowship of a church seldom goes away by itself, and it often gets worse. Christians intuitively know this, yet many are reluctant to do anything about it. An example of this is found in Corinth. Because of their arrogance and pride, the Corinthian Christians were not only unwilling to address a serious sin within their fellowship, but they had also become so callous that they were tolerating this serious offense as if there were no sin at all. Like a cancer eating away at the health of a physical body, the Corinthians' sin was destroying the health and vitality of their church. Left unchecked, the sin of a few members had the potential to affect every member within the body adversely. Paul could not be clearer in how he expected the church to respond:

> *When you are assembled in the name of our Lord Jesus with my spirit and with the power of our Lord Jesus, turn that one over to Satan for the destruction of the flesh, so that his spirit may be saved in the Day of the Lord.*
>
> *Your boasting is not good. Don't you know that a little yeast permeates the whole batch of dough?* (1 Cor 5:4-6)

Paul expected the church to treat the matter of sin seriously, even to the point of excluding the offender from the fellowship. Pursuing such a course of action was not for the faint of heart. It would require the resolve of the entire church.

Turning back to Thessalonica, Paul's charge not to "grow weary in doing good" may very well be a call for the Thessalonians to have the tenacity and resolve to deal with the busybodies in the church. In verses 14 and 15 Paul calls on the entire church to deal with this matter. A failure to address the issue of sin had serious ramifications for the testimony of the church. The Thessalonians could not abdicate their responsibility to practice church discipline. Greg Wills makes an important point:

> The unintended consequences of abandoning church discipline are great. It implicitly condones sin and obscures the church's vision regarding sin and righteousness. It demonstrates a lack of faith in the teaching of the Bible and the explicit command of Christ. And it weakens the testimony of the church to the outside world. (Wills, "Historical Analysis," 270)

Don't Be Negligent
2 THESSALONIANS 3:6,14-15

Sin in the church is a serious matter. God expects His people to take an active role in maintaining the purity and guarding the integrity of His church. He has thus prescribed a means of discipline by which the church should respond to sin in its fellowship. Thomas Schreiner explains why God's people cannot turn their backs on the issue of sin:

> Discipline is necessary so the church retains its purity and power. If sin is tolerated in the community, the difference between the church and the world is erased. If the church's purity is compromised, then the message of the gospel is diluted, and the message of salvation and the glory of God are besmirched. (Schreiner, "Biblical Basis," 225)

Since the consequences of inaction threatened to derail the ongoing work of the Thessalonian church, Paul called on the Thessalonians to take action. The church could not turn its back on the matter. According to Stott, this section of 2 Thessalonians contains "some of the most important teaching in the New Testament on the subject of church discipline" (Stott, *Gospel and the End*, 193). In this passage are three key principles of church discipline: hold fast, take note and keep away, and seek restoration.

Hold Fast (2 Thess 3:6b,14)

The Thessalonians recognized the authority of God's Word as the standard by which believers evaluate everything in the church (1 Thess 2:13). Paul therefore reminds them that the "tradition" and "our instruction in this letter" must be the starting point for church discipline. Those whose lives reflect habitual and willful disregard for God's Word must be made aware of the serious implications of their disobedience. In the case of the Thessalonians, the sin of the unruly and lazy Christians had become public and disruptive, and therefore detrimental to the health of the church. Furthermore, because these individuals remained unrepentant, inaction by the entire church was not an option. God demands obedience to His Word. Scripture is replete with instruction concerning how God expects those who belong to him to obey His Word and with repercussions that result from disobeying His Word (Deut 11:26-28; 1 Sam 15:22-23; 1 Kgs 13:11-26; John 14:15,21; Jas 1:22-25; 1 John 5:2-3).

Obviously, proper church discipline can only occur within the context of a biblically grounded church. From the outset of his ministry in Thessalonica, Paul exposed the Thessalonians to truth. They were saved by the truth (1 Thess 1:5; 2 Thess 2:14), they were being sanctified by the truth (1 Thess 5:23-24; 2 Thess 2:13), and their future security was resting on the truth (1 Thess 4:13-18; 2 Thess 2:5). He therefore praised them for their obedience to this truth (1 Thess 1:6; 2:13), and he corrected them for their disobedience to it (1 Thess 5:14). The Thessalonians could not claim ignorance concerning God's standards for how they were to conduct their lives. It is against this backdrop that Paul instructs them how to respond to the "irresponsible" in the fellowship.

Take Note and Keep Away (2 Thess 3:6,14)

Although Paul is not specific as to the exact manner by which the church was to approach the sinning members, the implication is that when the church would "take note" of those individuals, they would be served public notice that their unbiblical conduct and lifestyle was unacceptable to God. In the spirit of Matthew 18:15-16 Paul suggests to the church such action that these individuals would experience the shame of their sin and thus repent and be restored prior to any further action. Martin believes this to be the case:

> The punishment was not to alienate the person and make him an enemy of the church but to make the person aware of the wrongness of his actions by demonstrating the church's unanimous condemnation of his behavior. (Martin, *1, 2 Thessalonians*, 286)

Green adds,

> The concern that motivated this call to separation is not that the rest of the church will be infected by the behavior of the unruly, but that the unruly will respond to the discipline. . . . In a society oriented primarily toward the group rather than the individual and in which honor and shame were fundamental motivations for human action, the prescribed social separation that provoked shame would have been a powerful discipline. (Green, *Letters*, 355)

To underscore the public nature of this discipline, Paul commanded the entire church to "keep away from" the sinning individuals and to avoid associating with them (3:6,14; see also 1 Cor 5:9,11). Since his previous attempts to bring them back in line had failed (1 Thess 4:11-12; 5:14), the matter was now before the church. At this point, Paul's desire is that the issue would not escalate to the level of excommunication (Matt 18:17; 1 Cor 5:5). But in order to avoid such a fate, the Thessalonians needed to make the difficult choice to withhold fellowship from some of their own. While such an action may sound judgmental and cruel, its ultimate purpose is remedial and redemptive. In fact, the cruelest thing that we can do to a sinning brother or sister is to refuse to warn them of the consequences of traveling down a road that will ultimately lead to their ruin and destruction (Ezek 3:16-21; 33:1-9).

Seek Restoration (2 Thess 3:15)

The purpose of church discipline is never punitive; it is always redemptive. The erring brother or sister is not an enemy of the church. They are a brother or sister for whom Christ died. Believers have the solemn responsibility of holding one another accountable, even to the point of taking the drastic measure of withholding fellowship from an unrepentant church brother or sister. The focus is not on retribution or rebuke but on reestablishing the individual within the fellowship of God's people. As Schreiner so aptly sums it up,

> The primary reason for discipline is the purity of the church and hence the glory of God. If the church tolerates blatant sin in its midst, then sin will spread like an infection, and the church will lose its witness to the world. The great deliverance accomplished by Christ in His Passover sacrifice will be compromised. Hence, Paul calls upon the believers to be what they are in Christ. Therefore, they must judge those who are in sin and refuse to repent by removing them from the church. Such judgment does not violate what Jesus said about judging (Matt 7:1-5). Indeed, it fulfills Jesus' instructions on discipline (Matt 18:15-20). Self-righteous judgment violates Jesus' words in Matt 7:1-6. Those who reprove others must be gentle (Gal 6:1) and beware of being puffed up with their own "righteousness." True discipline comes from a humble heart, and the motive of discipline is the salvation of the one who strayed. Those who give way to sin and fail to repent are in danger of final destruction. Discipline is a shock treatment designed to provoke those who are rebellious to return to the Lord. (Schreiner, "Biblical Basis," 220–21)

Clearly, the act of church discipline is not a matter that a church entertains lightly. When handled correctly, we have the opportunity not only to "win" your brother or sister (Matt 18:15), but also to convey God's message of redemption to a watching world.

Don't Be Forgetful
2 THESSALONIANS 3:16-18

This final section marks Paul's fourth prayer in 2 Thessalonians (1:11-12; 2:16-17; 3:5). Throughout his letters, Paul's prayers on behalf of the Thessalonians are pointed and purposeful. He recognized that the Thessalonians were going to need divine enablement to live in the manner set forth in his letters. So, concerning their ability to view their present suffering through the lens of God's greater purpose, he prays that God would endow them with power (1:11). With regard to his challenging teaching on the antichrist and the Day of the Lord, he prays that God would fill them with comfort (2:17). Concerning their ongoing persecution from evil people, he prays that God would enable them to endure (3:5). Finally, knowing the challenges of dealing with unrepentant and recalcitrant church members, he prays for God to give them peace (3:16).

With a final note of peace and grace, the letter ends in the exact way that it began. As Fee observes, considering the weighty subject matter contained within the letter, Paul could strike no more appropriate note on which to conclude:

> In light of the preceding content (God's coming judgment on their enemies; the timing of the day of the Lord; and unrest caused by the disruptive-idle), this prayer is precisely what is needed. So quite in keeping with what will become his lifelong habit, the "grace" at the end of the letter focuses altogether on their *shalom.* And quite in keeping with the overall Christological focus in this letter, the prayer is for "the Lord of peace" to give them peace. (Fee, *First and Second Letters,* 340)

God's peace and grace keep you firmly planted amid the challenges of living out your faith. Paul places the emphasis on God Himself as the source of your peace. Hence, to have a relationship with God is to know His peace. Even as his world was caving in around him, King David knew that he had the security of God's peace. His words should serve as a comfort to you:

I lift my eyes toward the mountains.
Where will my help come from?
My help comes from the Lord,
the Maker of heaven and earth.

He will not allow your foot to slip;
your Protector will not slumber.
Indeed, the Protector of Israel
does not slumber or sleep.

The Lord *protects you;*
the Lord *is a shelter right by your side.*
The sun will not strike you by day
or the moon by night.

The Lord *will protect you from all harm;*
He will protect your life.
The Lord *will protect your coming and going*
both now and forever. (Ps 121)

Because God's peace is impossible without God's presence, Paul adds these words to his prayer: "The Lord be with all of you" (3:16). What comfort the Thessalonians could take in knowing that God was not going to abandon them. With God's presence, Jesus' grace, the Spirit's enablement, and reliable words from Paul's own pen (3:17), these young believers had every resource necessary to pursue their mission until the coming of Christ.

Conclusion

A number of years ago I invited some friends to join me on a trout fishing trip in the Great Smokey Mountains National Park. On the planned day, we arrived early at the park entrance, unloaded our gear, hiked several miles upstream into the park, and fished our way back downstream to where we were parked. Although we did not catch many fish, we enjoyed the scenery and one another's company. As the day drew to a close we made our way back to the entrance and prepared to load my truck for the journey home. Reaching into my pocket to get my keys, I made the startling discovery that they were gone. After searching all of my pockets I informed my friends of the situation. For the next hour we retraced our steps back up the trail in what would ultimately prove to be a futile attempt at finding my keys. I can vividly recall my friends repeatedly asking me if I was sure that I did not have my keys. "Of course not," I replied. "I have searched every conceivable pocket, and besides do you think I would have us search for keys that I knew were not lost?" With the daylight and our hopes fading, we prepared to spend a long cold night under the stars. As we stood alongside my truck discussing our next move for the evening, I reached into my back pocket and removed my billfold. As I did, I noticed that my "lost" truck key was in my pocket behind my billfold. I had it with me the entire time! Needless to say, my friends did not have many kind words for me that evening. But we all learned a valuable lesson: it is fruitless to search for something that you already have.

God has provided every conceivable resource necessary for the health and well-being of His people and His church. Through the inspired pens of the biblical authors, He has given us His completely trustworthy and perfectly reliable Word. Armed with "the tradition" to guide us and His presence within us, He provides sufficient peace and grace to endure any suffering, meet any challenge, and overcome any obstacle. As Peter puts it, God has provided for His people "everything required for life and godliness" (2 Pet 1:3). We therefore don't need to look for something that we already have. Instead, we would do well to obey the commandments and appropriate the resources that God has already given us. When the Thessalonians embraced the gospel, they left behind their gods to follow the one true and living God. They were eagerly waiting for the day when God would give Jesus the command to gather His people. Although that day was delayed, the Thessalonians could rest knowing that God Himself was fully committed to completing the work that He began in them. The gospel was doing its work in them, but the gospel was also doing its work through them. That is what the gospel does. And that is why we don't have to look for anything new. It is more than sufficient.

Reflect and Discuss

1. Based on your understanding of 1 and 2 Thessalonians, what do you think was the sin of the "irresponsible" Christians?
2. What is the connection between spiritual rest in our relationship with Christ and the pursuit of productive work?
3. What are some biblical reasons that Christians should be excellent workers at any job they have?

4. Describe how Paul, Silas, and Timothy demonstrated a strong work ethic.

5. Describe a situation in which the behavior of others might make you "weary." What can you do about it?

6. Why do the "strong" church members often fail at holding the "irresponsible" members accountable?

7. What are the consequences of a church failing to practice church discipline?

8. What is the primary foundation for church discipline?

9. What is the ultimate purpose of church discipline?

10. What is the primary purpose of Paul's four prayers in 2 Thessalonians? How can studying his prayers help you to be more intentional in your prayer life?

WORKS CITED

Aristotle. *The Rhetoric and Poetics of Aristotle*. Translated by W. Rhys Roberts. New York: Modern Library, 1984.

Asghar, Rob. "Ranking the 9 Toughest Leadership Roles." *Forbes*. February 25, 2014. Accessed February 26, 2014. http://www.forbes.com/sites/robasghar/2014/02/25/ranking-the-9-toughest-leadership-roles.

Barclay, William. *The Letters to the Philippians, Colossians, and Philemon*. Philadelphia: Westminster Press, 1957.

———. "A Comparison of Paul's Missionary Preaching and Preaching to the Church." Pages 165–75 in *Apostolic History and the Gospel: Biblical and Historical Essays Presented to F. F. Bruce on His 60th Birthday*. Edited by W. Ward Gasque and Ralph P. Martin. Grand Rapids: Eerdmans, 1970.

Barnes, Albert. *Notes on the New Testament*. Edited by Robert Frew. Grand Rapids: Baker, 1985.

Batterson, Mark. *The Circle Maker: Praying Circles Around Your Biggest Dreams and Greatest Fears*. Grand Rapids: Zondervan, 2011.

Beale, G. K. *1–2 Thessalonians*. Downers Grove: InterVarsity, 2003.

Bonhoeffer, Dietrich. *Discipleship*. Translated by Barbara Green and Reinhard Krauss. Minneapolis: Fortress, 2003.

Bounds, Edward M. *Power through Prayer*. Springdale, PA: Whitaker House, 1982.

Bruce, F. F. *1 and 2 Thessalonians*. Word Biblical Commentary. Waco, TX: Word, 1982.

Calvin, John. *1 and 2 Thessalonians*. Edited by Alister McGrath and J. I. Packer. Wheaton: Crossway, 1999.

———. *Commentaries on the Epistles of Paul the Apostle to the Philippians, Colossians, and Thessalonians*. Translated by John Pringle. Grand Rapids: Baker, 1996.

Carson, D. A. *Collected Writings on Scripture*. Compiled by Andrew David Naselli. Wheaton: Crossway, 2010.

Comfort, Ray. "Tips for a Biblical Altar Call." *The Comfort Zone.* Accessed May 14, 2014. http://www.onthebox.us/2012/09/tips-for-biblical -altar-call.html.

Criswell, W. A. "The Pattern of the Servant of God" (December 1, 1957). The W. A. Criswell Sermon Library. Accessed February 4, 2014. http:// www.wacriswell.org/index.cfm/FuseAction/Search.Transcripts /sermon/1123.cfm.

Erickson, Millard J. *Christian Theology.* Second edition. Grand Rapids: Baker, 1983.

Fee, Gordon D. *The First and Second Letters to the Thessalonians.* The New International Commentary on the New Testament. Grand Rapids: Eerdmans, 2009.

Finzel, Hans. *Empowered Leaders: The Ten Principles of Christian Leadership.* Nashville: Thomas Nelson, 1998.

Grant, James H., Jr. *1 and 2 Thessalonians: The Hope of Salvation.* Preaching the Word. Edited by R. Kent Hughes. Wheaton: Crossway, 2011.

Green, Gene L. *The Letters to the Thessalonians.* Pillar New Testament Commentary. Grand Rapids: Eerdmans, 2002.

Gundry, Robert Horton. *The Church and the Tribulation: A Biblical Examination of Posttribulationalism.* Grand Rapids: Zondervan, 1973.

Gundry, Stan, ed. *Three Views on the Rapture: Pre-, Mid-, or Post-Tribulation?* Grand Rapids: Zondervan, 1996.

Hiebert, D. Edmond. *1 and 2 Thessalonians.* Chicago: Moody, 1992.

Kaiser, Walter C. *The Christian and the Old Testament.* Pasadena, CA: William Carey Library, 1998.

————. *Toward an Exegetical Theology: Biblical Exegesis for Preaching and Teaching.* Grand Rapids: Baker, 1981.

Keller, Timothy J. *Counterfeit Gods: The Empty Promises of Money, Sex, and Power, and the Only Hope That Matters.* New York: Dutton, 2009.

————. *Every Good Endeavor: Connecting Your Work to God's Work.* New York: Dutton, 2012.

————. *Walking with God through Pain and Suffering.* New York: Dutton, 2013.

Lambert, Heath. *Finally Free: Fighting for Purity with the Power of Grace.* Grand Rapids: Zondervan, 2013.

Lawlor, George L. *Translation and Exposition of the Epistle of Jude.* Nutley, NJ: P&R, 1972.

Lee, R. G. "Payday Someday." Accessed April 30, 2014. http://www.jesus -is-savior.com/Books,%20Tracts%20&%20Preaching/Printed%20 Sermons/Pay_day_someday_r_g_lee.htm.

Lewis, C. S. *God in the Dock*. Edited by Walter Hooper. Grand Rapids: Wm. B. Eerdmans, 1970.

———. *The Problem of Pain*. New York: Harper Collins, 1996.

MacArthur, John. *1 and 2 Thessalonians*. MacArthur New Testament Commentary. Chicago: Moody, 2002.

———. "Principles for an Effective Missionary." Accessed April 30, 2014. http://www.gty.org/resources/sermons/2277/principles-for-an-effective-missionary-part-1.

———. *Slave: The Hidden Truth about Your Identity in Christ*. Nashville: Thomas Nelson, 2010.

MacDonald, James. *Vertical Church: What Every Heart Longs For, What Every Church Can Be*. Colorado Springs: David C Cook, 2012.

Marshall, I. Howard. *1 and 2 Thessalonians*. New Century Bible Commentary. Grand Rapids: Eerdmans, 1983.

Martin, D. Michael. *1, 2 Thessalonians*. New American Commentary. Nashville: B&H, 1995.

Mayhue, Richard. *1 and 2 Thessalonians: Triumphs and Trials of a Consecrated Church*. Focus on the Bible. Fearn, Scotland: Christian Focus, 2005.

Moreland, James Porter, and William Lane Craig. *Philosophical Foundations for a Christian Worldview*. Downers Grove: InterVarsity, 2003.

Morris, Leon. *The Epistles of Paul to the Thessalonians: An Introduction and Commentary*. Tyndale New Testament Commentaries. Grand Rapids: Eerdmans, 1978.

———. *The First and Second Epistles to the Thessalonians*. New International Commentary on the New Testament. Grand Rapids: Eerdmans, 1991.

Packer, J. I. "Providence." Pages 990–91 in *The New Bible Dictionary*. Second edition. Edited by J. D. Douglas. Wheaton: Tyndale, 1982.

Paton, John G. *John G. Paton: Missionary to the New Hebrides: An Autobiography*. Edited by James Paton. Edinburgh: Banner of Truth Trust, 1994.

Patterson, Paige. *Revelation*. New American Commentary. Nashville: B&H, 2012.

Phillips, John. *Exploring 1 and 2 Thessalonians: An Expository Commentary.* The John Phillips Commentary. Grand Rapids: Kregel, 2005.

———. *Exploring Acts.* Volume 1: Acts 1–12. Chicago: Moody, 1986.

Polhill, John B. *Paul and His Letters.* Nashville: B&H, 1999.

Rienecker, Fritz, and Cleon L. Rogers. *A Linguistic Key to the Greek New Testament.* Grand Rapids: Zondervan, 1976.

Robinson, Jeff. "Q&A with Bryan Chapell on Christ-Centered Preaching." *Southern News* of The Southern Baptist Theological Seminary, June 3, 2010. Accessed April 15, 2014. https://news.sbts.edu/2010/06/03 /qa-with-bryan-chapell-on-christ-centered-preaching.

Ryrie, Charles Caldwell. *First and Second Thessalonians.* Everyman's Bible Commentary. New edition. Chicago: Moody, 2001.

Schreiner, Thomas R. "The Biblical Basis for Church Discipline." Pages 105–30 in *Those Who Must Give an Account: A Study of Church Membership and Church Discipline.* Edited by John S. Hammett and Benjamin L. Merkle. Nashville: B&H Academic, 2012.

Stott, John R. W. *The Gospel and the End of Time: The Message of 1 and 2 Thessalonians.* Downers Grove: InterVarsity, 1991.

Swindoll, Charles R. *Contagious Christianity: A Study of 1 Thessalonians.* Dallas: Word, 1985.

Taylor, Thomas R. W. "I'm But a Stranger Here." In *The Lutheran Hymnal,* 660. St. Louis: Concordia, 1941.

Third Day. "Revelation" (song lyrics). Accessed April 15, 2014. https:// www.thirdday. com/music/songs/revelation.

Thomas, Robert L. "Imminence in the NT, Especially in Paul's Thessalonian Epistles." *The Master's Seminary Journal* 13, no. 2 (Fall 2002): 191–214.

Tozer, A. W. *The Knowledge of the Holy: The Attributes of God, Their Meaning in the Christian Life.* New York: Harper & Row, 1961.

Why Go to Work? Knoxville, TN: Vision Foundation, 1987.

Wiersbe, Warren W. *Be Ready: Living in Light of Christ's Return.* The Bible Exposition Commentary, vol. 2. Wheaton: Victor, 1989.

Wills, Gregory A. "A Historical Analysis of Church Discipline." Pages 131–56 in *Those Who Must Give an Account: A Study of Church Membership and Church Discipline.* Edited by John S. Hammett and Benjamin L. Merkle. Nashville: B&H Academic, 2012.

Yancey, Philip. *Where Is God When It Hurts?* Grand Rapids: Zondervan, 1977.

SCRIPTURE INDEX